Doing the Right Thing:
A Guide to Business Ethics

By
Michael P. Harden

ISBN: 1-59453-034-3

Table of Contents

Introduction to Ethics

Contrary to what some people believe, it is not unethical for a corporation to make a profit. Moreover, it is not unethical to make a *big* profit. In fact, it is not even unethical to make an *outrageous* profit. The issue of ethics only comes into play when we analyze *how* the profit was made. Business ethics deals with how we make profits, not with how much profit we make. This concept is completely misunderstood by many people.

A business exists first and foremost to generate a return for its shareholders. This is a basic concept of the free market and the foundation of our capitalist society. However, we are often hammered by naive but well-meaning people who believe that profits are evil. They believe that corporations are inherently bad and that corporations conduct their business based on nefarious underlying motives such as greed and avarice. It may be difficult for honest executives to counter this perception when recent events have added credence to these beliefs.

We see CEOs and CFOs handcuffed and carted off to jail where they easily post millions of dollars in bond, and then go home to await trial. How can we disagree with the "anti-capitalists" who rail against corporate greed when there are now so many visible and shocking examples paraded before us every evening on the nightly news? When the front page of *The Wall Street Journal* reads more like a police blotter, we have to question what is going on in our corporations.

We often hear the argument that these "rotten apples" make up a relatively small percentage of corporate management. This is certainly true since the number of corporations that are not guilty of financial corruption outnumber the others by something like a million-to-one. Yet the sheer size of the dollars involved, and the maddening amount of individual greed we are witnessing, leaves us wondering if this is indeed how business is conducted in the United States.

To add more fuel to the fire, a 1999 survey[1] of convicts and MBA students showed that both were pretty equal in their ethical standards. In fact, in some cases, the convicts' answers demonstrated a higher level of ethical standards than those of the MBAs. Is this what we can expect from our future CEOs and titans of industry — that their ethical standards are lower than convicts' ethical standards? Interestingly, the inmates prioritized customers first, while the MBAs put shareholders first. This is certainly not an insignificant difference.

It is easy to see why people are mistrustful of businesses and their executives today. When companies, one after the other, announce massive losses due to questionable accounting practices, we ponder on how pervasive these practices really are. When we see officers of companies like Enron, WorldCom, Adelphia Communications, and many others, gut their companies to enrich themselves at the expense of their shareholders and employees, we sit back and wait for the next one to turn up. When we see people who are worth hundreds of millions of dollars engaging in insider trading to save a few thousand dollars, we wonder about how much greed is out there. When we realize that nearly one out of every three publicly traded companies has major discrepancies between its earnings and its cash flow, we wonder if there is a pervasive practice of "cooking the books" to pump up shareholder value.[2] When we see politicians uncaringly discuss keeping the economy in the tank in order to enhance their chances of winning a majority of seats in the next Congressional election, we question whose interests they are really protecting. We even question the motives behind the outrageously lucrative "retirement" deal of Jack Welch, one of the more beloved and respected CEOs our country has produced. We live in a time when ethics seems to be nothing more than a theory; something that is laughed at in corporate boardrooms and in private jets. After all, didn't Enron have an ethics code that *all* employees were supposed to follow?

This explosion of unethical conduct in our corporations is not new. It is just so much larger than anything we have seen before. There were scandals in the 1980s too, and they were often publicized. Here is an excerpt from a *Time* magazine article that appeared in 1987:

"Not since the reckless 1920s and desperate 1930s have the financial columns carried such unrelenting tales of vivid scandals, rascally characters and creative new means for dirty-dealing (insider trading, money laundering, greenmailing). Consider these episodes, all hard to believe, all matters of record: — A widely admired investment banker with a yearly income said to exceed $1 million sneaks into Wall Street alleys to sell insider tips, for which he later collects a briefcase stuffed with $700,000. — Savings and loan officers in Texas, all with six-figure salaries and bonuses, loot their institution to buy Rolls-Royces and trips to Paris. — A defense contractor with $11 billion in annual sales charges the Government $1,118.26 for the plastic cap on a stool leg."[3]

It is the audacity of the corporate miscreants and the obscene amount of money involved that makes recent transgressions so notorious and so much more shocking than previous scandals. Aside from the 1980 amounts, which seem almost laughable when compared to the enormous figures involved in our current scandals, the words in the *Time* article sound like something we would likely read today in the same magazine.

What is more astonishing to us is not the monumental level of greed and corruption we have witnessed in recent corporate scandals, but the idea that these executives conducted themselves with such a deep and abiding belief in their own impunity. Many of these corrupt executives believed that they would be able to get away with their felonious actions. Many believe that even though they have been arrested, they will never serve a day in jail. But what is truly amazing is that a significant number of these looters, embezzlers, and swindlers don't really think that they did anything wrong! How did it all come to this?

As human beings, we want to believe in a greater good. We want to believe that humans will act in such a way that they will show respect for one another and that we all can count on the integrity of others. We need to believe this to remain sane and feel like we have some control over our lives. In essence, believing in ethical principles and the conviction that others do too, helps us function without constantly double-checking on everything and feeling as though we can never trust anyone. We need to be able to trust others so we can live without fear.

Ethics is the "Great Equalizer." No matter what competitive advantages or disadvantages a company possesses, ethical business principles assure us that everyone is playing by the same rules. Ethics sets the tone and establishes a level of trust between the parties involved in a transaction. This doesn't just pertain to business dealings, but applies to all types of dealings, such as personal relationships and even politics. In politics, we have partisan squabbles all of the time. This is to be expected since politics is *supposed* to be partisan. Each party is dedicated to advocating and advancing its ideals and policies, so this will naturally conflict with the other party's ideals and policies. Having rules, written or unwritten, allows these partisan politicians to work together and get things accomplished in a civil and hopefully constructive manner. If they can trust each other, even though they are opponents, the playing field is level, and each party can push its agenda based strictly on its merits and appeal to constituents. When one party's members take it upon themselves to disregard the rules in order to advance their cause, they corrupt the process and create a situation where only one party is playing by the rules. They have broken the *social contract*,[4] and by attempting to tilt the previously level playing field in their favor, they have engaged in unethical behavior.

Here is a good example: When Senate Democrats decided to use a filibuster to hold up judicial nominees from an up or down vote because they knew that the nominees would be approved by a majority, they changed the "rules" in the middle of the game. Never before in the history of the Senate has a nominee had to obtain 60% of the Senate's votes (the amount needed to break a filibuster) to be approved. In fact, their tactics are contrary to their own previous comments about using filibusters to prevent up or down votes on nominees. Listed here are several statements by Senate Democrats that were made prior to their own filibuster:

"I find it simply baffling that a Senator would vote against even voting on a judicial nomination." Tom Daschle (D-SD)

"Have the guts to come out and vote up or down…And once and for all, put behind us this filibuster procedure on nominations…" Tom Harkin (D-IA)

"If our…colleagues don't like them, vote against them. But give them a vote." Edward Kennedy (D-MA)

The filibuster "has unfortunately become a commonplace tactic to thwart the will of the majority." Joseph Lieberman (D-CT)

The Senate Democrats have violated their social contract with their Republican colleagues by changing the rules in the middle of the game. These are rules that have been in practice for approximately 200 years and allowed the two parties to function on a level playing field. Although the Constitution allows for a filibuster, previously accepted practices followed the "advise and consent" clause of requiring a simple majority vote to approve a nominee. In fact, when it suited their goals, the Senate Democrats condemned the filibuster and expected the Republicans to play by the rules.

By any measure, attempting to change or disregard accepted rules (written or otherwise) is cheating. Anyone who gambles, plays sports, or competes in any game, instinctively knows this. It is a fundamental axiom. And of course, we all can accept the fact that cheating is unethical.

In a business situation, if we assume that all parties are playing by the same rules, we can rely on our competitive advantages and competencies in our business dealings without the fear that someone on the other side of the table will try to cheat us or steal from us. In ethical dealings, even a small company (provided they have some kind of distinctive competencies) can compete effectively or negotiate successfully with much larger companies. Obviously, unethical companies and immoral managers can use this trust to their advantage. This corrupts the environment and creates distrust, which leads to chaos. Managers instinctively understand this. They realize that honesty and fairness is important to business being conducted successfully. Believe it or not, corporate managers and employees actually want their leaders to be honest and ethical because they know that everything works better under ethical conditions.

"Employees today are looking for strength of character in their leaders," said Chris Pierce-Cooke, Director of Rights Management Consultants' organizational consulting practice. His comments were based on a survey that Rights conducted of 570 fulltime white collar employees in the U.S.[5] Of the 28 attributes that survey respondents considered most important in their leaders, the top four were honesty, integrity/ethics, compassion, and fairness. These traits ranked well above typical business attributes such as flexibility, decisiveness, creativity, and attention to detail, which were at the bottom of the 28 attributes.

Pierce-Cooke added, "...when it comes to hiring and developing leaders, the ideal leader will already have an internal moral compass that is guided by ethics and caring." Clearly, employees want their leaders to be honest and fair. There is a desire to have moral leadership at the top. No rational person could seriously argue that Jeffrey Skilling (Enron), Andrew Fastow (Enron), or Bernie Ebbers (World-Com) are heroic figures.

Why do we feel this way? Perhaps it comes from our innate belief in good and evil. No matter what cynics say, human beings have a strong belief in the ongoing battle between good and evil, and we want good to triumph. We can see this in our movies. Movies that do well are morality plays where good fights evil, and good wins. There are classics like *High Noon*, where one decent man, through his own efforts and without the help of his cowardly neighbors, defeats an entire gang of evil villains. Another example is *The Natural*, where an aging baseball player overcomes a variety of evil characters, along with his own faults; to single-handedly help his team win the pennant. And more recently, fantasy movies like *Harry Potter* and *The Lord of the Rings* have beaten many other big movies at the box office because they represent the quintessential battle of good vs. evil...and of course, good triumphs in the end for both of these movies. The list of similar movies could go on for pages.[6]

We relish these fictional accounts of good triumphing over evil because we honestly believe that this is how it *ought* to be. We expect good people to rise up and defeat evil people, and we are willing to pay money to see it unfold on the movie screen because we believe that these movies reflect real life. After all, good people *should* triumph over bad people. Movies simply reinforce this instinctive belief. At some level, we accept the notion that "The only thing necessary for the triumph of evil, is for good men to do nothing."[7] So we are drawn to people, both real and fictional, who are willing to stand up to evil, battle it head-on, and defeat it.

This powerful urge to believe in the morality of others is demonstrated by the fact that nine out of ten U.S. employees indicate that they expect their companies to do what is right, not necessarily what is profitable.[8] Furthermore, nine out of ten employees say that they work with people who believe in their organization's standards. Yet, these beliefs seem to be inconsistent with reality because in the same survey, 31 percent of the employees who were surveyed reported that they had observed misconduct on the job, either often or occasionally during the past year. Most of this misconduct went unreported by them.

We are uncomfortable with the ethical scandals we see unfolding before us because we instinctively understand that we need to have ethics to keep our social contract intact. That is one of the reasons we look for ethical heroes. They represent the best in us. They show us that the social contract is being upheld, and that is something we earnestly need to believe in.

Sadly, in spite of our built-in need for moral reassurance, it is no longer surprising to see major ethical lapses in corporations, either among high-level executives, or among the rank and file employees. It seems as though many of us come into our jobs lacking certain minimal ethical standards. This can easily be seen in the Josephson Institute of Ethics survey that found the following:

- Two thirds of high school students and one-third of college students have cheated on an exam at least one time.

- One-third of the college-aged men and one-fifth of the college-aged women said that they would lie to land a job.

- 39 percent of high school boys and 26 percent of high school girls say that they have stolen something from a store.

- One-fifth of the boys and one-fourth of the girls surveyed admit to having stolen something from a family member.

This decline in ethical standards has a direct impact on the way we conduct business. Employers must constantly be on guard for ethical violations by employees, while at the same time, implementing measures to ensure that the organization itself follows strict ethical guidelines, not just because it is the right thing to do, but to avoid lawsuits and declines in employee morale. On the other hand, employees must be careful to follow the corporation's ethical guidelines, while at the same time being vigilant about possible corporate violations. The ethical relationship between employer and employee is both symbiotic and adversarial. As much as they wish to trust each other, current conditions do not nurture this kind of certitude.

The ultimate goal of the organization's managers and employees is to make sure that everyone from the board of directors down to the newest employee does the "right thing." Not just because it is morally correct, but also because it is profitable. Although it may surprise some people, companies that stress ethical behavior tend to be more profitable than those companies that only stress profits.

In 1992, two Harvard Business School professors, John Kotter and James Heskett, published an eleven-year study of 207 large U.S. companies. Kotter and Heskett found that companies that took a balanced approach (ethics and profits) rather than a narrow approach (profits) had greater increases in revenue (682% vs. 166%), size of workforce (282% vs. 36%), net income (756% vs. 1%), and stock price (901% vs. 74%). These increases are so substantial that they cannot be anomalies or aberrations. They are genuine and significant differences.

Additional studies have shown the same effects. The KPMG 2000 Organizational Integrity Study that surveyed almost 2,400 workers found that firms in which management is perceived as being ethical by both its employees and its customers often outperform other companies. One of the interesting statistics of the study is that 81% of the workers who believed their management to be ethical said they would recommend their own company to potential customers or new hires. On the other hand, only 21% of the employees who believed their firm's management to be unethical said they would recommend their company. Obviously, when employees believe that their management is ethical, they will feel much more confident in recommending their firm to potential clients and recruits. Ultimately, this condition results in higher morale, less turnover, decreased costs, and increased profits.

Another statistic from the study revealed that 80% of the workers who believed their management to be ethical, also believed that their customers would recommend the firm to other potential customers.

What these studies and their statistics demonstrate is that companies that practice good ethical standards will, on average, do better than companies that don't follow ethical principles. Management should seriously consider this when determining how to implement ethical practices throughout the firm. Therefore, getting management and employees, across the board, to understand the need for ethical practices, and to promote ethical standards, is an important factor in being successful.

We must realize that ethical behavior is a precious commodity. It is a thing to be treasured because it holds everything together in our personal and business relationships. Most importantly, ethical behavior and following ethical standards allows us to operate in an environment of trust. Yet we take this wonderful concept and slowly chip away at it through rationalizations and the lowering of our standards. There is a story about a farmer and a pig that demonstrates what is happening to our ethical principles. It goes like this:

A traveling salesman was driving through the country when he stopped at a farmhouse to see if he could get some directions. The old farmer was sitting in his rocking chair on the front porch, rocking back and forth, when the salesman approached him. As they were discussing directions, the weather, and other small talk, a pig with a wooden leg came out of the front door and hobbled over to the farmer. The salesman was amazed because he had never seen a pig with a wooden leg before.

"How did that pig get a wooden leg?" he asked curiously.

The farmer slowly replied: "That's not just any pig, Mister. That's a damn special pig. It saved my life."

"It saved your life?" asked the salesman. "How?"

"One day when I was plowing the field," replied the farmer, "my tractor hit a rut and turned over on top of me. I broke three ribs and was pinned under the tractor. I couldn't breathe. I thought I was going to die. Then that there pig came along and pulled me out from under the tractor. Then he ran five miles into town to get an ambulance for me."

"That's amazing," said the salesman. "But how did he get a wooden leg?"

"I'm getting there," drawled the farmer. "Another time, he saved my son's life. The boy was swimming in the pond and got a cramp and went under. That there pig dove in after him, pulled him out, and gave him mouth-to-mouth resuscitation. My son wouldn't be alive today if it weren't for that there pig."

"That's great," replied the salesman, getting a little annoyed that he couldn't get his question answered. "But how did he get the wooden leg?"

"I'm getting there," said the farmer. "One night our house caught fire while we were all asleep. That there pig woke us all up, dragged all of us out of the house, and then ran into town to get the fire department. He saved our lives and our house too."

"That's terrific!" said the salesman, now completely annoyed with the farmer. "But how did he get the wooden leg?"

The farmer replied slowly, "Well that's my point, Mister. When you've got a pig that smart, you don't eat him all at once."

And that is what is happening with our ethical and moral principles. We take something that is wonderful and beneficial, and slowly eat away at it, without fully understanding what it is we are destroying. Just like the farmer with his miraculous pig (who he slowly eats because he values the short-term enjoyment of eating ham more than he values the long-term benefits of a heroic pig), we sacrifice our ethical principles in order to achieve short-term, yet highly enjoyable benefits. This is what we have seen in many of the recent corporate scandals. This is what we have seen when the President of the United States claims that oral sex isn't really sex, and then agonizingly redefines what the word "is" means.

Our societal retreat from ethical and moral behavior is not unstoppable. We can improve our ethical behavior and learn to make ethical decisions so that we minimize hurting others. We can establish ethical standards and follow them, making the way we conduct business beneficial to ourselves and to others.

This book will help.

Notes

[1] James M. Stearns and Shaheen Borna. "A Comparison of the Ethics of Convicted Felons and Graduate Business Students: Implications for Business Practice and Business Ethics Education," Ball State University, Muncie, Indiana (1999).

[2] Martin D. Weiss, *The Ultimate Safe Money Guide* noted that 1,697 out of more than 6,000 companies listed on U.S. stock exchanges had such discrepancies.

[3] Stephen Koepp, "Having it all, then throwing it away. (scandals and punishment on Wall Street)," *Time* (May 25, 1987): v. 129, p. 22(2).

[4] Social contract theory proposes that we would live under a constant state of war of competing self-interests if we didn't have a set of rules to govern our mutual behavior. Since this environment of competing self-interests is not a healthy environment in which to live or conduct business, our own selfishness motivates us to adopt a set of rules that protects us from being hurt by others. See Chapter Six and the section covering the social contract for a more detailed explanation.

[5] The survey was conducted of 570 employees in December 2002 by Right Management Consultants. 24% of the respondents listed honesty as the most important character trait, while only .4% listed attention to detail as the most important.

[6] It isn't just movies, but popular plays and books throughout history have had this same moral struggle at their heart.

[7] This quote is often attributed to Edmund Burke, although it cannot be found in any of his writings.

[8] Findings from the Ethics Resource Center's 2000 National Business Ethics Survey, Volume I: *How Employees Perceive Ethics at Work.*

Others Books by Michael P. Harden

Forget Everything You Ever Learned

Section One: Understanding Ethics

Mark Twain once said, "Always do right. This will gratify some people, and astonish the rest." He was correct on several counts. First, we should always do right. Second, some people will certainly be gratified by our ethical behavior. And third, there will always be many people who will be truly astounded when they see ethical behavior. But why is it this way? Shouldn't we expect ethical behavior all of the time and be astounded when we *don't* see it?

The problem is that we are no longer taught ethical behavior on any substantial level, and we are bombarded by so much unethical behavior that we have begun to accept bad behavior as the norm and good behavior as the exception. Prominent people behave badly, corporations cheat their shareholders, and politicians put party politics and re-election above the wellbeing of their constituents. Seldom do we see someone "fall on his sword" over a principle. We have become desensitized to immoral behavior.

If we are to put ethics back into business, we must first understand what ethics really means. We must understand the various ethical principles that have been developed, studied, refined, and practiced for thousands of years before us. Knowing and understanding ethical principles and theories is the foundation we need to be able to identify ethical dilemmas and to make solid ethical decisions that keep us out of trouble.

This section covers many of the commonly accepted ethical theories that we use to determine ethically and morally correct courses of action. Once we understand and learn how to apply these theories, we will be armed with the tools we need to operate our organizations in an ethical manner.

Michael P. Harden

Chapter One: The Free Market System

The free market system is a wonderful mechanism that creates wealth, jobs, and goods. It developed naturally over thousands of years through the incessant desire of human beings to seek personal gain. Although many tyrants, as well as innumerable misguided socialists, have tried throughout history to quash it, the free market cannot be suppressed. Even totalitarian societies that are able to wield terribly oppressive measures to shut it down, ultimately fail. In every case, the free market ideal will creep in, manifesting itself through black markets and bartering, even when punishments are swift and harsh. Its nature is so fundamental to human beings, that it cannot be repressed. The Soviet Union tried to enforce communism over capitalism. So where is the Soviet Union today? Even the most ardent proponents of Marxist ideology must be scratching their heads in befuddlement as they are forced to watch one communist country after another fall to capitalism. It seems that no matter how hard they try to stop it, capitalism always triumphs over other economic systems.

Businesses are an integral part of the free market system, and as long as they operate within the scope of the law and practice an acceptable level of ethical standards, they are free to pursue profits in any number of ways in a competitive economic environment. Businesses will typically make their competitive decisions based on two factors: the law and economics. Economics guides our ability to generate profits while the law restricts what we do to achieve that profit. Nevertheless, in our capitalist system, we require that businesses go beyond the law. We expect our businesses to compete on a level playing field, and that field is generally defined by our ethical expectations.

In order to better understand the role of business in the free market, we must first understand what the free market really is...and how it really works.

Supply and demand typically rules in a free market society. These two forces govern what takes place in the marketplace, and businesses operate within these forces to achieve their ultimate purpose, specifically, to make a profit and generate a return for their shareholders. This concept is not new. It was originally proposed over 200 years ago by Adam Smith (1776).

In *The Wealth of Nations*, Adam Smith pointed out that seeking a profit is morally justified based on the notion that pursuing a profit by one organization ultimately results in a benefit to society as a whole. There is no doubt that we, as a society, believe that our capitalist system is superior to any other economic system in the world. We believe this because our system produces more goods and services, at a lower price, and of a higher quality, than any other economic system in practice. This alone would seem to justify a free market economy. Yet we go even further and justify our system on other factors as well. One of these factors is that we believe the nature of our system to be *moral*. By moral, we simply mean that it is ethically justified to make a profit by producing goods and services that benefit others. In common sense terms, this seems both logical and rational.

Free trade in a free society means one thing: that we have the ability to trade something we own for something someone else owns, provided we both want (or need) what the other has. For example, if I have food, and you have money, and I desire to have money while you need food, then a trade seems to make perfect sense and satisfies both of our needs. This is how free trade is morally justified. Our *voluntary* trade results in a benefit for both parties, allows us to satisfy our needs, and does so without conflict. Therefore, a system that is based on a free trade arrangement benefits society as a whole. This makes it morally acceptable. On a larger scale, entire economies are based on this free trade principle.

The Invisible Hand

Although we justify our free trade (capitalist) economic system on the basis of its contribution to society as a whole, we also accept the theory of an "invisible hand" that was originally introduced by Adam Smith in *The Wealth of Nations*. This theory proposes that as individuals, we act in our own best interests seeking personal gain; and by seeking personal gain and not the welfare of others, we end up creating an efficient system in which competition flourishes and prices are kept at low levels. This, according to Adam Smith, is where an individual is "led by an invisible hand to promote an end which was no part of his intention." Smith further argues in *The Wealth of Nations* that "By pursuing his own interests he frequently promotes that of society more effectually than when he really intends to promote it." What Smith is saying is that although our economic system is based on individual desires to promote self-interest, it results nonetheless in a benefit to society by creating a system that works for us all.

Reviewing this argument, we can easily see the working of the "invisible hand" and the moral basis for our free market system:

1. Individuals act in their own personal interests, seeking personal gain.
2. By seeking personal gain, individuals create a competitive system that results in lower prices, better quality, and more production of goods.
3. The lower prices, higher quality, and increased production of goods benefits society as a whole.
4. If the system benefits society as a whole, it is morally justified and ethically acceptable.

So, we morally justify our economic system, not *in spite* of the fact that it is based on satisfying self-interests, but precisely *because* it is based on satisfying self-interests.

In a free trade society, people will trade with each other, making the best deals they can, in order to obtain the goods and services they want. This is typically called "exchange." Whereas in previous centuries, much of the exchange was made up of trading goods for other goods, i.e., bartering, today we usually exchange money for goods (buying), or goods for money (selling). In either case, the exchange transaction has the same purpose — to give up something that is owned in exchange for something that is desired.

The market is a "free" market in the sense that the role of government is not to create or manage the market, but simply to establish a "level playing field" for everyone through the enactment of appropriate regulations. By creating laws and regulations that prevent fraud and theft, the government ensures that the proper economic conditions are present to facilitate a free market system. Anything that goes beyond these laws falls into the realm of ethics.

In "planned economies," otherwise known as *communism*, or "mixed market economies," such as *socialism*, the government typically owns and operates the sources of production (or in the case of socialism, substantially influences or controls certain aspects of the economy). In "market economies," such as our free market or *capitalist* system, the government's role is simply that of rule-maker and enforcer. This role is absolutely essential to ensuring that the market operates fairly, and all participants play by the rules. This role is analogous to that of the governing bodies in various sports. Each major professional and amateur sport has its own governing body that establishes the game's rules and enforces them. As an example, professional football has the National Football League (NFL) as its governing body. The NFL establishes rules that all teams must follow. It develops rules for how the game is played, what the penalties are for offenses, and even provides referees to enforce its rules. Although each NFL team is free to develop and call its own plays, choose its own players and coaches, and follow its own business strategies and on-field game tactics, it must do so within a set of rules that ensures that all teams compete on a "level playing field." This makes the game fair, rewarding compliance with the rules and punishing offenders. This is particularly evident during the game itself where every aspect of the game has some kind of rule, and referees and line judges are scattered about to ensure compliance. Without this oversight of the way the game is played, each team could do whatever it wants, quickly leading to chaos and injuries in a wild free-for-all. Asking football teams to play fairly without providing them with the appropriate rules and referees, is asking them to do the impossible. How many "roughing the passer," "roughing the kicker," "face mask," "chop block," "clipping," or "unsportsmanlike conduct" incidents would there be in a typical NFL game if there were no referees to impose 15-yard penalties for this behavior?

The government assumes a similar role in business. It acts as a governing body, creating and enforcing rules that ensure that all businesses play by the same rules. Instead of referees, the government has "regulators" that enforce compliance and punish offenders. To the extent possible, the government tries to prevent one business from gaining an unfair advantage over another through illegal or unethical means. It does not, however, prevent businesses from using their strategies, resources, and innovations to gain competitive advantages over other businesses, which is the true mark of a capitalist system. The government's role as referee ensures that the social contract[1] is enforced.

The Labor Theory of Property

There are other arguments for the free market system besides those of Adam Smith. John Locke's labor theory of property[2] provides a basis for the free market as well...one that greatly influenced our Founding Fathers in the establishment of property rights in this country. Locke asserted that individuals have a right to the product of their labor, and that this is a natural right, in essence, given to them by God, not by man. Because this right is natural, Locke believed that it should also be protected by law.

In Locke's labor theory of property, an individual has the right to the goods produced by his labor. So, if a man farms a field, toiling and putting in long hours, he is entitled to the crops that the field (and his labor) produces for him. He is entitled to the crops because they would not be there had he not worked to produce them. If someone were to come along and take the crops without restitution, then that would be theft of the man's property. The same rationale applies to the work performed by laborers working in mines or factories (or offices). The result of their labor is their property, except that in these cases they have chosen to exchange it for wages, which is their right to do so in a free market system.

Under Locke's natural right to property, we utilize our labor to produce something that belongs to us. We can exchange that product for anything else we want simply because it is ours to do with as we choose. So an individual can choose to work in a factory, and in doing so, sell his or her labor to the factory owner for an hourly wage. This is a fundamental principle of the free trade market. In fact, laborers who seek higher wages must typically produce more or contribute more to their employer. This contributes to the efficiency and productivity of the business, which results in a benefit to consumers and society. Conversely, when consumers, pursuing their own self-interests, seek to purchase goods that they need or desire at the lowest price possible, they are forcing businesses to be more competitive. This results in a competitive market that is characterized by lower prices and the most efficient utilization of resources. In the case of the laborer and the consumer, both are operating in their own self-interests and without regard for the welfare of others. Each is being led by the "invisible hand" to satisfy their personal needs, but in the process, they are creating market conditions that do indeed benefit the rest of society.

Even the owner of the factory has the right to the profits that flow directly from the labor of his employees. He is entitled to whatever wealth his factory brings him even though he did not perform the labor himself. The owner would not have been able to acquire the wealth generated by his factory had he not invested his own capital and resources in the factory. So individuals who invest in businesses, commonly called shareholders, are entitled to the profits of their capital investment. These people, who fund the means of production, are appropriately referred to as "capitalists." If it were not for their willingness to accept the risk of investing their capital, the rest of us would not benefit from their businesses' products and services. Nor would we have jobs that provide us with the income we need to live and prosper. They deserve the rewards their investments bring them, just as we deserve the wages we are paid for our labor.

In both Smith's and Locke's theories, there are three common characteristics that define the free market system. These are:

1. The private ownership of goods and services that are produced by someone's labor.

2. The desire for personal gain by trading the labor or goods for something that contributes to our wellbeing or creates a profit.
3. The ability to engage in the voluntary exchange of labor, goods, or services with other individuals seeking the same personal gains.

It is easy to see how this capitalist version of the market differs from other socio-economic systems, such as socialism and communism, where the rights of individuals to own their own labor and to pursue their own self-interests, are limited or prohibited.

So, although we may find people, who for various reasons, believe that our free market (capitalist) system is immoral, unfair, or hedonistic, the truth is that by promoting our own self-interests, we have created a system that is efficient, effective, and contributes to the wellbeing of society as a whole. There is no reason for any of us to feel guilty or apologetic about being a part of such a wonderfully beneficial and fair system.

Notes

1 See Chapter Six and the section covering the social contract for an explanation.
2 John Locke, Second Treatise Concerning Civil Government, Chapter V, 1690

Chapter Two: Social Responsibility

Debates take place on an incessant basis about the role of corporations in society. More specifically, these debates often focus fervently upon the social responsibility of corporations. Proponents of corporate social responsibility want corporations to be "socially conscious" (although many of these proponents seem to have their own definition of what this term means). To fully understand the impact of requiring corporations to exercise some level of social "consciousness," we must first explore what the purpose of a corporation really is.

Corporations exist to deliver value to their shareholders. That's pretty much it. Any other activity that does not contribute to this goal ultimately detracts from it.

According to Milton Friedman, social responsibility of corporations is a "fundamentally subversive doctrine." In his 1962 book, *Capitalism and Freedom*, Friedman proclaims "Few trends could so thoroughly undermine the very foundations of our free society as the acceptance by corporate officials of a social responsibility other than making as much money for their stockholders as possible."[1] What Friedman is saying is that corporations have a singular purpose, and that purpose is to generate a return for their shareholders. In a free economy, "there is one and only one social responsibility of business — to use its resources and engage in activities designed to increase its profits so long as it stays within the rules of the game, which is to say, engages in open and free competition, without deception and fraud."[2]

So, as long as a company plays by the rules, it is expected to pursue the goal of generating as much profit as it can for its shareholders. That is the reason a business exists. Therefore, if a business manager spends the corporation's money or utilizes its resources to promote some social issue other than those imposed by laws and regulations, then that manager is not acting under economic motives, but social motives, and is consequently not acting in the best interests of the shareholders.

When managers act in such a way that they assume the burden of social costs, and use corporate funds to provide for those costs, then they are acting in a role that has traditionally been ascribed to our elected officials, i.e., imposing taxes and then deciding which social programs should be funded. Corporate officers are elected by shareholders but not by the general public. Therefore, the right to impose taxes and indulge in social spending programs is not their responsibility. If we expect our corporate officers to engage in public policy issues such as taxation and social spending, we should elect them to the U.S. Congress but not to the board of directors. Friedman addresses the issue of social responsibility in more detail when he says:

> What does it mean to say that the corporate executive has a "social responsibility" in his capacity as businessman? If this statement is not pure rhetoric, it must mean that he is to act in some way that is not in the interest of his employer. For example, that he is to refrain from increasing the price of the product in order to contribute to the social objective of preventing inflation, even though a price increase would be in the best interests of the corporation. Or that he is to make expenditures on reducing pollution beyond the amount that is in the best interests of the corporation or that is required by law in order to contribute to the social objective of improving the environment. Or that, at the expense of corporate profits, he is to hire "hardcore" unemployed instead of better-qualified available workmen to contribute to the social objective of reducing poverty.
>
> In each of these cases, the corporate executive would be spending someone else's money for a general social interest. Insofar as his actions in accord with his "social responsibility" reduce returns to stockholders, he is spending their money. Insofar as his actions raise the price to customers, he is spending the customers' money. Insofar as his actions lower the wages of some employees, he is spending their money.[3]

Friedman's comments make sense. It is not the responsibility of corporate executives to allocate funds to social programs that would have otherwise gone to shareholders or employees. To do so is to have unelected agents engage in taxation. We reserve this right for our elected officials at the local, state, and federal levels, but not at the corporate level. When corporate officers spend the corporation's money on things that do not contribute to the profits of the corporation, they are violating their responsibility to the corporation's shareholders and imposing a specious form of taxation on those shareholders.

We can better understand this concept if we look at the allocation of corporate resources (capital) to social programs and where that money comes from. A corporation is a legally created entity that acts as a person. It can be taxed, prosecuted, fined, sued, and held responsible just as an individual may be. Therefore, a corporation is a *fictitious* person. But what we fail to understand is that this fictitious person's assets are really the assets of others. Unlike *real* people, corporations are *owned* by other people and have stakeholders. This distinction should not be taken lightly. When a corporation takes its hard-earned capital, usually from its profits, and uses it to fund social programs, we have to realize that this money must come from somewhere. Money taken out of a corporation reduces the amount of capital that can be used to operate or grow that corporation. This non-productive use of capital hurts the stockholders, employees, and other stakeholders in the corporation. Basically, corporations get the money to fund social programs through one or more of three areas:

Dividends — Money that goes into social programs is money that will not be paid in dividends. This could mean lost income to shareholders or reduced stock prices. Shareholders are the big losers here.

Higher Prices — Money that flows out of the corporation must be made up somewhere. Prices might be raised to cover the additional capital outflow. Or conversely, if capital had not been allocated to social programs, that additional capital could have been used to keep prices down. In either case, the consumer loses.

Lower Wages — Money that is used to fund social programs means that the corporation has less money for other operating expenses. Employees may have to work for wages that are lower because there is less capital available for wages. In the worst case, some jobs may be cut over time to make up for the loss of capital that went to social programs. Employees are losers when money is spent on social programs.

It doesn't take a genius to figure out that any amount of capital that flows out of a corporation for social programs is capital that is no longer available to enhance the growth or productivity of the corporation.

Another theory on the responsibilities of business comes from Archie Carroll. Carroll's model of business responsibility deals with more than just the economic aspect that was the basis of Friedman's view of business responsibility. Carroll's view takes into account four different responsibilities of business. He proposes that businesses have economic, legal, ethical, and discretionary responsibilities, and that these responsibilities are prioritized in that order.[4]

To understand Carroll's model of business responsibility, a definition of each of the four specific responsibilities is provided here:

Economic — The responsibility of management to produce goods and services that have a value so the business can generate money and pay its creditors to stay in business.

Legal — The responsibility to obey those laws and regulations promulgated by the government, whether they are anti-pollution laws, equal opportunity laws, or fair business practice regulations.

Ethical — The responsibility to act in accordance with generally held beliefs of society and the prevailing ethical values of that society.

Discretionary — The responsibility that deals with philanthropic and voluntary obligations assumed by the corporation.

These four responsibilities are listed in the order of their priority. Carroll and Friedman agree on the first two of these responsibilities: that a corporation has an economic responsibility to its shareholders to produce a profit; and that a corporation must follow the law when doing so. But even these two responsibilities have different priorities. Economic responsibilities come first, because if a company cannot generate a profit to stay in business, it will cease to exist. This makes economic responsibility a "must do" responsibility of business. If a firm can continue to exist, it has to do so by obeying the law and complying with government regulations. This makes the legal responsibility a "have to do" responsibility of business. The business must make a profit to remain in existence, and it has to do so under the rule of law.

But this is where Friedman and Carroll part company. Carroll takes the responsibility of business further by stressing that businesses have two more responsibilities beyond their economic and legal responsibilities.

Once the basic responsibilities have been met, the company has lower priority social responsibilities to fulfill. The first of these is the company's ethical responsibility. Ethical responsibilities go beyond the law by having a corporation follow the values of the society or local community. For example, having management consult with employees before implementing a new vacation policy or holding meetings with the community prior to deciding to move a plant or implement layoffs, would be a way of exercising ethical responsibilities. This ethical responsibility is an "ought to do" responsibility of business.

Once a firm has satisfied its ethical requirements, it can focus on discretionary responsibilities that are voluntary, such as donating money to various charities, establishing scholarship funds, adopting a highway for cleanup, or sponsoring a training program for handicapped workers. This discretionary responsibility is a "nice to do" responsibility of business.

15

In the case of social responsibilities, Friedman cautions us to recognize those that are really disguised forms of corporate self-interest. When a corporation donates money to a local hospital, a community action group, or to the town's orchestra, it may be doing so in order to gain a benefit, such as an enhanced reputation, good public relations, a better image, etc. Friedman cautions us to recognize that these types of philanthropic actions may really be based on the economic responsibility of making a profit by undertaking these so-called "voluntary" actions. In essence, the corporation hopes that these social actions will result in some economic gain at some point.

The concept that a corporation exists to provide a return first and foremost to its shareholders has long been held as an integral component of the "property rights theory." In 1919, the Michigan Supreme Court issued its ruling in the case of *Dodge v. Ford Motor Co.*[5] The basis of the case was that Henry Ford, who was running Ford Motor Company, believed that the company had made too much profit and should therefore lower its prices in order to share the wealth with the public. The Dodge brothers, who were major shareholders, wanted the profits paid out as dividends to the shareholders. The court ruled in favor of the Dodge brothers, and by doing so it affirmed that the purpose of a corporation was to return a profit to its shareholders. It assumed, and rightly so, that shareholders were the investors in the company and that made them owners of the corporation. As owners, they were entitled to the profits of the business. Investors had a natural expectation that the profits generated by the resources of the corporation were their property. Henry Ford could not use the resources of the company for other purposes, such as social or philanthropic endeavors, which would deprive the shareholders of their dividends.

This concept has been modified over the years as the growth in the number of shareholders has diluted their control of the company. As management exercises more control, shareholders become more passive owners. In modern corporations, shareholders have relinquished control to management, but they have done so in the expectation that management will make decisions that benefit the shareholders. Ownership and control have been separated, making the ownership of corporate property a passive role.[6]

Whether this concept is valid is still being debated. Managers and directors do have fiduciary responsibilities to their corporation's shareholders, regardless of any social responsibilities they may undertake on their own. And although individual shareholders may own so little stock that they can exercise no control or influence over management, the role of corporate managers still requires that they operate in the best interests of their collective shareholders. Failure to do so is one of the leading ethical issues faced by most corporations.

It is widely accepted that management does not have the unrestrained right to do whatever it wants with the corporation's resources. Unless shareholders specifically direct management to allocate resources for endeavors that will have a social or philanthropic function and not a profit-generating function, then how far can management go before it has abused its fiduciary responsibilities? This is where management must walk a fine line, balancing the interests of its shareholders with the interests of other competing stakeholders. Managers often allocate resources to social and philanthropic programs, but as Freidman said, they may be doing so to actually gain some kind of corporate advantage. Managers who use corporate resources for social and philanthropic purposes that do not, at least indirectly, benefit the corporation, create an ethical dilemma for themselves.

Businesses that engage in social programs are not engaging in capitalism, but socialism, which conflicts with the free market system that makes everything work. Often times, the economic responsibility to shareholders conflicts with social responsibilities. Because of the competing nature of economic and social "investments," business responsibilities and social responsibilities are naturally at odds with each other. However, business managers must also be aware of where they are compatible.

There are many instances of corporations that voluntarily undertook social responsibilities by implementing various pollution controls, recycling efforts, energy conservation, or labor reforms, and in doing so achieved significant savings or increased their profits.

What does all of this mean? It means that corporations must not lose sight of why they exist — to generate the greatest return that they can for their shareholders. And they must do this by staying within the law. As long as managers act this way, they are performing their responsibilities in an ethical manner and have nothing to feel guilty about. If, on the other hand, the corporation chooses to go beyond this and participate in social or philanthropic programs, it does so voluntarily with the knowledge that any capital or resources used for social programs is at the expense of its stockholders, customers, or employees. Optimally, managers would consider those programs that have the capability to add something to the bottom line, either due to enhanced image, reputation, or publicity; or through the implementation of voluntary social programs that have the potential to deliver tangible benefits to the company's operations.

We must not confuse social responsibility with ethics, because there is another aspect that often fails to gain consideration, and that is the idea of the "level playing field." Although shareholder value is the foremost responsibility of a corporate manager (and most business school students learn this during their MBA program), the infusion of ethics (which is not the same as social responsibility) with the drive for profits, is necessary to keep the playing field level for everyone: stockholders, employees, management, and customers. Without the glue that is ethics, the business of the corporation will begin to unravel. This is evident in situations like Enron, WorldCom, and so many other corporations we have seen self-destruct. Executives can run their companies and strive for profits, but they must do so by "playing by the rules." This is where ethics comes into play. Ethics is the way we guarantee that the game is being played fairly.

Notes

[1] Milton Friedman, *Capitalism and Freedom* (Chicago: University of Chicago Press, 1962) p. 133.

[2] Friedman.

[3] Milton Friedman, "The Social Responsibility of Business Is to Increase Its Profits," *New York Times Magazine* (September 13, 1970): p. 33.

[4] A.B. Carroll, "A Three-Dimensional Conceptual Model of Corporate Performance," *Academy of Management Review* (October 1979): pp. 497-504.

[5] *Dodge v. Ford Motor Co.*, 170 N.W. 668, 685 (1919).

[6] Adolf A. Berle and Gardiner Means. *The Modern Corporation and Private Property,* (New York: Macmillan, 1932).

Michael P. Harden

Chapter Three: Ambiguity

In 1878, an outbreak of yellow fever occurred in the city of New Orleans. It quickly spread through the city and proved itself to be very deadly. Soon afterward, it began to spread up the Mississippi River basin toward the city of Memphis. In those days, no one knew what caused yellow fever (it was thought to be caused by *miasma*, or bad air), but everyone knew that it could kill you. The people in the city of Memphis heard that it was coming their way. Based on reports coming in from other cities along the Mississippi, they could predict approximately when it would arrive. Yet they did almost nothing to protect themselves.

The local merchants in Memphis, not wanting to see a loss of trade along the river or the prospect of customers leaving town, assured everyone that business would go on as usual. The business community pressured the local government to quell any possible panic, and the government obliged. Soon, the city government, in its attempts to protect business in Memphis, assured everyone that there was still plenty of time; that everything would be fine; that they shouldn't leave town; and most of all, they should not panic. The people believed them and complied.

So business went on as usual. A few people left town, but most stayed. Those that tried to leave were ridiculed and taunted as cowards. Not wanting to appear timid, many people changed their minds and stayed anyway. Everybody continued to work and conduct business as if nothing was going to happen.

Then one day, just about on schedule, a laborer dropped dead down on the wharf. The cause: yellow fever.

People immediately began to panic. They wondered aloud how such a thing could have been allowed to happen. Hadn't the government promised to protect them? Hadn't they been assured that there was no reason to leave town? The government and businesses wouldn't lie to them. What would they do now?

As the fever spread through the town, some of the population hurried and got out in time. Thousands fled in unbridled panic. But in short time, as the government tried to contain the epidemic, the city was quarantined, and armed guards ringed the city. The order went out: anyone attempting to leave would be shot on site. Even so, many caring individuals who could have left before the quarantine, stayed voluntarily to help the sick. Doctors, policemen, and even nuns did their duty. But they were no match for the deadly yellow fever.

The epidemic was worse than anyone predicted. Eventually, before the killer epidemic finally subsided, the city of Memphis had ceased to exist. 5,000 people, or about fifty-five percent of the population that remained in the city died. Every doctor died. Every policeman died. Most of the nuns that cared for the sick died, earning them the title "The Martyrs of Memphis." Ironically, most of the businesses that had been so worried earlier about losing money failed and eventually disappeared.

Finally, the city itself went bankrupt, and with so few citizens left inhabiting it, Memphis lost its charter as a city. It wouldn't regain its status as a city for another fourteen years. Until then, it would remain nothing more than a tax district.[1]

We can look back at this terrible episode in hindsight and question the ethical decisions that were made. It is easy to do so with the information we now have in hand. It is obvious to any of us reading this story that the business community and the government acted unethically by trying to protect businesses at the expense of the citizens. "Profits over lives," we might say. Of course, to us, this decision was absolutely wrong. However, at the time, the decision by the government (prompted by the local merchants) seemed to make perfect sense. There was no reason to believe that Memphis would be hit by an epidemic that was so far away. How could *miasma* (bad air) come all the way up the Mississippi River? And why cause a needless panic that could jeopardize lives and property? The city's life was based on business, and shutting that down would kill the city. The smart thing to do was to protect the city by protecting the business community from what seemed to be an unwarranted panic.

So, at that time, and based on the information available then, the decision was much more ambiguous than it appears to us now in hindsight. Often, ethical decisions are not based on right vs. wrong but on right vs. right, or at least on degrees of right. We are constantly faced with a difficult choice: when all alternatives seem to be right, which one is the most right? This is the dilemma that we face when making ethical decisions. We must often choose from a set of options in which all of them seem to be equally valid or appropriate.

Ambiguity pervades our business environment in a variety of issues. We make business decisions everyday based on information that may be incomplete, wrong, or questionable. Yet we do it...because we must. To do otherwise would cripple our ability to function. In business, we are always rowing upstream. If we stop rowing, we move backwards. So we often make decisions based on ambiguous information. It is the only way we can keep moving. Ethical decision-making is pretty much the same thing.

For many of us, identifying ethical issues is not easy. Very little of what we do as business people, or even as human beings, is straightforward or uncomplicated. We must often make value judgments that affect our business, our employees, our shareholders, and our customers. In many instances, the decision will favor one over the other. One party will receive some benefit, while another party experiences some harm. Making such a decision in a principled way is of great consequence. If we use bad judgment, poor problem-solving skills, or fail to follow generally accepted ethical concepts to make the decision, we place upon ourselves (and our organizations) a tremendous burden of risk. We can find ourselves involved in lawsuits, watch key customers go to our competitors, see productivity drop dramatically as employee morale plummets, or endure a decline in the market value of our company. Basically, none of us can afford to make a really bad decision. There is simply too much at stake.

This is where the ambiguity of ethical issues comes into play. We can all look at right vs. wrong and make the correct decision. But how many of us can look at right vs. right and still make the correct decision? That's because "right" can be in shades of gray rather than in black and white. Some things are more "right" than others. Also, what may be right for one stakeholder may be wrong for another.

Ambiguity also comes from new situations that have never been handled before — situations where we may have no pre-existing rules to guide us. We have seen a lot of this in recent years. No one really knew how to treat software when computers first became popular on our desktops. Could we copy it? Is it property? Who owns it? It took years to work our way through these seemingly easy questions. We also dealt with issues such as AIDS. Is it an illness or a disability? Can we inform other employees if one of their coworkers has it? Is there a right to privacy for the HIV positive worker? What about the right of his coworkers to know that they are working with someone that has a potentially fatal disease? Does HIV or AIDS infer a sexual preference that could cause problems at work?

Once again, we had to work our way through these issues, some of which are still being debated today. Ethical ambiguity is a recurrent problem as new technologies and social issues thrust themselves into the business world. The Internet alone has caused more ethical issues for businesses in recent times than any other single technological development. In fact, there are so many ethical issues spawned from the Internet that they will be discussed in a separate chapter.

Ambiguity can also be found in our inability to distinguish between competing interests. As human beings with various values and differing notions about what is right and what is wrong, we are often faced with some really tough choices. Those choices often involve right vs. right. They are tough because they involve choices where either alternative is based on one of our deeply rooted beliefs. Rushworth M. Kidder listed four such dilemmas that are so common to all of us that they serve as models or paradigms.[2] They are:

> **Truth vs. Loyalty** — We are often placed in situations where we possess some facts that, if revealed, could harm someone to whom we feel some loyalty. For example, we may know about some improper conduct or crucial mistakes made by our boss, but because we have worked for him for years and feel some loyalty toward him, we are conflicted. If the president of the company asks us if we know who is responsible for the problems, we are torn between our value of honesty, which requires us to provide the information, and our loyalty to our boss, which requires us not to cause him any harm. We can either

tell or not tell on our boss, but we cannot do both. Therefore we must choose between two "right" courses of action.

Individual vs. Community — This is a very common dilemma. We are often faced with the competing interests of the individual's rights versus the rights of the community at large. This issue has really come to the forefront with the implementation of Megan's Law[3] that allows authorities to notify communities that there are convicted pedophiles or sex offenders in the community, and identifies whom those offenders are. People have taken both sides of this issue. Some say that identifying sex offenders and making their names and addresses public is a violation of their individual privacy. Others claim that the safety of the community and the right of the community to know about the sex offenders is more important than the rights of the individual. Each side believes that their idea is right. An individual may be in a position where she must choose between the conflicting values of individual rights versus the rights of the community. Another example is whether HIV positive individuals should have their status kept confidential even if they are in a position or situation that could expose others to the HIV virus.

Short-term vs. Long-term — Sometimes we must weigh short-term gains versus long-term gains. For example, a family has three children and money is tight. The parents are faced with a decision as to whether the mother should go back to work to supplement the family's income, even if only for a couple of years. The extra money will allow the family to get out of its heavy debt and maybe even save for a down payment on a house of their own. So the long-term aspects of this decision are obvious — a better life. But the short-term aspects are that the children will have to go to day care rather than having their mother take care of them. This is not something that the parents had anticipated or desired, and they would prefer that the children be at home with their mother. Nevertheless, the parents have to make a choice, and both competing alternatives look equally right based on the circumstances.

Justice vs. Mercy — We are often faced with situations where we have been wronged by someone and have competing desires to punish or forgive. When a woman finds out that her best friend went out on a date with a guy she had been dating herself, she is right to want to punish her friend by not speaking to her, in essence, giving her the "cold shoulder." Yet she also feels a strong bond of friendship and could just as easily "have a talk" with her friend, putting it all behind her. She is right to want some kind of justice, but she is just as right to decide to forgive her longtime friend. She is conflicted between these two competing desires.

We are all faced with these common dilemmas throughout our lives. In each case, the alternatives seem equally right, yet we cannot do both. Having to choose between "right" and "right" is harder than it seems, particularly because there is nothing significant to distinguish between the two competing alternative courses of action.

In order to make the correct moral decision, we must first understand the ambiguity we face and apply solid ethical principles to our decision-making process. But even before that happens, we must first be able to identify that an ethical dilemma actually exists. For example, we can ask people if is it ethically wrong to steal food if their children are starving? Looking at the exact same information, some people will say "yes" while others will say "no." What would you say if you were the parent of a starving child? What if you were the owner of the store from which the food was stolen? The answers will likely be antithetical, as both parties tend to use different concepts and standards to determine the ethical correctness of the action. Only by giving each party a solid foundation in ethical concepts can we reduce the ambiguity and achieve a greater understanding of what is morally correct in a given situation.

Notes

---

[1] Much of this information comes from two sources: *The Yellow Fever Epidemic of 1878 in Memphis Tennessee* by J. M. Keating for the Howard Association, printed in 1879, and a personal account titled: *The Yellow Fever Epidemic of 1878* by Dr. H. A. Gant, 1879.

[2] Rushworth M. Kidder, *How Good People Make Tough Choices* (New York: William Morrow and Company, 1995) pp 18-22.

[3] Megan's Law originated in New Jersey, but versions have been adopted by many states. The statute requires that convicted sexual offenders register their addresses with state and/or local police upon their release from prison. Different state versions of the law also require that the local police take steps to notify the public about the presence of any sexual offenders in their communities.

Michael P. Harden

Chapter Four: Defining Ethics

The term *ethics* has many different meanings. If we are to understand what makes up ethical (or moral) behavior and how to make ethical decisions, we must first establish a foundation by defining what we think ethics really means.

We interchangeably use the terms *moral* and *ethical*. Each word comes from a different root and a different language, yet both have become key words in our language. The word *ethics* derives from the Greek word *ethikos*, while *moral* comes from the Latin word *moralis.* Typically, there is no difference in describing conduct or actions as immoral or unethical since most things that are morally wrong are also ethically wrong. However, in our society, we tend to use the word moral in relation to social issues such as discrimination, racism, abortion, killing, stealing, child abuse, pornography, and other such issues. Ethics, on the other hand, deals with moral philosophy and a more systematic approach to using our moral beliefs. Ethics is really the study of morality and how we use our moral beliefs to establish standards and codes of conduct. Webster offers us these brief definitions:

Ethical — relating to morality of behavior.

Ethics — that branch of philosophy which studies the principles of right or wrong in human conduct...the moral principles which determine the rightness or wrongness of particular acts or activities.[1]

But these are simply definitions of what the words themselves mean. They do not accurately portray the full meaning of what ethics is — with all of its nuances and all of its interpretations. Ethics is a much broader concept requiring a more substantial definition. Practicing ethics often involves making tough decisions, sometimes based on ambiguous information, and weighing the amount of benefit that one party will receive vs. the amount of harm that another party will receive. In order to do this and arrive at the "correct" result, we have to understand the basic underlying philosophy of ethics.

As a college professor that teaches ethics, I often ask my students what they think ethics means. These are the kinds of answers I have gotten:

"It's doing the right thing."
"It's following a moral philosophy."
"It's not hurting someone."
"It's knowing the difference between right and wrong."
"It's knowing what acceptable behavior is."
"It's being fair and honest with other people."
"It's not breaking the law."
"It's acting with integrity."

All of these answers are right to some degree. Yet no single answer is sweeping enough to truly define what ethics means. Perhaps if we roll all of these together, we might come closer to defining ethics.

Some people equate ethics with religion, and it is true that many religions teach us certain moral principles. But religion and ethics are very different, and in fact, may often conflict with each other. Certain religions sometimes teach or espouse philosophies that are acceptable to those that practice that religion, but are extremely offensive to people who practice other religions. Furthermore, if ethics was tied closely to religious beliefs, only those people that followed their religion could be ethical. What about everyone else? Also, religions, in their fervor of believing their religion to be more valid or "correct" than other religions, have often resorted to immoral tactics to impose their morality on others. Remember the Crusades, the Spanish Inquisition, and the Taliban?

Some people equate ethics with the law. Although ethical ideas form the basis for most laws (such as prohibitions against killing, stealing, fraud, and many others), the law often stops short of what ethics must resolve. Laws may not prohibit a corporation from withholding certain information from its employees or shareholders, yet doing so may be considered unethical. We can go to our boss and take credit for a project that our coworkers completed. This is not against the law but it is reasonable to assume that it is unethical. On a more profound scale, slavery was legal in this country for 200 years, yet few people will argue that slavery is morally acceptable. Obviously, not everything that is immoral is against the law. Ethics often goes beyond what the law establishes.

Some people equate ethics with societal values. Society does indeed try to establish values for its members and usually imposes or enforces those values through various sanctions. However, simply because a society establishes standards of behavior doesn't mean those standards are ethical. Moreover, moral beliefs may be shaped by society but that doesn't ensure that those beliefs are morally right. Some societies stone women for adultery. The Nazis persecuted and exterminated Jews. Some societies practice female circumcision. Some societies believe nudity is acceptable, while others completely cover women from head to toe so nothing but their eyes are exposed. So societal values do not necessarily reflect ethical values. People may follow their societal norms, but that does not mean that they should (see Chapter Ten on ethical relativism). Ethics concerns itself not so much with what people *should* do (which can be determined by society or the law), but with what they *ought* to do (which is determined by our moral values).

Because there are so many aspects to ethics, people often have a difficult time articulating anything beyond a very basic definition, for example, "the ability to know the difference between right and wrong." Although that is a good start, we can explore the concept of ethics a little further. Here are some key points that contribute to our understanding of the concept of ethics and ethical behavior:

- Ethics deals with the concept of minimizing the harm to other people. People can and do harm each other through their decisions and the actions that flow from those decisions. Machines, on the other hand, may also harm people, but there is no thought process involved so there are no ethical issues at stake. Machines can harm people because something goes wrong but not because the machine actually made a decision to harm someone. Ethics examines the effects that our decisions have on people. Ethical decisions should strive to minimize harm to others.[2]

- Ethical issues are always about human beings and what they do to each other. Ethics deals with human interactions, human interests, human harm, and conflicts between human beings. Ethical issues surface when something that is valued by human beings is at stake.[3] This is why we exclude machines and objects from ethical issues.[4]

- Making defensible decisions is a part of ethics. When we make decisions that affect others, we want to be sure that those decisions are based on sound moral principles, are well-reasoned, and are completely defensible in regard to ethical concepts and standards. What this means is that when we find ourselves in an ethical dilemma, we "rationally examine alternative options and choose the best one."[5] We make a judgment that is based on our values, the values of others, and the values of our institutions; and we do it in a logical and rational way by applying ethical principles so that our decision can be adequately defended. This is important because different people, looking at the same ethical dilemma, can come to different decisions, both of which may appear to be the "right" decision. The most "right" decision is the one that can be defended using sound ethical principles.

Ethics refers to making principle-based decisions that examine alternatives and makes a choice based on standards of right and wrong that prescribe what human beings *ought* to do. These standards are usually defined in terms of rights, obligations, benefits to society, fairness, or specific virtues. Ethics, for example, refers to those standards that impose the reasonable obligations to refrain from rape, stealing, murder, assault, slander, and fraud. Ethical standards also include those that enjoin virtues of honesty, compassion, and loyalty. And ethical standards include standards relating to rights, such as the right to life, the right to freedom from injury, and the right to privacy. Such standards are adequate standards of ethics because they are supported by consistent and well founded reasons."[6]

The field of ethics is often referred to as moral philosophy and "involves systematizing, defending, and recommending concepts of right and wrong behavior."[7] To do this effectively, we must understand the three subject areas under which different ethical theories fall. These are:

Metaethics — This examines what our ethical concepts and ideas mean, and where they come from. Metaethics explores such concepts as natural laws, universal truths, and what forms the basis for our ethical and moral beliefs.

Normative ethics — This is the practical aspect of ethics. It deals with arriving at moral standards that determine right and wrong behavior. To fully understand the normative concept, we can look to the Golden Rule: "Do unto others as you would have them do unto you." For example, if I would not want people to cheat me in a business deal, then I should not cheat others when dealing with them. If I would not want someone to fire me without cause, then I should not fire others without cause. Stated simply, normative ethics seeks to determine the proper behavior for a given ethical dilemma. Some normative theories that we will examine in this book are: deontological theory, consequentialist theory, and virtue theory. All three theories will be explained and examined in subsequent chapters of this book.

Applied ethics — This area of ethics deals with taking our ethical theories and applying them to specific issues that are of great moral concern and likely to be controversial. These can be issues such as racism, AIDS, abortion, capital punishment, animal rights, gun control, homosexuality, doctor-assisted suicide, and cloning. In a business environment, applied ethics can deal with issues such as insider trading, job discrimination, drug testing, whistle-blowing, workplace privacy, sexual harassment, employee rights, and business social responsibility.

As we examine ethics in more detail, all of these three subject areas will be covered.

Notes

---

[1] New Webster's Dictionary and Thesaurus of the English Language. Lexicon Publications. 1992.

[2] Corporations, which are "artificial" people because they are legally treated as such, can cause harm through the decisions they make. So when we talk about humans harming other humans, we naturally include corporations.

[3] Deborah G. Johnson, Computer Ethics, 3rd Edition (Prentice Hall, 2001) p. 17.

[4] See 2 above.

[5] Ernest A. Kallman and John P. Grillo. Ethical Decision Making and Information Technology. 2nd Edition (Irwin/McGraw Hill, 1996) p. 7.

[6] Santa Clara University, Markkula Center for Applied Ethics. www.scu.edu/ethics.

[7] The Internet Encyclopedia of Philosophy. www.utm.edu/research/iep/e/ethics.htm

Michael P. Harden

Chapter Five: Can Ethics Be Learned?

Suppose for a moment that you are recruiting new management trainees for your company. One of your candidates is a recent graduate of a top business school with the ink still wet on her MBA diploma. Another is a recently released ex-convict with the ink still wet on his parole. Who should you hire?

If you are looking for someone with high ethical standards, a sense of loyalty, and a desire to put the customer first, you should probably pick the ex-con over the MBA. It turns out that convicts have higher ethical standards than business school graduates in many situations. So, if your company is stressing ethical behavior, a convicted felon may be a better choice than an MBA. That may seem shocking, but a recent study confirms it.

In a Ball State University study[1] that compared the ethical values of convicted felons to those of MBA students, some interesting findings came to light. Although the prison inmates and MBAs scored fairly evenly in many categories, the survey found that:

- Convicts valued loyalty and group trust more than the MBAs valued those characteristics.

- While MBA students put the interests of the stockholders first, convicts put the needs of the customers first.

- 73 percent of the MBA students said they would hire a competitor's employees who had knowledge of a profitable discovery while only 59 percent of the convicts said they would do so.

In today's world of high profile ethical lapses where corporate executives gut their companies to enrich themselves at the expense of their shareholders and employees, many of us are questioning what has happened to good old-fashioned ethics. WorldCom, Enron, Tyco, and Adelphia Communications all had codes of conduct that were supposed to provide ethical guidelines for *all* of their employees. Yet, this didn't seem to matter to senior executives who didn't give a second thought to breaking any rule in their quest for personal enrichment. When we turn on the nightly news and see executives being taken away in handcuffs, we are flabbergasted. We ask ourselves whether our universities are teaching ethics anymore.

The days of MBA students idolizing the titans of industry have long since passed away. Recent opinion polls now rate business executives in lower esteem than politicians. A Harris Poll[2] conducted in 2002, found some interesting changes in the way people look at business executives. 87% of the adults surveyed said that top company managers are paid more than they deserve, and 87% also said that top managers become rich at the expense of ordinary workers. 85% said that they were *angry* about this situation, with the highest percentage in the 50 years and older group (93%). Clearly, the public is not happy with the greed they perceive in the top echelons of management in our corporations. These attitudes are creating a drop in the status to which CEOs and others have previously been accustomed. This drop in status can be seen in a Gallup Poll conducted after many of the corporate scandals came to light. While 84% of the people surveyed said that most teachers could be trusted, only 23% said the same for CEOs of large corporations. CEOs came out only slightly ahead of HMO managers and car dealers, and tied with stockbrokers. It is quite a statement about the status of our corporate executives when the survey showed that journalists, lawyers, government officials, rich people, and accountants scored higher in trust than did CEOs.[3]

This dramatic loss of status has forced business school students to become preoccupied with studying corporate responsibility and business ethics. MBAs may soon place less emphasis on traditional business skills and more emphasis on ethics and integrity as they try to offset the current stigma attached to corporate executives. The business schools themselves have figured out that imparting ethical values and moral leadership may be just as important as teaching someone how to read a balance sheet or do a SWOT analysis. William G. Christie, dean of the Owen Graduate School of Management at Vanderbilt University said: "If courses in ethics and moral leadership are not already part of the curriculum, they had better be."[4] Corporate recruiters are expecting business school graduates to have received some level of leadership and ethics instruction before receiving their diplomas.

In the past, business school students dreamt about the next dot-com company. Now, they have been dragged back into the real world, and their new watchword is "ethics." The excesses of the 1990s, where business school students looked at their future corporate roles as step-pingstones to self-enrichment, have given way to a more realistic view of their futures. Whereas, in the past, CEOs and other senior executives used their positions to amass great wealth through excessive salaries and obscene stock options, the recent spate of corporate scandals and prosecuted executives has begun to change the attitudes of students. We now realize that all of these executives who made millions of dollars, didn't do it because they were financial wizards or business geniuses, but because they were nothing more than dishonest crooks that manipulated their companies' numbers. As history has repeatedly shown us, dishonest people can make as much money as smart people.

During the 1990s, various studies showed a decline in ethics among business students. A 1996 role-playing experiment by business schools showed that 76 percent of MBA students were willing to commit fraud by understating a write-off that reduced their company's profits.[5] A 1995 study by professors at the University of Dayton and Wright State University[6] that surveyed approximately 3,000 business school students at 31 American colleges and universities, found that students highly assessed their own moral self-image, while concurrently demonstrating unethical conduct. On average, students rated themselves on an ethical scale as an 84 out of a possible 100. Yet, nearly one-half of the students in the survey admitted cheating and lying. Of these students, the average respondent confessed to cheating around 12% of the time and lying around 15% of the time. Moreover, of the entire group, only 5.2% said they did not cheat at all! There is an obvious disconnect here.

MBAs coming into the business world are responsible for much of the corporate fraud that is taking place. While the big scandals such as Enron, WorldCom, Adelphia, and Tyco get all of the publicity, the statistics show that smaller amounts of fraud are rampant among managers. Every two years, Ernst & Young conducts a worldwide survey of corporate fraud. The most recent survey found that more than two-thirds of the companies around the world report having been the victim of corporate crime. 85% of the fraud was committed by employees, but most shocking was the fact that 55% of the fraud came from management. Of those managers who committed fraud, *85% were new managers who had been in their jobs for less than a year.* This phenomenon, according to Nick Hodson, a partner at Ernst & Young, indicates that "it pays to keep a close eye on new management."[7] The study also revealed that there has been a significant jump in fraud since the last survey. Two years ago, only 33% of the fraud came from management. This year, 55% came from management. That's quite an increase. Clearly, business school graduates and others who are entering management are responsible for much of the fraud taking place in corporations today. We must ask ourselves why this epidemic of management-based fraud is becoming so widespread.

Elizabeth Kiss, director of Duke University's Kenan Institute for Ethics, says that she has noticed more of a "bottom-line mentality" among business students.[8] Kiss said that recent studies have shown an increase in cheating among college students and that "business majors are among the ones who cheat at the highest rates." It seems that the focus on producing a profit and the bottom-line orientation of business education fosters a lack of ethical judgment.

As a professor, I can personally attest to this phenomenon. The most alarming thing is that out all of the classes that I teach, the greatest amount of cheating and plagiarism takes place in my ethics classes. Perhaps there is some ironic message here that I haven't yet been able to decipher.

Why are we faced with this situation? Is it because ethics can't be taught? Even *The Wall Street Journal* bemoaned in an editorial the proposition that ethics courses in school are a waste of time since ethics isn't something that can be taught. You either have it or you don't. But if ethics is knowing what we should do in a given situation, then why can't we teach people the skills they need to make the morally correct decision?

Well, most ethicists think that we can.

Lawrence Kohlberg, the late Harvard psychologist, believed that a person's ability to make ethical decisions develops in stages and that this development could be influenced by providing education on ethical decision-making.[9] There are three levels of moral development for individuals, and each level is made up of two stages. In Kohlberg's reasoning, an individual's moral development is directly tied to that person's maturity and growth.

According to Kohlberg, the first stage of ethical or moral development takes place in childhood. Kohlberg called this the *preconventional* level. As children, we have no concept of right and wrong. We must therefore define right and wrong based on what our parents or other authority figures teach us. This has to do with rewards and punishment. As children, if we tell a lie or steal from our playmates, we are faced with certain consequences. So a child in this stage of moral development might say that telling a lie is wrong because Mommy says so or because Daddy may send him to his room without supper. Or even worse, the child might get spanked for his actions. In this stage, the child is guided by his fear of being punished. In the second stage of the *preconventional* level, the child begins to realize that good behavior is rewarded. Perhaps he receives praise or a treat for doing something good. The child is now motivated by his desire to receive a particular reward. Some people never get beyond the *preconventional* level. They consistently define right and wrong based on whether it will bring them rewards or inflict some harm upon them.

The second level of ethical development deals with group norms. It is called the *conventional* level. This is where adolescents fit. In the first stage, they tend to look at right and wrong based on group loyalties, i.e., loyalties to their friends, their families, their school, or even their country. They begin to appreciate the importance of social norms and moral rules. When confronted with an ethical decision, adolescents will behave based on how they believe their group or family would behave. This stage is often called the "Good Boy/Nice Girl" stage. In the second stage of this level, the adolescent begins to identify with laws, forming an understanding of what being a "good citizen" is all about. People who remain in the *conventional* level of ethical development will often make ethical or moral decisions based on what they believe society expects them to do.

The third and final level of ethical development is what Kohlberg called the *postconventional* level. Adults in this stage no longer define right and wrong based on societal norms or group loyalty. Instead, they define right and wrong in more universal principles. Concepts such as human rights and justice come into play. We do things not because society expects us to, but because we believe our actions to be the right thing to do. We do not require confirmation from society to motivate us to do the right thing. In fact, in some cases, we may make decisions that conflict with social norms because they are not consistent with our moral principles. The first stage is defined based on the concept of the social contract and governed by the "Golden Rule." We fully appreciate the importance of living up to our agreements, whatever they may be. The final stage of this level of moral development is where we begin to act on moral principles because they are also our own principles. In essence, adults in the *postconventional* stage look at ethical issues from a broader perspective of how they affect everyone's interests.

Kohlberg discovered that courses in ethics that stressed looking at issues from a more universal perspective would actually move people upward from one stage to another. Subsequent research has proven these findings to be valid. The bottom line is that we need to move people from a level where they look at ethical situations in terms of rewards vs. punishments, to a level where they can fully appreciate the bigger picture — how their decisions impact others, and what that impact means.

Many ethicists and moral philosophers concur with Kohlberg's conclusions that ethics, or at least ethical behavior, can be learned. Understanding that ethics can be learned, and therefore taught as well, is important, particularly when we look at the current situation in our business schools.

In 2001, the Aspen Institute did a study of 1,978 graduates of 13 of the top international business schools.[10] Some of the schools included in the survey were: the London Business School, Columbia, the University of Pennsylvania, Northwestern, the University of Virginia,

Yale, Notre Dame, and Carnegie Mellon. The findings were startling. The study found that business school education not only fails to improve the moral character of its students, but it actually weakens it.[11] Students' attitudes were examined at three different points during their MBA program: upon entering the school, at the end of year one, and upon their graduation. Here are some of the findings of the study:

- There is a shift in priorities during the two years of business school from customer needs and product quality to the importance of shareholder value. Upon entering business school, 68% of the students said that maximizing shareholder value was one of the primary responsibilities of a company. Two years later, the number had increased to 75%.

- MBA students are not sure as to whether and how social responsibility contributes to business success.

- MBAs do not believe that they can change the values or culture of a company. If there is a conflict between their values and their company's values, they would rather quit than try to change things in the organization.

- When entering business school, 43% said that producing useful and high quality products was one of the primary responsibilities of a company. Two years later, the number had dropped to 32%.

One of the issues that should give all of us concern is that so many of the MBAs in this survey said that they would leave their companies rather than try to change any unethical values. This means they have given up before even starting. It also means that they are unlikely to become whistle blowers and report any misconduct they observe. This trend is easily observed in the phenomenon that took place at Enron. There were hundreds of people who knew, or had an idea of what was going on within Enron, yet not a single person spoke up publicly or contacted any regulatory agencies. If this kind of action had occurred about a year before the company's implosion, it might have been avoided, saving shareholders and employees millions of dollars.

In the National Business Ethics Survey (NBES) conducted by the Ethics Resource Center[12] in 2000, 8% of senior and middle managers, and 15% of all other employees, said that they feel pressured to commit misconduct on the job. Of those people who said they felt pressured, 28% said the pressure came from coworkers, 39% said it came from supervisors, and 36% said the pressure came from top management. Environments where the pressure to commit misconduct is culturally pervasive are difficult to change from the bottom up. MBAs that were surveyed in the Aspen Institute study clearly appreciated this when they said they would rather leave than try to change their companies' values. Realizing the futility of trying to implement change when they are not in charge, these MBAs would rather take the easy way out. Should our top business school graduates join our corporate management teams with this kind of defeatist attitude? Do we not want ethically aware individuals working in our companies at all levels and helping to influence our corporate cultures? After all, a rising tide raises all ships.

If we truly want our employees and managers to act ethically, we need to teach them that ethical companies actually do better and are more profitable than unethical companies. This paradigm, which studies[13] have shown to be valid, would extinguish the conflict we experience between our desire to increase shareholder value (which is our corporate responsibility), and our need to be ethical (which is our social responsibility). We must teach ourselves that the two are more conjoined than they are conflicted. From a shareholder perspective, if ethical practices positively impact the bottom line, then our corporate responsibility to increase shareholder value includes acting ethically. To emphasize this point, take the following brief multiple-choice quiz:

1. Which of the following executives delivered long term value to their shareholders?

    a. Kenneth Lay (Enron)
    b. Dennis Koslowski (Tyco)
    c. John Rigas (Adelphia)
    d. Gary Winnick (Global Crossing)
    e. Bernie Ebbers (WorldCom)
    f. Martha Stewart (Martha Stewart Living Omnimedia)
    g. None of the above

2. Which of these executives cost their shareholders hundreds of millions of dollars?

    a. Kenneth Lay (Enron)
    b. Dennis Koslowski (Tyco)
    c. John Rigas (Adelphia)
    d. Gary Winnick (Global Crossing)
    e. Bernie Ebbers (WorldCom)
    f. Martha Stewart (Martha Stewart Living Omnimedia)
    g. All of the above

Of course, the answer is "g." in both cases. The unethical practices of these executives did not deliver any long-term value to their shareholders, and in fact, collectively cost their shareholders billions of dollars. If there was ever an argument that unethical practices are incompatible with shareholder value, these six people certainly prove it.

There are also numerous other examples of recent scandals dealing with questionable accounting practices and other questionable tactics devised to increase shareholder value by hiding losses or artificially inflating profits. Many companies are finding that they must now "restate their earnings." And there are also accounting firms, like Arthur Andersen, that have lost their credibility and subsequently disintegrated due to their inability to maintain a minimal ethical standard for their business practices. It is a sad commentary on our business ethics when the very organizations that are supposed to oversee the accounting practices of our corporations, fail to uphold even minimal ethical standards.

What is interesting in many of these companies is that the executives were so driven to increase the value of their companies for their shareholders (which also resulted in tremendous personal gains for them) that they resorted to unethical tactics to do so. The result was a short-term ride that dramatically drove up stock prices, but like a pyramid scheme, it can only last so long before it collapses. As smart as most of these executives were, they were not bright enough to figure out this obvious flaw in their plans. You can only hide losses and debt, or inflate sales and earnings, for so long before it eventually comes to light, either through an *honest* auditor, which seems to be rare, or through a financial catastrophe, which is more likely. In any case, these practices are destined to doom your company in the long run.

In other cases, the intent was not to deceive shareholders and the market about earnings, but was for a far more sinister reason. Executives decided to use their companies like personal piggy banks that they could reach into whenever they wanted cash and take out whatever they could with impunity.

In the case of Martha Stewart, her desire to avoid a *personal* loss of several thousand dollars on 3,928 shares of ImClone stock eventually cost her company's shareholders megabucks in lost value. It also cost her personally as well as financially. Her personal reputation and image has been tarnished, perhaps beyond repair. She has become a poster child for personal greed. Financially, she lost over $400 million on her 30 million shares of her company's stock as a result of the scandal. She was also indicted on nine counts, including securities fraud, conspiracy, and obstruction of justice.[14] All of this over ImClone stock whose value was only $228,000 (it is estimated she only saved $40,000 on the sale). We are forced to wonder: when you are worth hundreds of millions of dollars, why would you do something so stupid that it would jeopardize your personal fortune and your company's value to save such a small amount? The answer is not surprising. It is because people who have achieved such enormous wealth and power often feel that they can operate outside of normal moral and ethical restraints. This is an example of the *preconventional* stage described by Kohlberg. The rightness or wrongness of a situation is based on its possible rewards and punishments.

Executives find it relatively easy to manipulate their earnings through accounting tricks. Some of these "tricks" may even be legal in certain conditions (and are often taught in our business schools' finance courses), but are they ethical? Since earnings are one of the primary factors that influence the value of a company's stock, executives are more likely to manipulate these numbers to improve their corporation's value. What these executives fail to see is that this practice can only continue for so long before it is discovered. Here are some examples of companies that misstated their earnings, and what happened when it was discovered:

Enron — bankrupt
WorldCom — bankrupt
Tyco — stock fell 59%
Kmart — bankrupt
McKesson HBOC — stock fell 82%
Informix — stock fell 89%
Sunbeam — bankrupt
Safety-Kleen — stock fell 96%
Summit Medical — stock fell 90%

None of these companies returned any value to their shareholders in the long term, and in fact, cost their shareholders billions. When we are finally able to teach our MBAs this valuable lesson, they will be more likely to take a balanced approach to shareholder responsibilities and ethical responsibilities. If it has not become obvious to them yet, our business schools need to make it obvious that using unethical practices to increase shareholder value actually has the opposite effect of decreasing shareholder value. The lesson should be:

1. Shareholder value is your primary responsibility.
2. Unethical practices decrease shareholder value.

3. Therefore, you must maintain acceptable ethical standards to satisfy your primary responsibility.
4. Conclusion: Shareholder value and ethical conduct are inseparable.

It is true that conducting business in an ethical manner is no guarantee of success. A poor business strategy, lack of capital, an inferior product, or any of a million other factors can prevent a business from becoming successful. *Nothing can guarantee success.* However, the empirical and anecdotal data does demonstrate strongly that unethical conduct will hurt a business, not necessarily in the near term, but certainly in the long term. This is the message that business schools and ethics training programs should be sending to our students and corporate managers.

Although it may be difficult to teach someone to become ethical or moral if they are not, it is relatively easy to teach someone how to make an ethical decision. While teaching someone how to *be* ethical requires changing his or her values, which is not an easy task, teaching someone how to recognize an ethical dilemma and come to a defensible decision is much easier. Ethical decision-making is a systematic process that can be learned and practiced. Teaching this process in our business schools (and in our corporations) makes sense because providing someone with the appropriate ethical tools allows them to make the best ethical decisions.

Jeffrey Skilling, the former CEO of Enron (and a Harvard MBA), spent agonizing hours in front of Congressional committees denying he even knew anything unethical was going on under his watch. From his performance before the committee, we are forced to conclude that he is either incompetent or dishonest. There seems to be no other rational reason for his amnesia before the committee. Shouldn't we expect MBAs from prestigious schools like Harvard to have a better grasp of what is ethical and what is not? As a minimum, they should at least be smart enough to know what is going on in the corporations they run. Claiming: "I didn't know what they were doing," isn't going to be good enough anymore.

MBAs should take note of the fact that in just a little more than a year since the fall of Enron, executives from WorldCom, Adelphia Communications, Kmart, Qwest Communications, Tyco International, ImClone Systems, and Enron have been charged with various crimes and face heavy fines and long prison terms if found guilty. As an example, at the date of the writing of this book, Andrew Fastow, the 41 year-old former CFO of Enron, has 109 charges in his indictment. His wife and nine other Enron executives also face numerous charges for fraud, money laundering, and filing false tax returns. Sam Waksal, former head of ImClone, pleaded guilty to six felony counts related to insider trading, and was sentenced to 87 months in prison, $3 million in fines, and forced to pay an additional $1.26 million in restitution.

In a final bit of chutzpah, Enron, Qwest, WorldCom, and several other companies are now seeking millions in tax refunds for the income taxes they overpaid on the bogus earnings they falsely claimed.

There are many lessons to be learned from the business scandals with which we have become so familiar. Our business schools need to teach history as well as strategic planning. It would be a great benefit to our future CEOs and the companies they will eventually run if we could teach them that "Those who cannot remember the past are condemned to repeat it."[15]

Notes

[1] James M. Stearns and Shaheen Borna. *A Comparison of the Ethics of Convicted Felons and Graduate Business Students: Implications for Business Practice and Business Ethics Education.* Ball State University, Muncie, Indiana, 1999.

[2] The Harris Poll, #55 (October 18, 2002) survey of 2,023 adults.

[3] The Gallup Poll survey (July 2002) also showed that middle class people and people who run small businesses scored near the top with 75% saying they can be trusted.

[4] Jennifer Merritt, "For MBAs, Soul-Searching 101; B-schools are emphasizing ethics and responsibility," *Business Week* (Sept 16, 2002): p. 64

[5] Cathy Lazere, "Ethically Challenged," *CFO, The Magazine for Senior Financial Executives* (April 1997): p. 40

[6] Philip H. Varherr, Joseph A. Petrick, John F. Quinn, and Thomas J. Brady. "The Impact of Gender and Major on Ethical Perceptions of Business Students: Management Implications for the Accounting Profession," *Journal of Academy of Business Administration I* (Spring 1995) p. 46.

[7] "It's an inside job — Majority of corporate fraudsters on the payroll," Ernst & Young press release, Toronto (February 20, 2003).

[8] Patrick O'Neill, "Corporate scandals spotlight need for ethics training; business schools foster bottom-line mentality that sidelines issues of right and wrong, some say," *National Catholic Reporter* (August 2, 2002): p. 15

[9] Lawrence Kohlberg, *The Psychology of Moral Development: The Nature and Validity of Moral Stages* (New York: Harper & Row, 2000).

[10] "Where Will They Lead? MBA Student Attitudes About Business & Society." Aspen Initiative for Social Innovation through Business, 2001.

[11] Amitai Etzioni, "When It Comes to Ethics, B-Schools Get an F," *Washington Post* (August 4, 2002): p. B04

[12] The survey included 1,500 employees in the U.S.

---

[13] See Introduction: 1992 Kotter and Heskett study, and 2000 KPMG study.

[14] Martha Stewart was not indicted on the originally alleged offense of insider trading, but was indicted on criminal charges based on her "cover-up" including conspiracy, obstruction of justice, and securities fraud. The SEC has filed a separate civil suit alleging securities fraud and insider trading.

[15] Geroge Santayana, (1863—1952), U.S. philosopher, poet. "Reason in Common Sense," *Life of Reason,* ch. 12 (1905-6).

Michael P. Harden

Chapter Six: Teleological Theory

Teleological theories of ethics hold that what makes an action right or wrong is determined strictly by the *consequences* of that action. This is often referred to as *consequentialism*, but the main teleological ethics theory is known as *utilitarianism*.

Utilitarianism

Utilitarianism, which derives its name from the word utility, stresses the outcomes of behavior or actions and the amount of good those actions produce. In utilitarian theory, actions are morally right and justified if they produce more good than evil. In essence, utilitarians would suggest that our actions as human beings should be based on achieving the greatest amount of good for the greatest amount of people. This can be better defined by looking at the differences between benefits and harm. If an action benefits people and promotes their wellbeing, it is basically good, and therefore morally right. If an action harms people and makes them worse off, it is considered evil or bad, and is morally wrong. Looking at it in these terms, utilitarianism is a fairly simple principle.

Utilitarianism, and its consequential basis, provides us with a fairly objective method for making ethical decisions. We must simply ask ourselves whether the actions we are taking will generate benefits or harm to the greatest amount of people. This particular aspect of utilitarianism is not only relevant for our personal lives, but relevant for business dealings as well. In both personal situations and business situations, we can look at our possible choices of actions and their likely consequences, and by determining whether those consequences produce the most good for the most people, we can make the morally correct decision.

One of the easiest examples of looking at the consequences of an action is the very act of lying. We generally believe that lying is morally wrong because if lying were commonplace, i.e., if everyone did it, society in general would be harmed, and that consequence is what makes lying morally wrong.

On the other hand, there are times when lying is justified in a teleological context. For example, during World War II, the Allies went to great lengths to give false information to the Nazis prior to the D-Day invasion in order to protect allied soldiers' lives and to provide a strategic advantage for the invasion. Few people would suggest that this "lying" was not justified based on its outcome. At a more local level, we realize and accept the fact that police often lie about evidence (or withhold information) during an investigation in order to protect their sources or to keep information from suspects who might use it to escape arrest. And finally, on a personal level, we might lie to our spouses in order to keep from hurting their feelings. When a wife tells her overweight husband that he doesn't look fat in his new pants, or a husband tells his wife that her new hair style makes her look younger, the lies are morally justified because they produce happiness for our spouses and do no harm to anyone. And in fact, the lies may even make our lives better as well since we will not have to deal with the wrath of a hurt and upset spouse for the next week. So the lies produce happiness for our spouses and ourselves, and they reduce the amount of possible harm to us as well. Everybody wins.

To carry the examples even further, we can ask ourselves if it is morally justified for an out-of-work father to steal food from the local grocery store in order to feed his starving children. A utilitarian would most likely say "yes." The good consequences of the action (feeding starving children) far outweigh any bad actions (stealing). Furthermore, the loss to the grocer is nominal compared to the benefit provided to the starving children. It should be noted, however, that the law typically makes no such moral distinction.

Utilitarianism works well in determining morally correct actions as long as the consequences of the action are easily measured. Sometimes it is hard to determine how the consequences may affect all of the various stakeholders involved. Since utilitarianism is basically a balancing act — attempting to balance the level of pain, harm, or happiness against the level of pleasure, benefit, or sadness — it is not always clear as to which consequences are good and which ones are bad.

We must be careful, however, when we use utilitarian principles to justify our actions without weighing other factors as well. If we go by the strictest definition of utilitarianism, we could easily justify morally wrong actions. In a utilitarian world, the practice of slavery can be justified as morally acceptable. If a society determines that holding a small number of people as slaves so that they can produce more products and provide the rest of us with more leisure time, then we could say that slavery produces the most good for the greatest amount of people. Obviously, some people (the slaves) would be harmed by it, but they are relatively few in number, and the vast majority of us would benefit greatly. Yet we all know that slavery is morally reprehensible and can never be justified in an enlightened society. This is the basic weakness of utilitarian theory. Some critics of utilitarianism suggest that following utilitarian principles can lead to the sacrifice of a few for the benefit of many. This is not necessarily an incorrect assumption. The real issue is at what level would these sacrifices be made. For example, should a manager terminate six mediocre employees so that their salaries could be redirected into a better health insurance plan for all of the remaining employees? If this creates a better situation for the remaining workers and helps the company retain good employees, isn't the "sacrifice" of the six employees morally justified? Haven't more people benefited from this action than were harmed?

Utilitarian principles, which make sense when we look at their underlying philosophy of creating the greatest benefit for the most people, have been used to justify terrible actions. The Nazis justified their medical experiments on helpless concentration camp prisoners by claiming that the results of their barbarous experiments would benefit mankind. Their utilitarian approach was based on the small sacrifice of a few for the benefit of many. The Nazi leadership decided that it was morally justified to put the state ahead of the individual. Doctors, who believed they were acting for the benefit of the state, took it upon themselves to conduct experiments that would supposedly improve the health of the nation. They gladly relinquished their roles as caretakers and healers, abandoning the Hippocratic Oath (and any moral reservations in the process) in order to serve the state.

After the fall of the Third Reich, the victorious nations drafted the *Nuremberg Code*. This code of conduct expressly forbade the experimentation on subjects without their voluntary consent, meaning "...without the intervention of any element of force, fraud, deceit, duress, over-reaching, or other ulterior form of constraint or coercion; and [he] should have sufficient knowledge and comprehension of the elements of the subject matter involved as to enable him to make an understanding and enlightened decision."[1] The purpose of the Nuremberg Code was to prevent future abuses of the utilitarian principle as a justification for forced or involuntary experimentation.

Politicians, in particular, have a hard time using the utilitarian approach correctly. Their measurement of pleasure (benefit) vs. pain (harm) is not objective, being tainted by political considerations, and therefore leads to a corruption of the utilitarian ethical principle. For example, let's assume that there is a political party that wants to gain control of the Senate, and there are upcoming elections that will determine this control. This party may go to great lengths to hold up vital economic or trade legislation in order to keep the current economy stalled. They believe that a poor economy reflects on the opposing party and would therefore give them a political advantage in the upcoming elections. So they will morally justify their actions in holding up necessary legislation, even though the poor economy will have a detrimental effect on their constituents, in the belief that the good consequences of their actions outweigh the Machiavellian means. Stated more simply, they believe that winning the elections and gaining control of the Senate is more important than improving the economy. Therefore, keeping the economy "in the tank" is justified because the benefits (pleasure) of having their party in control, is greater than the harm (pain) of a poor economy.

The problem here is that this is a purely subjective judgment on their part. These politicians have lost their ability to objectively measure the pain vs. pleasure of this situation. Their belief that their party must gain control of the Senate at all costs in order to be able to advance their agenda, which they believe is the right agenda for the country, means that everything else is less important. The perceived benefit of their party being in control and able to implement their policies (pleasure) far outweighs any injurious effects of a poor economy (pain). But this belief may not reflect the true situation or the beliefs of the people affected by the poor economy. Can the ideology of any party outweigh the impact of a poor economy on 290 million people? If you think so, you probably have not talked to any of the 290 million people who are dealing with the economic downturn. These politicians have lost sight of what is really important, and in doing so, have used the utilitarian approach to justify actions based on an incorrect measurement of pleasure vs. pain. Their subjective measurement of pleasure, which is based solely on political goals, has skewed their judgment in favor of winning an election over improving the economy. People who are neither politicians nor worried about who controls the Senate, might measure things differently and propose that improving the economy provides more benefit (pleasure) to the country than a particular party gaining control of the Senate.

Although politicians are more likely to subjectively measure pain vs. pleasure, corporate management is not immune from losing objectivity either. Therefore, business managers must be careful to ensure that they do not fall into this same subjective trap in measuring the consequences of their actions in business decisions.

The theory of utilitarianism proposes that actions are right if they produce a greater balance of pleasure over pain. This does not mean that we are required to produce pleasure with the absence of pain. It simply means that pain may be produced by our actions, but in weighing the pain against the pleasure that the actions achieve, the balance should be in favor of the pleasure. Few actions will achieve 100% pleasure for all parties involved. Typically, in any transaction — personal or business — someone will be harmed while someone else will receive some benefit. It is the measure of the amount of harm against the amount of benefit that determines the moral or ethical correctness of the action.

In a business situation, we can look at utilitarianism as a cost-benefit analysis. This is easy for any businessperson to understand. In a cost-benefit analysis, we weigh the cost of an investment or program against the return it generates for the business. This is typically done in monetary terms. If the return is greater than the cost, we can assume that the investment is generally acceptable, based on corporate parameters. Utilitarianism is much the same except that evaluations are not done using monetary calculations —although money may come into play as part of the ethical decision. In a utilitarian approach, we could compare the corporate financial cost-benefit analysis to the act of weighing the needs of customers against the needs of shareholders, or the needs of shareholders against the needs of employees. These comparisons deal more with human consequences, although monetary factors may be an element of the outcome.

Monetary considerations may take the form of measuring corporate benefits vs. those of the community or the employees. This often happens when management must decide on implementing a lay-off to cut costs or moving a plant to Mexico to take advantage of cheaper labor rates. The moral dilemma takes shape when we look at the cost-benefit analysis of the benefit to the stockholders (reduced operating expenses and improved earnings) to the cost to the community (lost jobs, lower retail sales, and lower tax revenues). The utilitarian theory proposes that we evaluate the benefits and harm to these two groups of stakeholders in order to determine the ethically correct course of action. In a larger sense, we may take into account other stakeholders such as management, employees, suppliers, and customers; and the harm or benefit that might befall each of them if the proposed action is taken.

Nevertheless, we must be careful in looking strictly at monetary considerations in a cost-benefit analysis. The problems it creates can be easily seen in the following questions:

If it were possible to do so:

- Should a corporation pay $100 to make its plants 100% safe from accidents?
- Should a corporation pay $100,000 to make its plants 100% safe from accidents?
- Should a corporation pay $100,000,000 to make its plants 100% safe from accidents?

In a utilitarian argument, any rational person would say that paying $100 for a 100% safe environment is a great bargain and is ethically justified. But as the price goes up, the balance may begin to shift. Would a corporation pay $100 million to create an accident-free environment? It isn't likely. The extreme cost far outweighs the likely benefits. In fact, corporations make this kind of decision every day. It is called "risk management." The business is willing to take the risk associated with possible accidents because it cannot afford the exorbitant cost to mitigate the risk. The utilitarian argument defends this decision on the basis of a cost-benefit analysis. The amount of harm caused to the stockholders by spending such a large amount of corporate money is greater than the benefit to the employees of the assurance against possible injuries. Therefore, the ethical decision is to not make the investment, regardless of the possibility of accidents and likely bodily injury to employees.

This is where cost-benefit analysis gets a bad name. Although it makes logical sense to use it in such circumstances, many people are concerned that it places a monetary value on human life. In reality, it does place a monetary value on human life. We should not be ashamed of this or feel guilty, regardless of what "socially-conscious" people may say. There are certain restrictions, which are ethically defensible, that we make on valuing human life. Should we all donate 100% of our incomes to a fund that would provide organ transplants to anybody that needs one? A utilitarian would say "no." The harm caused to society and to all of us by having no money to support ourselves or buy food would far outweigh the good that the organ transplants would provide to the smaller number of people who need them. On the other hand, if each of us could donate just $5.00 and achieve the same results, wouldn't we all want to do so? In essence, we are putting a value on the lives of the patients in need of organ transplants. It is somewhere between $5.00 and our entire income.

The cost-benefit analysis proposition can have particularly bad connotations when we see real life examples like the now infamous decision made by Ford Motor Company many years ago to allow the Pinto to be produced with an obvious design flaw that could cause explosions and severe fires when the car was rear-ended.[2]

In the strong competition that was taking place between the U.S. and Japanese car manufacturers in the 1960s, Ford felt pressured to rush its newest car into production. The Pinto was put into production in almost half of the time typically required for most cars. However, before production, Ford's engineers identified a serious flaw in the design of the Pinto. It was found, through rear-end collision tests, that the Pinto's fuel system easily ruptured, resulting in explosions and fires. Even though Ford owned the patent on a much safer gas tank, top management decided to manufacture the car anyway. This decision came from a cost-benefit analysis. Lee Iococca, who was in charge of the Pinto's production, had design specifications that were firm and could not be changed. Part of that specification was that the car would not cost more than $2,000. Adding safety features, which would also add cost to the car, were not acceptable. The cost to fix the fuel system problem was $11 per automobile.

Not wanting to delay production, Ford used a cost-benefit analysis to determine the cost of altering the fuel tanks. According to Ford's estimates, the unsafe tanks would cause 180 burn deaths, 180 serious burn injuries, and 2,100 burned vehicles each year. Ford calculated that it would have to pay approximately $200,000 per each death, $67,000 per each injury, and $700 per each vehicle. The total cost would be $49.5 million. Conversely, the cost of adding the $11 alteration to the Pinto and other small cars and light trucks (which would have resulted in the saving of lives and injuries) was much higher. It came to $137 million per year. To Ford, the decision was obvious.

It is precisely this kind of notorious cost-benefit analysis that tarnishes the image of businesses and corporate management, implying that greed supersedes concerns for the safety and welfare of the consumer. So, although the cost-benefit aspect of the utilitarian approach to ethical decision-making has very strong features that can assist us in making the morally correct decision, we must be careful to not let every decision come down to a strictly financial-based equation or we will continue to justify the public perception of corporate greed. Weighing *all* of the factors, both human and financial, makes the utilitarian approach much more feasible.

The Social Contract

There is another profound consequentialist theory known as the social contract theory. This theory was originally proposed by Thomas Hobbes.[3] Social contract theory aligns itself very well with the laws of nature, which were previously discussed. Basically, social contract theory argues that we are all motivated by our own selfish interests (note the similarities with Smith and Locke), and it is these selfish interests that compel us to create a moral world in which to live.

Hobbes believed that we create moral rules because it is in our own selfish interests to live in a world that is governed by morality. If we had no moral rules that we could all live and operate under, we would all be subject to the actions of others who were only trying to fulfill their own selfish interests. We would live under a constant state of war of competing self-interests. Since this environment is not in our best interests, our own selfishness motivates us to adopt a set of rules that protects us from being hurt by others. These rules may prohibit lying, cheating, stealing, killing, etc. But these rules only protect us if they are enforced. Hobbes believed that as selfish creatures, each of us would plunder our neighbor's property once their guards were down. In this environment, each of us would always be at risk from our neighbors' desire to steal our property. Therefore, for selfish reasons alone, we devise a means of enforcing these rules — we create a policing agency that punishes us if we violate these rules.[4]

In a business situation, it is in our mutual interests to follow morally binding rules that protect us from the selfish interests of others. For example, it is in the mutual best interests of Company A and Company B to not cheat each other. This social contract, which applies to personal self-interests as well as business self-interests, requires that Company A give up its right to cheat Company B, and Company B agrees to the same. By transferring these rights to each other, both companies become obligated to not cheat the other. Although the rule against cheating is morally binding because it is in our best interests to operate in a world that enforces the rule, each company still has a natural fear that the other may violate this unwritten contract. Therefore, policing agencies are established to enforce these rules. Laws governing contracts, theft, and fraud are ways in which we enforce the basic social contract. On a greater scale, all of our laws (laws against stealing, killing, assault, slander, etc.) are devised to enforce our social contract with each other to not do these things. We realize that if we break our mutually beneficial rules and hurt someone, we will in turn be hurt by others (punished). So, for purely selfish reasons, we abide by the rules we create.

The social contract helps to eliminate uncertainty and suspicion. It makes us feel more secure. By giving up some of our freedoms, we gain security. We create a moral obligation for everyone to not harm each other. Even so, there are people who believe that they can violate these moral obligations, and by being clever, not risk being punished. The executives from companies like Enron and Adelphia are examples. They acted completely in their own selfish interests, violating the social contract they have with the rest of us. Since the contract exists as a mutual obligation to protect us all, violating the social contract is a highly unethical and immoral act. It creates insecurity and uncertainty. This is why we create agencies to enforce our social contract through the application of laws and punishments. It is in our own selfish interests to do so.

Notes

[1] THE NUREMBERG CODE from *Trials of War Criminals before the Nuremberg Military Tribunals under Control Council Law No. 10.* Nuremberg, October 1946—April 1949. Washington, D.C.: U.S. G.P.O, 1949—1953, often referred to as the "Doctor Trial."

[2] Information obtained from the following sources: *Design Defects of the Ford Pinto Gas Tank: Engineering Disaster*, www.fordpinto.com/blowup.htm, "Engineering Disaster: The Ford Pinto Case." *A Study in Applied Ethics, Business, and Technology* by Sajjad Haroon, University of Guelph, and *Mother Jones.*

[3] Social contract theory was described by Hobbes in chapters 13, 14, and 15 of *Leviathan.*

[4] James Fieser, "Social Contract Theory," from *The Internet Enclyclopedia of Philosophy.* www.utm.edu/research/iep/e/ethics.htm. January 2003.

Michael P. Harden

Chapter Seven: Deontological Theory

Utilitarianism proposes that an action, behavior, or rule is morally correct if its consequences produce the greatest amount of goodness or pleasure. In contract to this teleological approach, deontological theories of ethics propose that the consequences are irrelevant in making an ethical decision. The deontological approach emphasizes the nature of the action itself or the rule governing the behavior. Stated another way, teleological theories such as utilitarianism place the ethical emphasis on the *ends*, while deontological theories place the ethical emphasis on the *means*. Deontologists are more concerned with the *motive* behind the action rather than the result of the action.

As an example, suppose two teenagers volunteer to work weekends with handicapped children. One does it because she believes in helping the handicapped, while the other does it to satisfy a requirement for "community service" on her college admission application. Although the results are the same to the handicapped children that have been helped, the motives of the two volunteers are quite different. One is motivated by a sense of *duty*, while the other is motivated by a self-serving need. The first is a morally good action while the latter is a morally bad action.

The word "deontology" comes from the Greek words *deon*, which means duty, and *logos*, which means science. So deontology is, in essence, the "science of duty." Knowing this helps us to better understand the nature of deontology. Deontologists believe that people should act from a sense of duty or obligation. These rules are rather absolute. For example, if I tell the truth because I know it is the right thing for me to do, and not because I am afraid of being caught in a lie, then I am basing my action on a duty, and that makes it morally correct. If I tell the truth only because I fear being caught lying, then my action does not come from a sense of duty, but from a sense of self-protection, thereby making it morally wrong.

In 1930, W.D. Ross, a British philosopher, developed seven absolute rules of duty that fit into the deontological theory of ethical behavior.[1] Those seven duties are listed here:

1. Duties of fidelity — The duty to keep our promises and to always tell the truth.
2. Duties of reparation — The duty to provide compensation to people when we have injured or harmed them.
3. Duties of gratitude — The duty to return favors to people who have done things for us.
4. Duties of justice — The duty to ensure that goods are distributed fairly according to people's merits.
5. Duties of beneficence — The duty to do whatever we can to improve the condition of other people.
6. Duties of self-improvement — The duty to improve ourselves in regards to intelligence and virtue.
7. Duties of nonmaleficence — The duty to avoid harming others.

It is easy to see that these seven rules hold a lot in common with the Golden Rule: "Do unto others as you would have them do unto you." Much of what deontologists believe fits well into this rule.

In determining moral correctness, utilitarians take into account the circumstances under which an action is taken, e.g., lying is correct under some circumstances depending on the outcome of the situation. However, since deontologists believe that right and wrong are not dependent on the consequences or outcome of an action, they can hold that certain actions are *always* wrong. For example, lying and cheating are never right because they violate the duty of fidelity — to always tell the truth.

The Categorical Imperative

Perhaps the most famous of all deontologists is Immanuel Kant, an 18th century German philosopher. Kant wrote three books that describe the deontological ethics tradition and lays out Kant's concepts of morality: The *Foundations of the Metaphysics of Morals* (1785), *The Critique of Practical Reason* (1788), and *The Metaphysics of*

Morals (1798). Kant's main moral proposition is known as the *categorical imperative.*

Kant believed that moral action should be based on reason and not on consequences. In fact, to Kant, consequences were irrelevant to the morality of the decision or action. Any action should be taken because it is the right thing to do, because it has a basis in reason, and that rational people would do it from a sense of duty or moral obligation. This sounds a little confusing; so let's discuss this in a more relevant way.

There are two imperatives that individuals have: *hypothetical* and *categorical*. The differences are based on the use of the word *ought*. In a hypothetical imperative, we do things because we have a desire to do them. Here are two examples:

- I am putting on too much weight, so I *ought* to go on a diet.
- I am having trouble reading, so I *ought* to have my eyes examined and get glasses.

In both of these examples, we use the word *ought* to express a desire. If gaining weight isn't a problem to me, then there is nothing that I *ought* to do about it. It only matters if I have a desire to do something about it. In no case does the word *ought* indicate that there is any firm moral obligation for me to do something I do not want to do.

In the categorical imperative, we do things not in a hypothetical fashion, but in a categorical fashion. The categorical imperative is an absolute command that has nothing to do with desire or any other subjective considerations. In essence, a categorical imperative is something that *must* be done from a sense of duty. For example, "Do not lie," or "Tell the truth," are imperatives that Kant would propose we must follow because it is our duty as rational beings to follow them. We treat categorical imperatives as if they were unquestionable truths.

How do we know, as rational people, which imperatives are categorical, i.e., which ones must we follow without condition or subjective considerations? Kant helps us determine this through his *Formula of the Law of Nature,*[2] which states:

"Act as if the maxim of your action was to become through your will a universal law of nature."

This statement requires us to think about our actions in universal terms. We are forced to ask ourselves what would happen if everyone did this. For example, if we look at the categorical imperative "I must tell the truth," we can see how this might be universalized. Suppose no one ever told the truth. What would the world be like? Certainly, there would be no trust. We would not be able to accept anything as being true. Our business and personal dealings would always be suspect. We would be suspicious of everything we are told. Clearly, a world where everyone lies would be a terrible place in which to live. On the other hand, suppose that everyone always told the truth. What would the world be like? In this environment, it would be logical to assume that we would be able to trust everyone and always know that what we are being told is the truth. All of our decisions could be made with correct and reliable information. It would be a wonderful world indeed.

So, by putting a moral judgment in a universal setting (what if everyone did this?), we can determine if it is a categorical imperative, i.e., a universal or consistent moral principle. This consistency allows us to utilize the moral judgment without making exceptions. As an example, suppose you apply for a bank loan, and in doing so, inflate your gross income on the application form in order to help qualify for the loan. After the loan is granted, you find out that the interest rate is a point higher than you had been led to believe. You are outraged that the loan officer misled you! In your mind, you are able to justify the lie that you told, but unable to accept the lie told to you. If you thought of this in terms of a categorical imperative, you would see that there is no rational difference in the two situations and that neither of you should have lied to the other.

We find similar situations like this where one party is dishonest, yet at the same time is outraged when someone else lies. As an example, suppose corporate management strictly enforces a code of conduct for its employees, firing any individuals that violate its rules; yet it allows executives to freely flaunt those same rules? Enron had a code of ethics that they enforced upon their employees, yet the company's senior management made egregious exceptions for its executives. This violates Kant's principles of consistency and universality.

To use the categorical imperative in ethical decision-making, we simply have to ask ourselves "what if everyone did this?" to determine the correct course of action.

But Kant went further in his categorical imperative. He also believed that we should make ethical decisions based on respect for other people. His *Formula for the End Itself*[3] states that you should:

"Act in such a way that you always treat humanity, whether in your own person or in the person of any other, never simply as a means, but at the same time as an end."

Kant is expressing his belief that we must never treat people as a means to an end, but as an end in themselves. We do not use people for our own gains. The basic principle here is respect for others. Although we do use other people everyday in our work and personal environments (we have secretaries, bus drivers, delivery people, and employees), we must always look at others as more than objects or things. This differs somewhat with utilitarians, who may treat people as a means if it provides the greatest amount of good or benefit for everyone. For utilitarians, it depends on the outcome.

In Kant's categorical imperative, we make moral decisions by asking ourselves whether our actions will respect other people and not use those people for our own gains. As an example, if a software salesman sells an unsuspecting customer a new software application before it is fully tested or debugged simply in order to meet his annual quota before the end of the year, then he has treated that customer as a means, whereas the customer should actually be the end. The salesman's action also shows no respect for the individual involved.

We can determine the moral validity of our decisions by asking ourselves whether we are using the person involved as a means to achieve our own ends, and whether our contemplated actions demonstrate respect for that person. Employees that are treated with respect and paid a decent wage would meet Kant's moral test, but slaves or sweatshop laborers would not be morally acceptable because they are used solely as a means, and without respect for their humanity.

Duty Theory

A *duty* is a moral obligation that a person has towards another person, such as the duty not to lie to him or the duty not to harm him. From an etymological perspective, duties are actions that are *due* to somebody, such as paying money that one owes to a creditor. However, in a broader philosophical sense of the term, *duties* are actions that are morally mandatory. Medieval philosophers, among them Saint Thomas Aquinas (1225-1274), proposed that we have specific duties or obligations to avoid committing certain sins. Since sins such as theft are absolute, then our duty to avoid stealing is also absolute, irrespective of any good consequences that might arise from particular acts of theft. From the 17th to the 19th centuries, many philosophers held the normative theory that moral conduct is conduct that follows a specific list of duties.[4]

The Law of War and Peace (1625), written by the Dutch philosopher Hugo Grotius (1583-1645), gives us one of the first descriptions of this concept. Grotius believed that our duties are fixed features of the universe and therefore obligations of natural law. It was also common at the time to link duties to virtues.

Another philosopher, Samuel von Pufendorf (1632-1694), outlined three components of duty theory in *On the Law of Nature and of Nations* (1672) and his subsequent work *The Duty of Man and Citizen* (1673). The first component is his correlation of duties with rights. What this means is simply that if a person has a right, then other people have a duty to respect that right. As an example, if I have a right to live in peace, then you have a duty to respect that right and to leave me alone and not pick on me. Another example would be that if I have a right to own property, then you have a duty to respect that right and not steal my property away from me. So duties and rights are tied together.

The second component that Pufendorf described was the difference between perfect and imperfect duties. A perfect duty was one whose obligations were precisely defined. Consequently, perfect duties should be followed all of the time. Some examples would be the duty not to harm others, the duty not to steal, or the duty not to cheat. Following these perfect duties would ensure our proper behavior. Imperfect duties, on the other hand, are duties that are not as precisely fixed. These are duties that are open to when or how we perform them. Some examples are the duty to be loyal or the duty to be generous. Here is how Pufendorf discusses these "voluntary" obligations:

"But if things due us under an imperfect obligation merely are intercepted, it is not considered that a loss has been inflicted, which must be made good. For it would be unseemly to consider it a loss not to have received, or to demand compensation for, such things as I could not expect from another except as a voluntary gift, and things which I cannot reckon my own, until I have received them."[5]

Pufendorf's third component was a categorization of all duties into three groups. These groups were: duties to God, duties to oneself, and duties to others. It is primarily in the duties to others that we focus for business purposes. Pufendorf divides duties to others into absolute duties and conditional duties. Absolute duties are universally binding on us, and consist of:

1. Avoiding wronging others
2. Treating people as equals
3. Promoting the good of others

This concept can be seen in Pufendorf's own writings about absolute duties, for he felt that they were essential to society:

"Among the absolute duties, i.e., of anybody to anybody, the first place belongs to this one: *let no one injure another* (emphasis added). For this is the broadest of all duties, embracing all men as such. It is also the easiest, as consisting in mere refraining from action, unless the passions that resist reason have somehow to be checked at times. Again, it is likewise the most necessary duty, because without it the social life could in no way exist."[6]

Conditional duties result from the social contracts between people. These are, in essence, duties that we mutually agree upon between others and ourselves so that we can function as a civil society, making and keeping promises and agreements. Here is a brief section of Pufendorf's discussion of these duties:

"Therefore, in order that the mutual duties of men (the fruit, that is, of sociability) may be discharged more frequently and according to certain rules, it was necessary for men to agree among themselves, as to the mutual performance of all that they could not certainly promise themselves from others, on the basis of the law of humanity alone. And indeed it was necessary to determine in advance, what one was bound to perform for another, and what the latter should in turn expect and exact as his right from the former. And this is done by promises and agreements."[7]

Basically, duties are defined by these philosophers as our obligations to ourselves, to God, and to others. In today's world where religious beliefs are separated from those of business, we tend more to look at duties as those obligations we have to each other. Duty theory expresses the notion that all of us have absolute obligations or duties to behave toward others in a certain way, to avoid harming others, to keep our promises, and to respect the rights of others. It is easy to see how duty theory fits into deontological theories. Since the word *deon* is actually the Greek word for duty, then it is logical to assume that duty must be a basic component of deontological theories.

Notes

1 W.D. Ross, *The Right and the Good* (Oxford: Oxford University Press, 1930) p. 21

2 Immanuel Kant, *The Foundations of the Metaphysics of Morals* (1785).

3 Kant.

4 *Internet Encyclopedia of Philosophy*, (www.utm.edu/research/iep/e/ethics.htm).

5 Samuel von Pufendorf, *The Two Books on the Duty of Man and Citizen According to the Natural Law* (Translated by Frank Gardner Moore), p. 48.

6 Pufendorf, p. 42

7 Pufendorf, p. 53

Michael P. Harden

Chapter Eight: Justice and Fairness

Over 2000 years ago, Aristotle said, "equals should be treated equally and unequals unequally." This has become the basis for the principle of justice (or fairness). We often use the terms *justice* and *fairness* interchangeably because we tend to view justice as being fair in our decisions and treating everyone equally. Justice and fairness are very important ethical concepts.

We usually use the principle of justice when we are dealing with the distribution of something. This might be how we distribute money to shareholders, benefits to employees, or discounts to our customers. On a larger societal scale, justice may have to do with the fair distribution of things like criminal punishment. We establish punishments that "fit the crime" and try to ensure that those punishments are distributed fairly among convicted criminals who are being sentenced. Following the principle of "equals should be treated equally and unequals unequally," we would not expect a shoplifter to be sentenced to life in prison, nor would we expect a murderer to receive a sentence of 30 days of community service. Obviously, shoplifting and murder are not equal and should not be treated as if they are.

Since the principle of justice usually deals with the fairness of distribution, and most business decisions involve how something will be distributed (for example, jobs, resources, benefits, wages, workload, dividends, stock options, supplies, materials, etc.), then the principle of justice is particularly relevant to business.

In his writings in *Politics*, Aristotle stated, "All men think justice to be a sort of equality." Aristotle was able to devise an equation that expressed how this equality worked. In this equation, Aristotle simply demonstrated that people are not treated equally across the board (everyone gets the same amount of something), but equally in the sense of what they deserve. *Differences in what someone receives should be justified by differences that are relevant to the basis for the distribution.* For example, if an employee works harder or longer than others, then that employee should be paid more on a proportional basis. If a shareholder invests more capital than other shareholders, then he should be entitled to more dividends than the others, proportionate to the amount of stock he owns. If a customer buys more products than other customers, then she should be entitled to better discounts than the other customers. This is Aristotle's principle of distributive justice. This principle also infers that if there are no relevant differences between individuals, then there should be no differences in the equality of distribution. The substance of this concept is that if two people are performing the same job, working the same amount of hours, and are equally productive, then they should be paid the same.

When an employer shows some kind of *favoritism* to an employee or customer, the principle of fairness and justice is violated because someone receives a benefit that is not justified on some relevant difference. Other employees or customers will not consider this fair. Conversely, if an employer *discriminates* against someone, they are depriving that person of something without basing that decision on a relevant difference. Favoritism bestows unequal benefits to someone and discrimination imparts unequal harm to someone. Neither situation is fair based on the principle of justice. When one or the other occurs, we have an *injustice.*

The sense of unfairness among employees is easily aroused when favoritism is demonstrated by a manager. If an employee receives a raise or promotion simply because the boss "likes" him, rest assured that the other employees will resent this. Their concept of justice and fairness has been piqued.

Discrimination can have similar effects. When someone fails to receive a raise or promotion for a reason that is not a relevant difference, they know that they have been treated unfairly. For example, if a person is not promoted because of his race, we know that this is not a relevant difference and is therefore unfair. If a woman is not selected for a job because management believes it is a "man's" job — even though she may be perfectly capable of performing just as well as the man — we inherently realize that this is unfair.

When there are no relevant differences, the concept of justice argues that everyone should be treated equally. To pay someone less than others when everyone is doing the same job and everyone is equally productive is patently unfair. This is one of the problems that employers have when they pay women less than men for the same jobs. If productivity and other factors are all equal then there is no justification for this action under the principle of justice. In fact, the principle of justice was codified when the Equal Pay Act (EPA) of 1963 was enacted. This law specifies that employers are forbidden from paying different wages to men and women who are performing the same or similar work unless there is a difference that is relevant (other than sex).

The concept of justice, often credited to the ancient Greeks, can be traced back much earlier to almost 1,500 years before Aristotle. Hammurabi (1795-1750 BC) was one of the first rulers to put into effect a code of laws that reflected the principles of justice and fairness. Hammurabi ruled Babylon, the world's first metropolis. He is often considered by historians to have been a wise and just ruler. As the Babylonian empire grew, Hammurabi realized the need to establish a code of laws that could be clearly understood by his people. He created a code, which bears his name today (the "Hammurabi Code"), that covers many different areas of social and business life. It outlines and numbers both the offenses and the appropriate punishments for those offenses. Hammurabi had it carved into a huge black stone monument that was eight feet tall, and placed in a public area so all of the Babylonian citizens could read it. The stone was carried off after the fall of Babylon, and was not found until 1901.

The Hammurabi Code is clearly based on the concept of fitting the punishment to the crime and ensuring that everyone be treated the same. Listed here are several of the 282 offenses and their respective punishments:

21.   If anyone breaks a hole into a house (breaks in to steal), he shall be put to death before that hole and be buried.

22.   If anyone is committing a robbery and is caught, then he shall be put to death.

44.   If anyone take over a waste-lying field to make it arable, but is lazy, and does not make it arable, he shall plow the

fallow field in the fourth year, harrow it and till it, and give it back to its owner, and for each ten gan (a measure of area) ten gur of grain shall be paid.

57. If a shepherd, without the permission of the owner of the field, and without the knowledge of the owner of the sheep, lets the sheep into a field to graze, then the owner of the field shall harvest his crop, and the shepherd, who had pastured his flock there without permission of the owner of the field, shall pay to the owner twenty gur of corn for every ten gan.

102. If a merchant entrust money to an agent (broker) for some investment, and the broker suffer a loss in the place to which he goes, he shall make good the capital to the merchant.

108. If a female tavern-keeper does not accept corn according to gross weight in payment of drink, but takes money, and the price of the drink is less than that of the corn, she shall be convicted and thrown into the water.

113. If anyone have consignment of corn or money, and he take from the granary or box without the knowledge of the owner, then shall he who took corn without the knowledge of the owner out of the granary or money out of the box be legally convicted, and repay the corn he has taken. And he shall lose whatever commission was paid to him, or due him.

124. If anyone deliver silver, gold, or anything else to another for safe keeping, before a witness, but he deny it, he shall be brought before a judge, and all that he has denied he shall pay in full.

127. If anyone "point the finger" (slander) at a sister of a god or the wife of anyone, and cannot prove it, this man shall be taken before the judges and his brow shall be marked.

129. If a man's wife be surprised (in a sexual act) with another man, both shall be tied and thrown into the water, but the husband may pardon his wife, and the king his slaves.

157. If anyone be guilty of incest with his mother after his father, both shall be burned.

185. If a man adopt a child and to his name as son, and rear him, this grown son cannot be demanded back again.

195. If a son strikes his father, his hands shall be hewn off.

196. If a man put out the eye of another man, his eye shall be put out. (An eye for an eye)

197. If he breaks another man's bone, his bone shall be broken.

200. If a man knocks out the teeth of his equal, his teeth shall be knocked out. (A tooth for a tooth)

218. If a physician make a large incision with the operating knife, and kill him, or open a tumor with the operating knife, and cut out the eye, his hands shall be cut off.

229 If a builder build a house for some one, and does not construct it properly, and the house which he built falls in and kills its owner, then that builder shall be put to death.

230. If it kills the son of the owner, the son of that builder shall be put to death.

In Hammurabi's code of laws, all people were treated the same. The punishments were literally "written in stone" and there were no deviations from these based on extenuating circumstances, i.e., there were no excuses. This rigidity made certain that all transgressors were treated equally, which would be fair. Although some of the punishments may seem harsh for our enlightened time, we cannot argue that a system built on this principle would not be considered a just system.

Hammurabi, Aristotle, and Plato are just a few of the ancient wise men who understood the inherent value of justice in maintaining an orderly society and ensuring that all people are treated fairly. Subsequent philosophers have realized that justice is fundamental to our concept of morality since ethical decisions often take into consideration whether an action or a behavior is fair. In our own interactions with others, the principle of justice forces us to ask ourselves the following questions:

1. Am I treating everyone equally?
2. If not, is the difference in treatment justified by some relevant differences?

By being able to answer these questions when we are faced with potential ethical issues, we can prevent someone from being treated unfairly.

Chapter Nine: Virtue Ethics

"In spite of everything, I still believe that people are really good at heart."
- Anne Frank (1929-1945)

"The primitive simplicity of their minds renders them a more easy prey to a big lie than a small one..."
- Adolf Hitler (1889-1945)

Deontological and teleological theories of ethics deal with actions. They ask the question: are certain actions right, based on their consequences or the motives behind them? Virtue ethics deals more with our moral character. Instead of being concerned with our actions, virtue ethics is more concerned with the kind of person we should be. Virtue ethics asks: Are we of good character? Do we live virtuous lives?

The concept of virtue ethics goes way back to ancient Greece. It is the oldest of all normative theories of ethics. Both Plato and Aristotle were concerned with the virtue of people. They considered virtue to be fundamental to a good life. They spent much of their time trying to understand or define what makes a good person and what virtues a good person would possess. Aristotle expressed the role of virtue and described various virtues in great detail in his *Nicomachean Ethics*. In Aristotle's notion of ethics, only people who led virtuous lives could enjoy success and happiness.

During the same period of time that Aristotle was formulating his ideas about ethics and virtues, the Cynic[1] school of philosophy was developing. The basic ethical doctrine of the Cynics was inspired by Socrates. They believed that living a virtuous life was necessary for attaining happiness. They also believed that a virtuous life was all that anyone needed to be happy, and so they disdained such values as social status, beauty, and wealth. According to the Cynics' philosophy, living a virtuous life *guaranteed* happiness. Their philosophy argued that virtues can be taught and do not require studying worthless things like music, geometry, literature, and science. Ethics was the only subject that really mattered in life. To prove their point, Cynics typically lived like beggars, completely abandoning anything of value. They would often approach strangers and attempt to persuade them to abandon their materialistic ways of life and accept the virtuous life instead.

Perhaps the most famous of all the Cynics was Diogenes of Sinope. It is said that he roamed the streets of Athens with a lantern. When asked what he was looking for, he would reply, "An honest man." Legend says he never found one.

By the 17th century, proponents of virtue ethics theory had developed a list of approximately one hundred character traits that they believed a good person should acquire.[2] However, philosophers do not agree on what makes something a virtue, and therefore, there is also disagreement on what characteristics are indeed virtues. The list of possible virtues is very long, but most people agree that it should at least include:

- Honesty
- Courage
- Generosity
- Compassion
- Loyalty
- Dependability
- Self-control
- Benevolence
- Tolerance
- Courtesy
- Fairness

Aristotle also believed that virtues should include traits such as pride, which many people say is a vice, not a virtue. But Aristotle believed that we should be genuinely proud of our accomplishments and achievements, and as long as we weren't arrogant about them, this would be virtuous. On the other hand, Aristotle also believed that shame was a virtue. In his concept of virtuous behavior, Aristotle felt that we should be ashamed of our failures and shortcomings. By being ashamed of our failings, we could strive to improve ourselves.

Aristotle believed that a virtue had to be something that was practiced habitually. For example, character traits like honesty, fairness, and compassion do little good if they can be turned on and off. They must be practiced all of the time. It does no good to be compassionate to one person and then to be unmerciful to another. What good would be accomplished by being honest in one situation and then being dishonest in another? Truly virtuous people cannot compartmentalize their virtues, calling upon them only when it suits their needs, and then ignoring them later. Truly honest people are, for the most part, honest all of the time. Caring people are, by and large, concerned for the wellbeing of others as a way of life. Generous people are typically generous in situations where someone is in need. When we say, "He would give you the shirt off his back," we are describing someone who is a generous person all of the time, not simply when it suits him.

Aristotle believed that virtues had to be learned over time. Virtues are not something that we are born with or miraculously appear as if in some epiphany. They are traits that we acquire over time…things we learn from our caretakers and others as we grow up. And once we learn them, we must also practice them, for it does no good to know how to be courteous to others, yet be rude in our dealings with co-workers. What good would come from knowing how to be honest but then lying whenever it gains us some advantage? This would not be a virtue. So knowing the virtue and practicing the virtue are necessary if we are to be virtuous people.

Aristotle described his philosophy succinctly when he said: "Excellence is an art won by training and habituation. We do not act rightly because we have virtue or excellence, but we rather have those because we have acted rightly. We are what we repeatedly do. Excellence, then is not an act, but a habit." He also said in another instance, "Moral excellence comes about as a result of habit. We become just by doing just acts, temperate by doing temperate acts, brave by doing brave acts."

General Charles (Chuck) Krulak, former Commandant of the Marine Corps, said this of character, which is the outward expression of virtues:

> "We are not born with character. It is developed by the experiences and decisions that guide our lives. Each individual creates, develops and nurtures his or her own character. Being a man or woman of character is no easy task. It requires tough decisions, many of which put you at odds with the more commonly accepted social morés of the times."[3]

Virtue ethics deals more with developing good habits of virtue rather than following rules. The idea is that once a person acquires a habit of good character, for example, honesty, that person will then act honestly by habit. Since virtuous character is developed in our youth, virtue theory stresses that adults are responsible for ensuring that children learn the proper virtuous character traits.

It seems that we know virtuous people when we see them in action. We almost sense this. We identify these people and we point them out to our children as examples and role models. We have a compelling need to identify moral heroes and admire them. This surely must come from our own innate beliefs that virtues are desirable characteristics. It may also come from our abiding sense that virtuous people are good, and people who lack virtues are bad. Our belief in the constant struggle of good vs. evil compels us to believe, on some level, that virtuous people are heroic and worthy of our praise and admiration.

One can easily see that virtues are analogous to class. If a person has class, that person is always classy. And moreover, class may be difficult to describe, but you know class when you see it. Virtues are the same way. If someone is virtuous, you will know it when you see it.

Virtues are also *universal* characteristics that can be useful in any situation. Honesty, loyalty, fairness, and self-control are just a few examples of virtues that provide us with great benefits in both our personal and our business lives.

Virtues that we practice in our personal lives easily carry over to our business lives as well. If virtues are truly universal, and they are traits that cannot be turned on and off at will, then a virtuous person would be virtuous in both his private life and his business life. If being virtuous in our private lives makes us happy and successful, why wouldn't being virtuous in our business lives make us happy and successful there too?

A truly virtuous person will carry her virtues into her business life. Virtues are virtues, and there is no differentiation between personal virtues and business virtues. Since virtuous character traits, by their very nature, are habitual, they *must* follow us into our business lives. However, we do understand that business situations are different than personal situations. For example, we do not want our competitors to know all of our trade secrets, so being completely honest isn't an option all of the time. When we are negotiating a contract, we are not expected to "lay all of our cards on the table," for our opponent to see. Similarly, we do not want to prematurely release information that may have a detrimental effect on our stock price until we are prepared to deal with it.

As businesspeople, we must fully understand what the goals of our business are in order to better understand the role of virtue in our business dealings. What this means is that we may "puff" things up in our marketing campaign to make us appear more attractive, but not be dishonest by presenting false or misleading information. When a restaurant says that it has the "best burgers in Chicago," that is a bit of puffery that most of us accept. If, however, the restaurant stated that "three out of four people rate our burgers as the best in Chicago," then that information had better come from a formal survey of local restaurant patrons.

In any case, most of us would readily agree that character traits that contribute to success in our private lives would also be valuable in our business lives as well. If we appreciate honesty in our personal dealings, we will likewise appreciate it in our business dealings.

Compartmentalization of Ethical Behavior

If a person lies, cheats, or fails to honor commitments in his personal life, we cannot expect him to behave differently in his business life. A virtuous person is virtuous all of the time, not when it suits him, and not when it is convenient. This on-and-off behavior defies the very definition of what a virtue is. Gen. Krulak makes this point: "Making the right ethical choices must become a habit. Decisions cannot be situational, based on other's actions or dependent upon whom is watching."[4]

A person either behaves virtuously because he has virtues, or he doesn't. Since virtues are learned and practiced, we assimilate them and integrate them into our very being. They are habitual. Therefore, virtues cannot be turned on and off at will. We call this notion of being able to be ethical in one situation and unethical in another, *situational* ethics. It is as if we can compartmentalize our behavior and our moral values, choosing which to use based on the situation in which we are placed.

The idea that ethical behavior can be compartmentalized — or turned on and off at will — reached its zenith during the 1990s with the scandals of the Clinton administration. When people began to say that whatever the President did in his personal life did not matter to them since he was a good President and did his job well, they were being naive at best or dishonest at worst. When people like Dan Rather[5] for example, stated categorically that the President was an honest man, even though he lied about something that was strictly personal, they were demonstrating a complete lack of understanding of what virtues like honesty and commitment really mean. Their argument that a person's behavior can be unethical in his personal life, but ethical in his public or business life is intellectually dishonest. Virtues such as honesty and integrity, the outward manifestations of ethical beliefs, are not virtues that are called forth only in certain situations. They are underlying beliefs that control all of our actions, not just our personal or public behavior.

You are either honest or you aren't. You either possess integrity or you don't. There are no degrees of either, and no situations in which they can be turned off or on at your convenience. When Rather said "I think you can be an honest person and lie about any number of things,"[6] he demonstrated a complete lack of understanding of how an honest person actually behaves. You cannot be regarded as honest and still lie. It is incongruous and defies logic. Honest people do not lie. If they lie, then they are not honest people. On the other hand, it is at least reasonable to assume that you can be *dishonest* and lie. Few people would disagree with that statement.

It is silly to propose that a person who shows little regard for ethical behavior in his personal life by lying, cheating, or breaking promises, would somehow be able to follow a completely different set of ethical principles in his public or business life and behave in a totally moral or ethical fashion (in absolute contrast to his personal behavior). To believe such a preposterous concept is neither rational nor defensible. People who believe this should be ashamed of themselves because they are either naive or disingenuous.

Ethical beliefs are either present or absent all of the time. They do not pick and choose which situation in which they will work. They cannot be turned on or off at will. The idea that a person could be unethical in her private life, yet follow ethical standards in her business life, defies logic. Not only is this argument illogical, but it is bogus on its face value alone. To validate this proposition, all someone has to do is ask this question: Should a reasonable person expect that people who act unethically or immorally with their family and friends — the very people they love and care about the most — will somehow hold themselves to higher ethical standards with business associates and strangers? No rational person could respond affirmatively to this question. If a person does not treat the people she cares about with ethical respect and solid moral values, then how can she do so with other people who mean even less to her?

To fully understand this point, we can ask ourselves some revealing questions. Could a person who cheats on his spouse — someone to whom a sacred commitment has been made — be expected to honor commitments he makes to strangers or business colleagues? To assume that he could is illogical. If a man will lie to his family, how can a rational person expect that he will tell the truth to others who mean far less to him? Can a person who lies to his family and friends be expected to deal honestly with business associates, employees, and shareholders? Can a person who cheats on her personal income taxes, be expected to be trustworthy in handling corporate financial matters?

Virtues, as you may recall, are characteristics,[7] such as courage, fidelity, honesty, loyalty, generosity, and compassion. If someone has the virtue of being courageous, can he be brave in some situations, but cowardly in others? If so, then he is not truly courageous. The same holds true for honesty. If someone is an honest person, can she be truthful when she feels like it, and yet lie when it suits her to do so? If that is the way she behaves, then she is not really a person who possesses the virtue of honesty. She cannot be trusted in *any* situation since she has demonstrated that she is capable of lying in *some* situations. She can pick the situation in which she chooses to be honest, as well as pick the situation in which she chooses to lie. How is the person with whom she is dealing to know which behavior was chosen in *this* particular situation? Because of this uncertainty, a person who demonstrates dishonesty in one situation can never be fully trusted in another.

This notion is not new to us. We have known this for years. Nathaniel Hawthorne wrote in *The Scarlet Letter*, "No man, for any considerable period, can wear one face to himself, and another to the multitude, without finally getting bewildered as to which may be the true."

Notes

[1] Cynicism believed that virtue can be won by self-control and austerity, not by owning property or following social conventions. Today, we label someone as a cynic if they believe that self-interest is the motive behind human conduct, or if they are a habitual scoffer. "Cynic" comes from the Greek word for "dog." It is unclear as to how this name was adopted for this philosophy, but one theory is that it is named after Diogenes' nickname, the "Dog," a name he acquired because of the lifestyle he followed.

[2] *Internet Encyclopedia of Philosophy.* www.utm.edu/research/iep/e/ethics.htm.

[3] "Marines Have to be Held to Higher Standards," *USA Today* August 11, 1998: Sec. A - 10

[4] "Marines."

[5] Dan Rather, in an interview with Bill O'Reilly on the "O'Reilly Factor," Fox News Channel, May 15, 2001, stated: "I think he's an honest man…I think at core he's an honest person…I think you can be an honest person and lie about any number of things."

[6] Rather.

[7] A characteristic is defined as "a quality typical of a person, place or object." *New Webster's Dictionary of the English Language.* Lexicon Publications (1992). Therefore, if a virtue, by its own definition, is typical, it cannot be sporadic or intermittent, and must be consistent.

Michael P. Harden

Chapter Ten: Ethical Relativism

Many people believe that ethics is not universal. Instead, they subscribe to the idea that ethics is "relative." What they are actually saying is that what may be morally right for you may not be right for them. Traditionally, this belief has applied primarily to cultural differences. *Ethical relativism* is a theory that presumes that morality differs based on cultural norms. For example, certain societies may hold that genocide, polygamy, slavery, racism, infanticide, torture, sexism, or even incest, are morally acceptable practices. Other societies may condemn all or some of these practices. Therefore, the belief that a practice is right or wrong (moral or immoral) depends on the society in which you live and what the cultural norms of that society are.

In certain societies, it is completely acceptable for a husband to kill his wife if she has an adulterous affair or embarrasses him. Fathers may be able to kill their children for a variety of different reasons, such as having too many female children in the family or having a child with a disability. In certain societies, children may be able to kill their parents if they have grown too old to support themselves. In some cultures, amputation is a rational punishment for theft, castration for rape, or beheading for religious heresy. And of course, there are some commonly held societal practices such as female circumcision and the right to sell your children into slavery or prostitution.

Ethical relativists explain that these practices, no matter how repugnant or morally unacceptable they are to us, should not be judged by us as morally wrong. Only the society that practices them can judge their morality based on their own ethical standards. Sometimes these standards developed from practical or religious reasons. For example, agrarian cultures needed more male children to help farm the land, so females (who used up valuable resources without contributing) were less desirable and could be killed by the father. In another example, if a tribal chief died, his slaves would be killed so they could accompany him into the afterlife. These practices, one coming from a practical need and the other stemming from a religious belief, may carry through many generations and eventually become societal norms where fathers can kill their children without condemnation and slave owners can kill their slaves without worrying about punishment.

The concept of social conformity dictates that a person living in a society must adhere to the moral code of that society. African tribesmen will subscribe to the ethical beliefs of their culture, just as Eskimos, Arabs, Koreans, or Germans will with their own cultures. Anthropologists spend their lives studying the practices of various cultures, how they developed, and how they have become societal norms.

Ethical relativism can also be viewed in historical contexts. Societies often evolve beyond crude or barbarous practices that were once considered ethical into more enlightened times where a previously moral practice eventually becomes morally wrong. Slavery in the United States is a good example. Slavery was once considered morally acceptable, and in fact, it was upheld in several Supreme Court decisions. Today, it would be difficult indeed to find a rational person who advocates the moral acceptability of slavery. Even apartheid in South Africa, a more recent phenomenon, has become a historically loathsome whisper from the past.

Gender roles in the United States have changed as well. Women are no longer considered the "property" of their husbands, and the word "obey" is now typically omitted from their wedding vows. After years of struggle, women gained the basic right to vote. They are no longer expected to stay at home and take care of the house. Moreover, in earlier times, secretaries were all male, and nurses were all female. Obviously, roles change as society changes.

Our culture develops new standards as it determines that certain practices are no longer ethical. Punishments were harsh for minor crimes in early colonial America. Hanging someone for stealing was acceptable (and expected), and long prison sentences were handed out for petty theft. Flogging and branding were sometimes used as punishments years ago, but are universally condemned here today. In fact, Thomas Jefferson once proposed in *A Bill for Proportioning Crimes and Punishments* that:

"Whosoever shall be guilty of rape, polygamy, or sodomy with a man or woman, shall be punished; if a man, by castration, a woman, by boring through the cartilage of her nose a hole of one half inch in diameter at the least."

(Perhaps it was good that Jefferson's criminal code was never accepted.)

So ethical relativists will easily say that we should not judge past people for their unethical practices because those practices were considered ethical *at that time.* What was morally acceptable in 2nd century Rome (gladiators and religious persecution), 16th century Spain (the Spanish Inquisition), or 18th century America (slavery) is not acceptable today. Relativists argue that since ethical beliefs have a tendency to change over prolonged periods of time, we should not condemn past generations for practicing what they thought was right during their times. In fact, moral relativists believe that it is arrogant for someone to judge people from other times or other places. Who says that we are right and they are wrong? Ethical relativists further argue that people who condemn other people's beliefs are intolerant. And intolerance is, of course, morally unacceptable and therefore should not be tolerated. (Doesn't this concept seem at least a little ironic?)

It is interesting to note that there are certain common beliefs among ethical relativists. Here are some statements that would easily identify a moral (ethical) relativist:

"I can only decide for myself, but I cannot tell others what to do."
"There are no universal rights or wrongs."
"What is right for me may not be right for you."
"Who am I to judge them?"
"Whether something is right or wrong depends on the circumstances."
"Ethics is relative."

One of the problems we face in today's world is that ethical relativism has been carried beyond the historical and cultural contexts into a new paradigm. We now have a widespread belief by many that ethical relativism is a way to promote tolerance and to be non-judgmental…and that being non-judgmental is good.

The same relativist quotations listed here can apply in situations that have nothing to do with diversity among cultures or historical periods. Ethical relativism is practiced by many as a form of *situational ethics*[1] or *rationalized dispassion*[2] where we do not accept our responsibility to pass moral judgments on others.

Somehow, we have accepted the politically correct proposition that we should not "judge" other people. In doing so, we have not only abdicated our responsibility, but our obligation to maintain society's ethical norms. Relativists who argue that we should not judge others based on our personal moral values fail to fully grasp the axiom that ethics and morals serve a necessary and useful purpose in our society. We are perfectly within our rights to condemn immoral and unethical behavior. In fact, in a moral society, we are obligated to do so. Imagine how Enron and WorldCom would have turned out had people stood up and condemned the unethical behavior of the executives early on in the scandal.

Yet people still have the misguided belief that we have no right to pass judgment on the unethical behavior of others. A great example was a recent television interview with a police officer about a convicted murderer. The police officer said, "It's not up to me to judge him…" The point that was missed by the officer is that it is *exactly* up to him to judge the person. It is up to all of us to judge and condemn morally indefensible behavior. If we cannot morally condemn a convicted murderer's behavior, then we are saying that our moral values are no more valid than are the twisted values of the murderer. Moral relativists equivocate two distinctly different and opposing value systems as if one was no better than the other. This idea should be illogical to any rational person.

We often hear people say, "Who am I to judge him?" What these people fail to understand is that by "judging," i.e., making a moral judgment about someone's behavior, we affirm and keep intact our society's values. They confuse being "judgmental" with being intolerant, and of course, intolerance is intolerable. What these people fail to grasp is that *we make moral judgments all of the time*. That is how we do the "right" thing rather than the "wrong" thing. That is how we pick our friends and associates. By using our judgment, we make discerning decisions about many things that may deeply affect our families, our businesses, and ourselves. By making moral judgments, we help to define our own moral character and establish our own ethical standards. Hopefully, we also help establish these standards for our employees, our children, and others around us as well.

If given a choice, how many of us would steal money from a church, even if we knew we would not get caught? We would not do it because we made a moral judgment that it is wrong. Conversely, we judge people who do steal from churches as immoral people. If given a choice, how many of us would gladly associate with a murderer, rapist, or pedophile? How many of us would tolerate their behavior and want them as our close friends? How many of us would allow them to baby-sit our children? We don't do this because we made a judgment that their behavior is morally wrong, and we voluntarily choose not to associate with immoral people. In a business setting, how many of us would hire a convicted embezzler to handle our cash and our accounting system? Would we hire someone who has committed securities fraud to work with our investors on a new stock offering? Of course we wouldn't…because we judge these people to be morally and ethically deficient. To keep our moral framework intact, we judge others all of the time.

Once we abdicate our ethical values by failing to use them to "judge" others' behavior, they lose their meaning and what was heretofore unacceptable moral behavior eventually becomes acceptable. It is the "use it or lose it" principle. If we choose not to maintain our moral and ethical standards, we will eventually see them vanish. It is much like the farmer with the partially eaten pig. We continue to eat away at something of great value until it is gone and we have nothing of value left.

We saw this to a great extend during the 1990s. It became quite common, particularly in light of the Clinton scandals, to excuse immoral or unethical behavior by claiming that it was none of our business. Many people had no problem saying ridiculous things like "What people do in their private lives is none of my business," or "Of

course he lied under oath. He didn't want to embarrass his family."
We found it easy to excuse bad behavior by demonstrating how non-
judgmental and tolerant we could be and by practicing moral relativism on a broad scale. We have even gone to such lengths to excuse
immoral behavior that we began to say that oral sex is not really sex at
all. Not surprisingly, this new concept did not go unnoticed by the
thousands of high school students who now regularly practice oral sex
as a "non-sexual" activity. This shows how easy it is to lower moral
standards by pretending that immoral behavior really isn't immoral,
even when we know otherwise.

During this period of denial, pundits and spin doctors on national
news programs often said things like: "I don't condone this kind of
conduct, but who am I to judge someone else's behavior?" or "What I
consider wrong may not be what someone else considers wrong."
They made these outrageous statements as if there were different degrees of right and wrong for the same behavior. Ethics is like life and
death. You are either alive or you are dead. Doctors have not been
able to find a middle ground. Similarly, a behavior is either ethical or
it is not.

The academic world has not been of much help either. A poll that
was conducted by Zogby International[3] for the National Association of
Scholars revealed that three-quarters of all college seniors reported
that their professors teach them that right and wrong depends upon
"differences in individual values and cultural diversity." The students
also reported that their professors teach them that corporate policies
that further social and political goals are more important than policies
that ensure accurate accounting to shareholders and creditors. This
was clearly demonstrated when the students were provided with a list
of business practices and 38% listed "recruiting a diverse workforce in
which women and minorities are advanced and promoted" as the *most*
important policy. Only 23% said that "providing clear and accurate
business statements to stockholders and creditors" was the most important policy. Tell this to the executives at Tyco, WorldCom, Kmart,
and Enron who are facing criminal charges.

The students also learned to have a negative, perhaps cynical, image of business. 28% listed business as the profession where "anything

goes" (a higher percentage than was given to journalism and law). And a whopping 56% of the seniors surveyed said that the only real difference between the executives at Enron and executives at other large companies is that the Enron executives got caught. Stephen Balch, the president of the National Association of Scholars, expressed concerns about the disturbing results of the survey. "The revitalization and politicization of ethical standards," said Balch, "plus cynicism about business in general, opens the way for such excuse making."

The study concluded that "…it seems reasonable to believe that when students leave college convinced that ethical standards are simply a matter of individual choice, they are less likely to be reliably ethical in their subsequent careers." The study reiterated that three-quarters of the respondents said that this was the "relativistic view of ethics" that their professors were teaching them. (This may explain why 85% of the corporate fraud committed by managers is committed by new managers who have only been on the job for less than a year.) What is more disturbing about this study is that 97% of the seniors said that college has prepared them to act ethically in their personal lives.

All of these politically correct arguments from professors, pundits, apologists, and other relativists, mirror the cultural and historical arguments for moral relativism. Once again, moral relativists do not want to appear arrogant by claiming that their values are better (or more right) than someone else's values. But there is a difference. Although ethical beliefs may differ *within* a society, they do not differ to such a degree that right becomes wrong and wrong becomes right. Moral relativists fail to realize that there are certain universal moral principles that transcend culture, historical periods, and rationalized dispassion.

From a consequential perspective, what are the end results of moral relativism in today's society? It is either an increased tolerance of immoral behavior, or the failure to maintain society's ethical values. Neither result sounds very good. In a utilitarian context, the end result does not appear to be a benefit to anyone, nor does it seem to provide the greatest amount of happiness. Moral relativists fail to see the need in society to both espouse and practice a visible level of ethical standards. These standards provide stability to our society and put us all on a level playing field where we can all expect the same ethical conduct from everyone else, or see them sanctioned for failing to behave in an ethical way. Even the most primitive societies that may have had barbaric practices, at least made all of their members subscribe to those practices in order to have societal cohesion and cultural norms they could all depend upon for stability.

Universal Moral Standards

Regardless of cultural or historical practices, we can accept the proposition that there are some moral standards that are universal. For example, we believe that murder is wrong, regardless of the circumstances. Our belief that murder is *always* wrong means that cultures that practice infanticide are not morally justified in doing so, even though their culture condones and encourages it. Just a few decades ago, apartheid was practiced in South Africa, yet we knew that it was morally wrong, regardless of the fact that it was a part of the South African culture. We know that slavery is abominable, yet there are still cultures that routinely practice it. We cannot overlook slavery simply because another society believes that it is acceptable. We condemn it regardless of the cultural norms of that society. The Nazis believed that killing Jews was morally acceptable, and radical Muslims believe that killing "infidels" is praiseworthy. We cannot accept either of these cultural beliefs as morally right, and in fact, we must vigorously condemn both as morally reprehensible behavior.

We can carry universal moral standards into business as well. We know that there is no moral justification for cheating a customer, stealing from an employer, lying to a government investigator, defrauding stockholders, or cooking the books. These actions are unethical regardless of the circumstances, and we must condemn them in *all* situations. They are universal moral standards for business.

Notes

[1] Situational ethics describes the ability to pick and choose the ethical principles that apply in a given situation. For example, lying about a sexual affair may be acceptable if I do not wish to be embarrassed, but it may not be acceptable to me if someone lies to me during a job interview.

[2] I call this *rationalized dispassion* because people who practice this often rationalize to themselves that they should refrain from making a judgment or having an interest in the moral behavior of others.

[3] Poll conducted of 400 randomly chosen seniors from colleges around the country, April, 2002.

Michael P. Harden

Chapter Eleven: Obligation of Reciprocity

How many times have you felt skeptical when you have heard a politician say, "Although I accepted gifts from lobbyists and support-ers, I can assure you that it had no influence on my vote"? There is a reason that you find this statement hard to believe and often feel dis-trustful of politicians. It is known as the *obligation of reciprocity*.

As human beings, we are brought up to understand the principle of reciprocity — I do something for you, and in return, you will do some-thing for me. We say "thank you" when someone does something nice for us. We do this out of politeness (and reciprocity) that has been taught to us by our parents and caregivers as we grow up. We develop a sense of reciprocity that stays with us. We know at a psychological level that we have an obligation to reciprocate, so when someone gives us something or does something for us, we feel obligated to "return the favor." If we don't, we feel uncomfortable and perhaps even guilty.

This obligation is a social contract. We can call it either the "rule of reciprocity" or the "rule of obligation." In either case, the principle is the same. Whenever we accept a gift from someone, regardless of the value, we incur an obligation to provide some form of reciprocity. To not recognize this is naive. As we grow up, we are taught that we have a *duty* to reciprocate. As adults, we feel this sense of duty in our dealings with others. In fact, the words *duty* and *contract* are syno-nyms for the word *obligation*.

Webster defines *obligate* as follows: to place (someone) under a moral or legal obligation; to cause (someone) to be indebted by render-ing him a service. *Obligation* is defined as: something which a person is bound to do or not do as a result of such an agreement or responsi-bility. Additionally, *reciprocate* is defined: to return in kind some-thing done, given, etc., and to give and receive mutually.[1]

From these basic definitions alone, it is easy for us to conceive the notion that when someone renders us a service, it obligates us, or binds us, to do something in return. We all naturally sense this and psycho-logically feel the obligation to reciprocate when someone does some-thing for us or gives us a gift. So, when a person in a position of responsibility, whether he is a politician, a government official, a business manager, or an employee, accepts a gift or favor, that person has now placed himself in a situation where he may be incapable of performing his duty properly and making an unbiased judgment.

We differentiate this obligation from the explicit expectation that occurs in bribery. Bribery is an example of the obligation to reciprocate on a broader and more legalistic scale. The term "bribery" has many legal definitions, which in some cases may actually include minimum dollar amounts, but the underlying concept of obligation is valid regardless of any legal definitions.

People will often do things out of a sense of obligation. They may feel obligated to protect a friend, repay a debt, or return a favor. This sense of obligation is a fundamental psychological duty that we follow. When someone gives us a ride to work while our car is in the repair shop, we almost always offer to pay for gas, even if they were going there anyway. We feel an obligation to make the offer. When we are invited to someone's house for dinner, we usually bring something along as a gift, perhaps a bottle of wine. And after dinner, we linger because we do not want to "eat-and-run." We owe it to our host to spend some time with them after they have gone to such an effort to provide us a nice meal. When we go out to lunch with a colleague and they pick up the check, we more than likely will say something like "I'll get the next one." These are all examples of how we follow the rule of reciprocity on a daily basis. We do it without even thinking about it because it is a fundamental aspect of our nature.

Those politicians and businesspeople that claim to be uninfluenced by gifts or favors, delude themselves. In their own minds, they may actually believe that they are not being influenced, but they are denying the underlying psychological aspects of their behavior. Unless they are sociopathic, there is no way that they can accept a gift and not incur some degree of obligation.

In fact, to accept a gift and not reciprocate is, in itself, an unethical act. When a gift is given, a transaction takes place. As in any transaction, there is an underlying presumption of trust. Once the gift is accepted, the receiver now has a moral obligation, no matter how unsavory, to fulfill the implied obligation. To do otherwise is to violate that trust, because if someone gives you a gift, they have a *right* to reasonably expect you to return the favor, and you have a *duty* to do so. It is the nature of the social contract. Through the mere act of accepting the gift, you have tacitly agreed to the contract.

Let's look at an example: If I accept two unsolicited tickets for a European trip from a vendor who is bidding on my contract, and I then award the contract to his competitor, I can rationalize to myself that his gift had no influence on my decision. However, to accept his gift and then not reciprocate in awarding him the contract means that I "stiffed" or "double-crossed" him. Basically, I *used* the vendor (who was obviously expecting some form of reciprocity) to gain something for myself. By not returning the favor, I have violated my *duty* to reciprocate, albeit a duty that I should never have allowed myself to incur in the first place. The fact that reciprocating in this case would be unethical does not relieve me of my duty to reciprocate. Therefore, by accepting the gift, I have dug myself into an ethical dilemma, no matter which way I respond. That is because using someone to get "freebies" is also an unethical practice. If I intend to provide no reciprocity, i.e., to not fulfill my obligation, then I should not accept his gift in the first place. Otherwise, I have accepted the gift under false pretences because people who are in a position to gain something from my obligation do not give me gifts without expecting an obligation to incur. What other possible reason can there be for the gift? To claim the gift was given to me for no other reason than the gift-giver *liked* me, but didn't expect anything in return from me, insults the intelligence of any reasonable person.

This situation shows that I have three alternatives from which to choose:

1. I can accept the gift and reciprocate in kind, which is clearly unethical.
2. I can accept the gift without providing any reciprocity, using the person for personal gains, which is also unethical.
3. I can choose not to accept the gift, which is the only ethical thing to do.

The major difference between the obligation of reciprocity and *bribery* is that bribery is overt. In a bribery scenario, the person receiving the gift makes a definitive agreement to do something in return. (Bribery is a legal term and has many different definitions and requirements. Typically, for a transaction to be considered bribery, the receiver must *know* that giver's intention was to influence him through the gift, and the receiver must fulfill the obligation *because* of the gift.) In an obligation to reciprocate scenario where the agreement is not definitive, it is at least tacit or implied, making it an agreement nonetheless. It simply does not meet the *legal* definition of bribery. Politicians, in particular, are keenly aware of this distinction, and as a rule, will claim that the gift was not *intended* to solicit a favor and that no favor was *granted* in return. Case closed. They ignore the rule of the obligation of reciprocity, claiming that nothing unethical transpired.

William Buchholz made an interesting point when he wrote: "I suppose, to the cynical among us, *any* form of gift-giving is bribery. Perhaps, in fact, the greatest modern bribe of all is the marketer's 'free' gift. Its invisible strings tug at us unconsciously. Its insistence that no obligation exists becomes the obligation itself."[2]

One thing to remember about taking gifts, whether you consciously reciprocate or not, is that both parties — the gift-giver and the receiver — are morally culpable.

Reciprocity in Action: A Case Study

Jack Grubman, an analyst for Salomon Smith Barney, a division of Citigroup, presents an excellent example of obligations and reciprocity in action. Eliot Spitzer, New York state attorney general, was conducting a probe of conflicts of interest on Wall Street when he discovered a series of emails from Grubman that demonstrate vividly the swapping of personal favors. Grubman said in an email to one of his friends that he had upgraded his opinion of AT&T in order to get Sanford Weill, Citigroup's co-CEO, to help get Grubman's children into a private school. As more emails came to light, the amount of favors and reciprocity expanded as well. Here is how all of the "favors," the obligations, and the reciprocation took place:

1. Sanford Weill asks Jack Grubman to "take a fresh look" at the neutral rating of AT&T. (Weill serves on AT&T's board, and AT&T CEO, Michael Armstrong, serves on Citigroup's board.)
2. Grubman informs Weill of his reassessment of AT&T, and asks for help getting his kids into a prestigious New York nursery school.
3. Weill makes a call to the school and pledges a $1 million donation from Citigroup.
4. Grubman turns bullish on AT&T and gives it a "buy" rating.
5. AT&T awards Solomon (Citigroup) a deal to underwrite a new stock offering for AT&T's wireless unit. The value of the deal to Citigroup is $45 million.
6. Michael Armstrong (AT&T) lends his support on the Citigroup board to Weill and helps to oust co-CEO John Reed. Weill becomes the Chairman and CEO of Citigroup. (An email from Grubman states that Weill needed Armstrong's support to "nuke" Reed.)
7. Citigroup starts meeting its $1 million donation commitment to the school (spread over five years).
8. The school enrolls Grubman's children.

The parties in this situation claim no favors were ever asked for or granted, and Grubman is adamant that his emails, which make all of these claims, were simply his bragging to friends to make himself look important. If these denials are true, then we are witnessing a series of coincidences that are remarkable in their scope, or we are indeed seeing the obligation of reciprocity in action. Since an obligation incurs whenever a favor is granted, one does not need to overtly ask for reciprocation. If we look closely at the sequence of events that took place with Grubman, Weill, and Armstrong, it is easy to see how each favor triggered a reciprocal favor. So even if Grubman's disclaimer of his own emails is true, the obligation to reciprocate was occurring nonetheless. Here is how it worked:

1. AT&T's CEO, Armstrong, and Weill, co-CEO of Citigroup serve on each other's boards.
2. Weill asks Grubman to re-evaluate AT&T's stock rating (Weill's favor *to* Armstrong, and a favor *from* Grubman).
3. Grubman asks Weill for help getting his children into a private school (favor *from* Weill).
4. Weill makes a call to the school and pledges a donation from Citigroup (favor *to* Grubman).
5. Grubman upgrades the AT&T's rating (Grubman's favor *to* Weill, and Weill's favor *to* Armstrong).
6. AT&T gives a $45 million deal to Citigroup (Armstrong's favor *to* Weill).
7. Armstrong supports Weill over Reed at Citigroup. Weill then gets the Chairmanship (Armstrong's favor *to* Weill).
8. Citigroup begins donating the $1 million to the school (Weill's favor *to* Grubman, and Weill's favor *to* the school).
9. The school enrolls Grubman's children (school's favor *to* Weill).

Although each favor may not have been asked for specifically, each favor still incurred an obligation from its recipient, and each recipient reciprocated in some way. In the above case study, you can draw your own conclusions as to whether the reciprocity is conscious or unconscious, however, it is undeniable to any reasonable person that favors were indeed given for favors received.

On April 28, 2003, the Securities and Exchange Commission, the New York Attorney General's Office, the New York Stock Exchange, and the NASD announced that Jack Grubman was permanently barred from the securities industry and that he must pay $15 million to settle all of the charges against him. The main charge against Grubman was that he issued fraudulent research reports that contained omissions and misstatements of facts about the companies, recommendations that were contrary to the actual views regarding the companies, and that he minimized the risk of investing in these companies (including AT&T).

Grubman did not admit or deny the allegations and findings. Citigroup was forced to pay $400 million in fines as well.

The obligation of reciprocity is not always unethical. There are many situations where the transactions have no moral implications. What makes a transaction unethical is how and why the gifts are given and the favors are returned. When they involve business issues, the receiver of the gift typically violates the corporate trust of management, shareholders, and employees. In a public policy situation, the receiver of the gift violates a much larger trust, that of her constituents, supporters, and colleagues, while also damaging public confidence in our elected officials and our system of government.

Notes

[1] *New Webster's Dictionary and Thesaurus* (Lexicon Publications, 1992).

[2] William James Buchholz, "A Vexing Conundrum: Bribery and Public Relations," This article first appeared in *The Challenge of Change: Managing Communications and Building Corporate Image in the 1990s: Proceedings of the Second Conference on Corporate Communications* (May 24-25, 1989). (Madison, NJ: Fairleigh Dickinson University), V1-V20.

Chapter Twelve: Ethical Lapses

Have you ever seen a coworker or friend that you personally believed to be ethical do something that was dishonest or morally wrong? It may have shocked you, but it happens. Strangely enough, even people with solid ethical values will lapse into unethical behavior or make decisions that do not uphold ethical principles. There are several reasons why this can happen.[1] Among these are:

Competitive Pressures — Some companies exist in highly competitive markets. The competition may be so fierce that the survival of the company is at stake. In cases like this, managers and employees may be under so much stress and pressure to perform that they lose sight of their ethical principles in order to reduce their fear of failing to achieve their objectives, or in the worst case, fear of losing their jobs. An otherwise ethical manager or employee, when faced with deadlines that cannot be met, objectives that cannot be achieved, or other situations that may jeopardize their company's survival, may disregard their own ethical beliefs and/or the company's ethical standards to "get the job done." After operating this way for some period of time, these managers and employees may begin to consider that the means justifies the ends. Goal attainment becomes a high priority with little consideration of the methods used to achieve them. The engineer, for example, who sacrifices safety by using inferior materials in order to satisfy a tight budget, is so focused on cost containment that he overlooks the underlying ethical issues of his decisions.

Opportunity Pressures — Sometimes, the temptation to take advantage of an opportunity, albeit through unethical means, is so great that people cannot resist. This is particularly true if the penalties for doing so are nominal and the rewards are great. A struggling sales rep that notices a confidential proposal from a competitor on a prospect's desk, may succumb to the temptation to "sneak a peak" and garner proprietary information in order to obtain a competitive advantage. If she wins the contract and her company rewards her resourcefulness, she is apt to do more of the same unethical behavior down the road.

Globalization — Businesses have become more globalized in recent years. This globalization has caused problems for companies that must operate within new and diverse cultures that hold different ethical standards. Cultural norms affect business practices. Although bribery is illegal in the U.S., it is widely practiced in many countries, particularly in the less developed nations. In fact, the practice is so common outside the U.S., that most other countries allow money paid in bribes to be tax deductible. The term "bribery" itself is vague. It can mean a host of different practices, ranging from giving small "gifts" to gain favor, to paying "commissions" for help in obtaining a meeting with a decision maker, or secretly paying huge "kickbacks" for landing a contract.

Although most governments do not visibly condone bribery, corruption is so widespread that doing business internationally is next to impossible if the company does not follow the practice. The Foreign and Corrupt Practices Act (FCPA) of 1977 prohibits U.S. companies from making certain kinds of payments, even outside of the United States.[2] Therefore, U.S. companies doing business overseas are placed at a considerable disadvantage when competing with firms from other countries that have no such prohibitions. The pressure on U.S. business managers, doing business overseas, to compete on an even playing field may create situations that promote unethical behavior.

Moral Blindness — There are times when the ethical implications of a situation are not clear to an otherwise ethical individual. Sometimes the ability to see an ethical dilemma is blinded by rationalization. For example, when somebody says, "All companies do it," they are rationalizing their unethical behavior. Or they may say something like, "It's my job to get things done, and the boss doesn't care how I make it happen." And of course, there is the competitive cop-out: "If I didn't do it to them first, they'd do it to me."

The Wrong People — Sometimes companies hire the wrong people. These "bad apples" may have little concern for ethical behavior, and by their nature, may just be corrupt individuals. If the company culture has been influenced by these bad apples or if the company has put tremendous pressure on its employees to produce results, unethical behavior may become systemic. In that case, the company may be faced with a "bad barrel" rather than just a solitary "bad apple," and the entire culture is operating without solid ethical standards.

Goal Displacement

Another reason that ethical lapses may occur is due to a phenomenon known as *goal displacement*. In goal displacement, we find that people lose sight of the true organizational goals because we have set up a situation where the wrong behavior is rewarded. They may begin to engage in unethical behavior to satisfy the wrong goals. One of the best examples of goal displacement occurring on a large scale was the case of Sears, Roebuck and Company.

In 1991, Sears, Roebuck and Company, faced with severe financial pressure, decided to revamp its compensation plan for mechanics in its Sears Auto Centers. Previously, mechanics were simply paid an hourly wage. But Sears' management wanted to increase productivity and profits, so it devised an incentive system that would supposedly pay mechanics a smaller hourly wage, but provide them with a performance bonus using quotas and commissions. Also, so much pressure was applied to the workforce, that many were directly or indirectly told that they would lose their jobs if they did not achieve their repair sales quotas. Soon, mechanics found out that the only way to achieve their goals and make money was to concentrate on selling more work rather than servicing the customer. The new program resulted in mechanics and service managers over-billing customers, charging for work that wasn't performed, and charging for work that wasn't needed.

The California Department of Consumer Affairs (DCA) conducted an undercover operation during 1991 and found 34 of 38 instances where Sears' employees had recommended repairs or services that were unnecessary or where they had charged for services that were not performed. When word of the results came out, New Jersey, Florida, New York, Illinois, and several other states decided to investigate Sears Automotive Centers for consumer fraud. The scandal rocked Sears. Its reputation was severely tarnished, and it ended up costing Sears $60 million in legal fees, restitution, and lost sales. Many consumers stayed away from Sears Auto Centers for years.

The phenomenon that took place at Sears Auto Centers is an excellent example of goal displacement. In goal displacement, the means are confused with the ends. It is commonly characterized when the activities that are intended to help achieve corporate objectives actually have the opposite effect. What happened at Sears is a form of goal displacement known as *behavior substitution*. Behavior substitution is a phenomenon where employees substitute activities that do not lead to accomplishing their assigned goals for activities that do lead to accomplishing those goals. They do this because management is rewarding the wrong activities. Employees will work for the rewards, not for the real objectives, which in Sears' case, was to properly service their customers. What management was measuring and rewarding had little to do with servicing the customer efficiently. Sears' management set up a program that they thought would increase productivity, but by establishing the wrong incentives, they inadvertently rewarded unethical behavior. As one of the deputy attorney generals for California said: "There was a deliberate decision by Sears management to set up a structure that made it totally inevitable that the consumer would be oversold."

Another example of goal displacement that was observed many years ago was a large corporation located in San Francisco. The interoffice mail system was so inefficient that it often took several days for a simple envelope to travel from one floor in the building to another. Because there was always pressure to get things done quickly, and managers could not be effective without the quick turnaround of documents, an ingenious system evolved whereby all of the important interoffice documents were sent from one floor to another via Federal Express. It worked this way: A Federal Express driver would show up and pick up the envelope or package, drive it to San Francisco International airport where it would be put on a Federal Express plane bound for Memphis, TN. When it got to the Federal Express center in Memphis, the package would be sorted and put back on a plane headed to San Francisco. It would arrive in San Francisco the next morning, be put on a truck, and delivered back to the corporation's offices and taken to the correct floor by 10:00am that morning. This process took substantially less time than simply dropping the package in the interoffice mail and waiting several days for it to be delivered. The problem was the cost incurred by the corporation in thousands of dollars of Federal Express charges. The managers responsible for this "Rube Goldberg" solution took the easy way out. They could have worked within the current system and tried to improve it, but it was easier to spend the company's money to make sure that they could achieve their business unit and individual objectives.

The situation with this company and Sears shows how easy it is for management to create an environment that leads to unethical behavior by establishing goals that conflict with ethical objectives and then rewarding the unethical behavior. Another way to look at it is that goals that are easily measured and rewarded will cause employees to substitute behaviors that meet the measurements and achieve the rewards. They will tend to ignore those behaviors that are not as easily measured or do not result in rewards, even if those behaviors would help achieve the corporation's goals. This is why management must be careful to set up programs that actually reward the desired behavior. Otherwise, management pressures employees to behave in an unethical manner in order to achieve their rewards.

Another form of goal displacement that takes place in companies is a phenomenon known as *suboptimization*. This occurs when a business unit within the corporation optimizes its goal accomplishment to the detriment of other units or the organization as a whole. Suboptimization will occur when a division, subsidiary, or functional unit (accounting, human resources, sales, production, etc.) begins to think of itself as a separate entity and chooses not to cooperate with other business units because that cooperation might have a negative impact on its performance measurement. An example would be when the sales department of a software company contractually commits to deliver the new version of a product early in order to win a big contract (even though the sales department knows that the product is not yet ready for delivery). Since the product is not finished, R&D must work overtime to test and debug the product to meet the deadline. The sales department is able to meet its sales quota (and its salespeople get their commissions) but it does so at the expense of the R&D department which has incurred significant labor and financial costs to meet the deadline. The sales department has optimized its goal accomplishment, but the corporation as a whole may have missed its profitability goals due to the increased costs in R&D.

Companies must be careful about how they measure their business units and whether those measurements are exclusive of other business units' performance. Emphasizing separate cost or profit centers can increase the tendency towards suboptimization. Since suboptimization harms the entire organization while only benefiting a small business unit, most people consider it to be unethical behavior.

Survival

Another reason executives will lapse into unethical behavior is to build or save their companies. They will often overlook what they consider to be a nominal ethical issue when the bigger picture has to do with much more pressing issues like survival. Michael Dell and the Dell Computer Company provide us with an example.

Dell, now a heroic figure in business schools and Corporate America, had to resort to some unethical practices in the early days of his fledgling company. When he originally started his company, Dell had to find a cheap source of machines if he wanted to build his business. He started the company by selling IBM computers that he purchased on the gray market. Back in those days, IBM was pretty restrictive, not allowing its dealers to sell its PCs to anyone who would resell them. But no dealer ever wants to get stuck with unsold stock, so when Dell or one of his buyers approached them offering to buy up all of their surplus PCs at cost, they simply couldn't pass it up. As one of Dell's former buyers tells it, "I would go to, say, a ComputerLand store and tell the salesman I needed 10 or 20 computers. He would ask: 'Are these for resale?' And I'd say, 'No, I'm buying these for my fraternity brothers.'" Dell would then take the PCs and enhance them with graphics cards and hard disks before reselling them.[3]

How many business people would forcefully argue that Dell did the "wrong" thing to get his company started? By most objective standards, both Dell's behavior and the behavior of the retailers was unethical. Yet most business people don't think so.

Covering Mistakes

People will often lapse into unethical behavior to falsely create success or to cover a mistake. In some cases, the culprits will throw good money after bad to try to extricate themselves from a bad situation. Two symptomatic examples are Nick Leeson at Barings Bank and John Rusnak at Allfirst Bank.

Barings PLC (Baring Investment Bank) was Britain's oldest merchant bank in 1995. It had been around for 223 years and had a history that would astound you. It had financed the Louisiana Purchase in 1803 for Thomas Jefferson, thereby doubling the size of the United States. Barings had also helped finance the British government's war against Napoleon by lending money to maintain the war effort, buy military equipment, and pay soldiers. More recently, Queen Elizabeth was one of its clients. By any standard, Barings was a solid and prestigious banking firm.

In spite of its illustrious history and solid reputation, Barings went down the tubes in 1995 thanks to the singular efforts of Nick Leeson, one of its employees at Baring Futures Singapore. Through his unethical trading practices, Leeson had created liabilities for the bank totaling $1.3 billion, far more than the entire capital and reserves of the bank. Thanks to Leeson, Barings was technically bankrupt. The Dutch bank, ING, agreed to acquire the institution and assume its debt for the token sum of £1.

Leeson had come to the Singapore operation in 1992, and quickly became successful trading futures on the Nikkei exchange. He was making millions for Barings. Or at least that is what his bosses at Barings thought. Actually, Leeson was losing money for the bank. Nick Leeson, who was only in his mid 20's, was trading futures based on the Nikkei-225, an index of the leading Japanese stocks. He appeared to be doing so well that he earned over $1 million in salaries and bonuses during 1992 —1993.

What Leeson was supposed to be doing was arbitrage, seeking profits by buying options on one exchange and simultaneously selling on another to take advantage of price differences. Soon, Leeson began to move beyond arbitrage, and gambled on the future direction of the Japanese markets. He ceased hedging his positions, and eventually bought $7 billion worth of stock index futures and sold $20 billion worth of bond and interest rate futures. Leeson began to sell straddles on the Nikkei-225 (selling put and call options with the same strike prices and maturities). This strategy only works when the market is not volatile. The Nikkei-225 had to stay within the 18,500 — 19,500 range for Leeson's strategy to work. When the Kobe earthquake struck, the market began to decline. Things soon began to unravel for Leeson.

By the end of 1994, Leeson had already experienced losses of over $512 million, which he hid in a special account to avoid detection. Rather than admit the losses had occurred and stop the bleeding, Leeson decided to invest even more, buying large amounts of futures in an attempt to single-handedly prop up the Nikkei-225. His hope was to "dig himself out of the hole" before the losses would be found. In just three months, Leeson bought more than 20,000 additional futures contracts at $180,000 apiece. Eventually, Leeson's efforts were fruitless. The market did not rebound, and Barings collapsed under the $1.4 billion it lost on Leeson's trades.

Although Leeson pleaded guilty in a Singapore court to forging documents and misleading the Singapore Monetary Exchange

(SIMEX), he said before his trial, "I don't think of myself as a criminal." He was found guilty and sentenced to six-and-a-half years in prison. Leeson eventually served only three-and-a-half years of the sentence. With the loss of $1.4 billion, that equates to one year of punishment for every $400 million that Leeson lost.

The second story is just as informative. In October 2002, John Rusnak, a former currency trader, pleaded guilty to bank fraud after he hid $691 million in trading losses at Allfirst Bank in Baltimore. It was one of the largest bank fraud cases in U.S. history, and the largest worldwide since Nick Leeson caused the collapse of Barings Bank.

Rusnak ran up the losses at Allfirst over a five-year period, trading Japanese yen. Apparently, after sustaining large losses in his trades, Rusnak resorted to fabricating trades in order to cover those losses and show a profit. Once again, we see someone who, rather than admit to mistakes and notify the bank of the losses, devised a scheme to hide the situation, eventually costing the bank far more than the original losses. Rusnak began to take more and more risks, eventually digging himself into a hole he could not climb out of. He was able to avoid being caught by entering false information into the bank's accounting and trading systems. Rusnak created fictitious trades that created assets on the books that offset his liabilities.

The false profits earned Rusnak bonuses of $650,000 over his $85,000 salary. When word of Rusnak's losses first came to light, Susan Keating, the head of Allfirst Bank, commented "Up until Monday he was an employee of good standing." Even his neighbors had good words about him. One neighbor even went so far as to say: "He seems like a really cool guy. His kids are cool. I'm kind of shocked."

Rusnak agreed to a plea bargain of seven-and-a-half years in prison for one count of bank fraud. He was found guilty and sentenced to that term and to pay restitution of $1,000 per month for five years. That equals $60,000 restitution for a loss of $691,000,000.

After the losses came to light, Allied Irish Bank (AIB), the parent of Allfirst, agreed to sell Allfirst to M&T Bank Corp. for $3.1 billion. Dublin-based AIB denied that the sale had anything to do with the massive losses that Allfirst sustained in the scandal.

Ethical Differences Among Managers

In order to better understand why certain managers behave ethically and others do not, we need to be cognizant of the types of ethical differences found in managers. There are three types of ethical differences among managers.[4] These are: immoral, moral, and amoral.

Immoral Management — When the behavior of managers is devoid of any ethical principles, it is called immoral management. Managers who practice immoral management believe that the corporation or themselves come first. They will do anything that contributes to the success of the corporation or their own personal success. This could be lying, cheating, stealing, falsifying documents, bribery, "cooking the books," inflating earnings, threatening subordinates, or embezzlement. Some of this can be seen in many of the recent corporate scandals. Codes of conduct, regulations, and laws mean nothing to immoral managers.

Moral Management — The opposite of immoral management is moral management. With moral management we see managers who follow ethical principles, codes of conduct, professional standards, and comply with existing regulations and laws. Although, as good managers, they are still concerned with generating profits, they do so within ethical boundaries.

Amoral Management — When managers are indifferent to ethical concepts, or when they appear to lack awareness of ethical issues, they are considered to be amoral managers. They tend to act without fully realizing what the impact of their actions may be on others. Amoral managers may make decisions without taking into account ethical principles, which would have otherwise influenced their decisions.

The type of management — immoral, moral, or amoral — will greatly influence whether ethical lapses occur in the organization.

Agency Theory

Agency theory argues that top managers in corporations are not the "owners" of the company, but are "hired agents" who are more concerned with their own self-interests than those of the shareholders. Managers, who are merely agents of the owners, will make decisions that are likely to increase their own power, salaries, or bonuses, often at the expense of the owners (shareholders). Actions that accomplish this can range from needless acquisitions to heavy debt burdens to creative accounting. The likelihood that this will happen is greatest when the managers own little stock in the company and when a high percentage of the board of directors are friends of management or managers themselves (inside directors).

The traditional way to reduce the impact of agency theory was to ensure that managers had a large stake in the company, i.e., they owned sufficient stock to more adequately align their own self-interests with that of the owners (shareholders). However, an interesting phenomenon has recently developed which demonstrates that self-interests, whether they align themselves with shareholders or not, will always take precedence for some people. This phenomenon is contrary to agency theory.

The rash of recent corporate scandals seems to have actually occurred *because* managers had significant stakes in their companies. Except for those executives that looted the corporate coffers of their companies by embezzling funds or paying themselves excessive salaries, much of the corporate shenanigans that have taken place were all intended to drive up the value of the company's stock. When managers obtained significant ownership stakes or enormous grants of options, their subsequent actions became focused on creating shareholder value. This is supposed to be the solution to the problems associated with agency theory. However, in their own self-interests, managers became *too* driven to increase shareholder value. The results were "cooked books," phony balance sheets, hidden liabilities, bogus information to analysts, and efforts to keep these actions hidden from the board, shareholders, the press, and employees. Once managers (who were previously agents) became owners, their tactics shifted to meet the new circumstances.

The bottom line is that it doesn't matter whether certain managers have a little or a lot of stock in the company. Managers who are basically immoral will use whatever tactics they can to satisfy their own self-interests. The factor of ownership vs. stewardship simply alters the tactics they use. We can logically presume that an unethical manager who had enormous stock options and used phony accounting practices to drive up the stock price, would, if placed in a position where his ownership was nominal, use quite different tactics to increase his salary and bonuses instead.

Notes

[1] C. Farrell and John Fraedrich. "Understanding Pressures That Cause Unethical Behavior in Business," *Business Insights* (Spring/Summer 1990): pp. 1-4

[2] It should be noted that the FCPA prohibits payments that are intended to corrupt. It does not prohibit certain kinds of "facilitating" payments that are meant to help expedite routine government services or are legal under the written laws of the host country.

[3] Stephanie Anderson Forest, Catherine Arnst, Kathy Rebello, and Peter Burrows. "The Education of Michael Dell," *Business Week* (March 22, 1993): p. 85.

[4] A.B. Carroll, "In Search of the Moral Manager," *Business Horizons* (March/April, 1987).

Michael P. Harden

Chapter Thirteen: Moral Courage

In expressing our nation's desire to go to the moon, President John F. Kennedy said, "We do these things not because they are easy, but because they are hard." The same can be said of moral courage.

When we discuss ethical behavior, the term *moral courage* is not used very often, or at least not often enough. It has a profound meaning that is important in determining ethical behavior. Often, the ability of someone to behave ethically, particularly in the face of intense opposition, requires a great deal of moral courage.

The dictionary defines courage as "the capacity to meet danger without giving way to fear."[1] So courage doesn't mean that we are fearless, it simply means that we act in spite of our fears. As a society, we acknowledge that brave people, i.e., people who demonstrate courage, are brave not because they are unafraid, but precisely because they *are* afraid and still act nonetheless.

Courage is a virtue. In fact, Aristotle believed that courage was the greatest of all virtues. When he said, "Courage is the first of human qualities because it is the quality which guarantees the others," Aristotle was proclaiming that other virtues are meaningless unless we have the courage to both exercise and protect them. If a person is not courageous, he may not be able to exercise his other virtues, such as honesty, in situations where he is faced with strong opposition. What good then are virtues that cannot be practiced due to a lack of courage to practice them? Obviously, virtues that cannot be practiced are not virtues at all.

This definition and description of courage is accepted by most people. Courage seems to be a characteristic trait that has been universally admired in every society and culture that has ever existed on earth. It would be hard indeed to find anyone who would argue that courage is not a trait that they admire in others. So what then is moral courage? Simply stated, moral courage is the ability to overcome the fear to do the right thing. Yet the concept of moral courage is much deeper and complicated than this simple definition can express. That is because exercising moral courage often requires us to risk losing those things that we value about ourselves.

In a white paper written for the Institute for Global Ethics, Rushworth Kidder and Martha Bracy provided this definition of moral courage:

"Moral courage is not about facing physical challenges that could harm the body. It's about facing mental challenges that could harm one's reputation, emotional wellbeing, self-esteem, or other characteristics. These challenges, as the term implies, are deeply connected with our moral sense — our core moral values."[2]

Sometimes moral courage gives us the ability to overcome our fear of being humiliated, of being punished, or of being rejected, so that we can take a moral stand. Moral courage also allows us to stand up against immoral behavior, even though taking such a stand may be unpopular or dangerous. Moral courage is a positive attribute we use to overcome negative behavior.

On March 6, 1983, a 21 year-old woman named Sarah Tobias was raped by three men on a pool table in Big Dan's Bar in New Bedford, Massachusetts.[3] Numerous men watched the rape take place and did nothing to stop it. No one tried to intervene; no one called the police; no one even yelled, "Stop!" In fact, some of the men actually cheered the rapists on. But more profound is the fact that no one exercised any moral courage to stand up and stop something they knew to be morally wrong. Nobody had the courage to stand up to evil, even though the risk of danger to themselves was nominal. The observers of the rape simply could not find moral courage when it was needed the most. Sadly, evil will always win when people do nothing to stop it. Failures of moral courage happen much too often, allowing immoral acts to go unreported and unpunished.

Failing to find moral courage also happens in business situations. People find it difficult to display moral courage in the workplace because they fear losing their jobs, being ridiculed by coworkers, or being thought of as a "squealer." They cannot overcome these fears and "do the right thing" or prevent someone else from doing the wrong thing. Obviously, the opposite of moral courage is moral cowardice. General Charles Krulak said this of moral cowardice:

"Cowardliness in character, manifested by a lack of integrity, or honor, will sooner or later manifest itself as cowardliness in other forms. People who have the courage to face up to the ethical challenges in their daily lives, to remain faithful to sacred oaths, have a reservoir of strength from which to draw upon in times of great stress—in the heat of battle."[4]

Moral courage in the face of terrible consequences has been demonstrated throughout history. There were Romans who hid Christians from persecution in ancient Rome. There were abolitionists who helped slaves travel north in the "Underground Railroad" in the 1850s. And there were Germans, French, and Dutch citizens who hid Jews from the Nazis in the 1930s and 40s. In spite of all of the other people who took the easy way out and did nothing, these brave people overcame their fear of being persecuted or killed, and found the moral courage to do what they knew to be right.

If anyone ever exemplified moral courage, it is Jeffrey Wigand. Wigand was the head of research and development at Brown & Williamson Tobacco Corporation (B&W), the third largest tobacco company in the U.S. While there, he was privy to the company's efforts to use cancer-causing additives to increase the flavor and addictive nature of cigarettes. He saw first-hand how B&W lied about the addictive nature of nicotine and how the company hid documents that could be used against it in smoker's lawsuits. But there appeared to be nothing he could do about it, so he wrote an internal memo about the situation to the CEO of B&W, Thomas Sandefur. Soon thereafter, Wigand was fired by Sandefur.

Wigand was faced with a moral dilemma. He could not go public with the information because he had a confidentiality agreement that, if violated, would terminate his severance benefits, including his medical insurance. He desperately needed the insurance because his daughter had spina bifida and required daily medical care. Wigand chose to keep quiet to protect himself and his family.

However, over a period of time, Wigand began to see the need to go public with his information about nicotine and B&W. One of the seminal events that pushed Wigand into becoming the quintessential whistle-blower was watching Sandefur and six other tobacco company CEOs testifying before Congress that nicotine was not addictive. Wigand knew from B&W internal documents that Sandefur was well aware of the addictive nature of nicotine. His testimony was an obvious lie. Finally, Wigand decided to act.

Wigand delivered a crushing deposition in the government's lawsuit against the tobacco industry and agreed to do an interview with Mike Wallace on *60 Minutes*. The tobacco industry eventually lost the suit, thanks in part to Wigand's testimony, and was forced to pay a settlement of nearly $250 billion. But during this tumultuous period, Wigand's life would take a dramatic turn. He was faced with lawsuits from B&W, anonymous death threats against himself and his family, and a highly orchestrated smear campaign by his former employer. He even found a bullet in his mailbox. Eventually, Wigand's wife divorced him and took their two children. His reputation was ruined and he was unable to find employment at the level at which he had previously worked. He ended up teaching high school for about $30,000 per year, far below the $300,000 he had been paid at B&W. Today, Wigand continues his campaign against tobacco, lecturing often about the addictive nature of nicotine and promoting his not-for-profit group, "Smoke-Free Kids." Obviously, his life has changed a great deal due to his actions.

It is interesting to note that Jeffrey Wigand does not consider Sherron Watkins of Enron a hero or a true whistle-blower.[5] According to Wigand, Watkins' only action was to write an internal memo to Ken Lay, Enron's CEO. She never went outside the company to the SEC or the media. After writing the memo and talking to Lay, "She turned around, sat back down, and shut up...I don't think what she did was right."[6]

Jeffrey Wigand's story was later made into a movie, *The Insider*, where Wigand at least had the satisfaction of having himself played by Russell Crowe.

In 1977, Major General John Singlaub, the Chief of Staff of the Eighth Army in Korea, demonstrated moral courage in a different way. President Jimmy Carter had proposed (and planned on) withdrawing U.S. troops from South Korea. Singlaub and most other senior military leaders knew this would be a dangerous move. On May 18, 1977, General Singlaub gave what he thought was an off-the-record interview to a *Washington Post* reporter. In that interview, Singlaub expressed the concerns of himself, as well as those of other military leaders, that any withdrawal of troops would send the wrong message to North Korea and could likely lead to war. Singlaub was later told by the reporter that the interview was not off-the-record, but on-the-record. He offered Singlaub a chance to retract or change what he had said, but Singlaub refused, saying, "I'm not going to retract anything I said because I don't believe in changing what I consider to be the truth."[7] Singalub held to his position even though he knew he would get into trouble for this.

The next day, the interview appeared in the *Washington Post*. President Carter was livid, and Singlaub was summoned to the White House. Senior Pentagon officials advised Singlaub to say that he was misquoted, but he refused to lie. High-ranking officers and Pentagon officials who knew that Singlaub was right, refused to defend him and ran for cover, leaving General Singlaub hanging out to dry. An angry President Carter relieved him of his duties in Korea. Later, when Singlaub spoke out about other disastrous defense policies of Carter, he voluntarily retired rather than embarrass the Army by embroiling it in a confrontation with the President. Congress eventually prevented Carter's ill-advised troop withdrawal from Korea, and history has since vindicated Singlaub's position over Carter's.

Many years later, I met Jack Singlaub at a party. By that time, few people remembered how he had sacrificed his career to attract attention to what he and others believed was a disastrous and dangerous policy. I asked him about the incident and told him that I admired his courage. He downplayed his sacrifice and told me, "Falling on your sword isn't really as tough to do as you think…if you know you're right." I thought that was good advice coming from someone who definitely knew what he was talking about.

If there is no risk of loss; no risk of paying a price; then there is no moral courage involved in making a decision or taking a stand. Moral courage comes only when there is little to gain (such as financial rewards), and a lot to lose (such as your job, your reputation, or your business associations). This is the situation often faced by whistle-blowers. They must decide whether to risk losing their jobs, being ridiculed by their peers, or facing the contempt of their organization's management in order to stop some unethical practice.

It is easy to be ethical when all around you are upholding ethical principles and are acting in an ethically responsible way. However, when those around you are behaving badly, it is more difficult to demonstrate ethically correct behavior. The urge to "fit in" is often hard to fight. But reaching deep within oneself and finding the moral courage to do the right thing while others are doing the wrong things, is what makes the difference — the difference in our workplace and the difference in how we feel about ourselves. The true test of moral courage is the ability to tell a coworker who is acting immorally to stop doing so, or to report unethical behavior to those people in a position to do something about it.

The 2000 National Business Ethics Survey (NBES) of 1,500 employees found that two out of every five employees who observed misconduct, failed to report it. Obviously, a fear of retaliation by management is one reason, but another reason is fear of retaliation by coworkers. One out of every three respondents said they believed that coworkers would see them as "snitches." Even though employees know what is right and what is ethical, they cannot overcome their fear of being labeled a "troublemaker" by management or a "snitch" by coworkers.[8] Since so much about ourselves is defined by our jobs — our self-image, or social relationships with coworkers, our status, and our income — finding the moral courage to overcome the fear of losing this is difficult for many people.

Notes

[1] *New Webster's Dictionary and Thesaurus of the English Language.* (Lexicon Publications, 1992).

[2] Rushworth M. Kidder and Martha Bracy. "Moral Courage, A White Paper," Institute for Global Ethics, (2001).

[3] This incident was used as the basis for the movie, *The Accused*, which starred Jodie Foster as Sarah Tobias.

[4] "Marines Have to be Held to Higher Standards," *USA Today* August 11, 1998: Sec. A - 10

[5] It can easily be argued that although Sherron Watkins has received much praise as a "whistle-blower," she does not meet the definition of a whistle-blower. Boatright's definition (see Chapter Twenty-Three) states: "Whistle-blowing is the voluntary release of nonpublic information, as a moral protest, by a member or former member of an organization outside of the normal channels of communication to an appropriate audience about illegal and/or immoral conduct in the organization or conduct in the organization that is opposed in some significant way to the public interest." Watkins did not release nonpublic information outside of the company, and in fact, was criticized by her fellow employees for not going to the SEC. Watkins' later Congressional testimony was not "voluntary" since it was under subpoena, and it occurred *after* the Enron bankruptcy had been filed and the scandal had already become a matter of some public knowledge. Her now famous memo to Ken Lay was not given by her to the government, but was discovered by Congressional staffers buried in 40 boxes of subpoenaed Enron documents, which then prompted her subpoena and testimony. Technically, you cannot be considered a whistle-blower if you are subpoenaed to testify.

[6] Information about Jeffrey Wigand was taken from an article by Chuck Salter. "Jeffrey Wigand: The Whistle-Blower," *Fast Company*. From Web-Exclusives (March 2002). www.fastcompany.com/articles/2002/05/wigand.html.

[7] John K. Singlaub with Malcolm McConnell. *Hazardous Duty* (New York: Summit Books, 1991) p. 389.

---

[8] Joshua Joseph, Lee Wan Veer, and Ann McFadden. "Ethics in the Workplace," *Executive Update Online* (October 2000).

Section Two: Business Ethics Issues

Businesses are complex entities, and because they are so complex, businesses are faced with ethical dilemmas each and every day. Some ethical issues may be more problematic than others, but the variety and number of possible ethical dilemmas can be staggering. Ethical dilemmas can spring from the many different relationships that businesses have with stakeholders. Every business must be cognizant of the relationships it has with its customers, employees, shareholders, directors, managers, suppliers, business partners, government agencies, the local community, bankers and lenders, and even its competitors. Businesses also deal regularly with controversial issues, such as sexual harassment, AIDS and HIV, privacy, employee monitoring, drug testing, discrimination, and whistle-blowing. Businesses also face ethical dilemmas dealing with day-to-day operational issues, e.g., Internet usage, software piracy, employee theft, lay-offs, trade secret protection, hiring and firing, promotions, raises, and conflicts of interest. And of course, businesses are faced with new and pervasive ethical dilemmas that naturally evolve from new and ubiquitous technologies, most recently the Internet and computers.

This section covers a wide range of ethical issues that organizations typically face. By identifying and analyzing these issues, we can gain a better insight into where ethical dilemmas are likely to occur and how we might be able to address these issues. We can also see how the ethical principles we studied can help solve these dilemmas and lead us to ethically correct decisions.

Michael P. Harden

Chapter Fourteen: Ethics and Technology

We can legitimately proclaim that ethics isn't what it used to be. Whereas in the past (no more than 20 years ago), business ethics dealt primarily with business deals and how companies treated their employees, customers, and shareholders; things have now changed. The reason things are different is because two new advances in technology added significant new moral issues to businesses. These two technological advances are the computer and its offspring, the Internet.

Until computers and the Internet came along, we did things the "old fashioned" way. We used paper files in locked filing cabinets. We used the U.S. Postal Service to send and receive mail. We used the telephone and fax machine (with all of its limitations) to communicate with each other. There was no such thing as "surfing the net" or downloading pornography. We couldn't send messages around the world in nanoseconds. We couldn't collect and retain the massive amounts of information we now keep on clients, employees, competitors, and suppliers. We were never able to do such massive mathematical and financial calculations in such a short period of time. We never had to worry about the prospect of "computer errors" wreaking havoc on people's lives. Nor have we ever been able to monitor so many different communications so easily without people knowing they are being monitored.

When technology advances, particularly as quickly as it did in the last twenty years, it is hard for ethical guidelines to keep up. Issues that were easy to deal with in the past, no longer seem to apply. One excellent example is software. When software came into common use, many people were unsure as to how it should be handled. Was it property? If so, who owned it? Could it be copyrighted? Could it be copied? These were all new issues. Some business, legal, and technology experts thought software should be owned and treated just like a written document (books, magazines, etc.). There should be copyrights, licenses, and fees. Property rights should apply because software was the fruit of someone's labor. Other experts advocated the position that software was not a tangible thing, so it couldn't be owned. It was nothing more than a string of electronic 1's and 0's. How could someone copyright or own electronic numbers? Moreover, if the underlying operation of software is nothing more than a series of various mathematical calculations, how could someone own those? Beyond these points, there were also well-meaning people who believed that since software could be reproduced so easily without loss of quality, it should be available to everyone, free of charge. Software could be written and reproduced in infinite quantities, allowing everyone on earth the opportunity to take advantage of it. The quality of human life could be dramatically improved.

With so many competing ideas about how to treat this new technological advancement, it was only through diligent analysis, numerous court cases, and much wrangling by legal scholars that we finally got to where we are today regarding the ownership of software. This process took years…and that is how new technology creates new ethical issues. More recently, we have seen technology create ethical issues in areas such as downloading music on the Internet, cloning human beings, conducting stem cell research, and monitoring employee emails. Resolving the ethics issues created by a new technology often lag behind the technology itself. This leaves a period of time, perhaps several years, where ethical and moral issues are ambiguous and we have to "feel" our way through them.

In the past, if you walked into an office and opened someone's private filing cabinet and read her personal correspondence, you knew that what you were doing was morally wrong. Today, many people agonize over the "rightness" or "wrongness" of reading someone's email or going though someone's computer files. It doesn't seem to be as clear-cut as breaking into a physical object like an office, filing cabinet, or safe. This is the dilemma that technology has thrust upon us.

As new technologies develop and roll out into the business community, we will inevitably find that new ethical issues will soon follow. If the technologies are revolutionary, much like the computer and the Internet were several years ago, we will find ourselves trying to fill the gap between our application of the technologies and our capability to define and solve the ethical dilemmas they create. This phenomenon will leave business managers and ethical philosophers scrambling to develop new policies and standards to ensure ethical practices. In the meantime, we will have to muddle through, applying the ethical principles we have learned to these new situations. Eventually, our ethical (and legal) practices will catch up. Then it will start all over again with the next new revolutionary technology.

In subsequent chapters, we will explore many of the common ethical issues faced by businesses today, particularly those that sprang from new technology.

Michael P. Harden

Chapter Fifteen: The Internet

Of all of the technological advancements that have occurred in the 20th Century, the one that has created the most ethical dilemmas for business is the Internet. To understand these problems, we must first look at how the Internet came about.

Few people realize that the Internet exists largely because of the U.S. government and a few major universities. The government's Advanced Research Projects Agency (ARPA) provided the original funding in the 1960s to a group of universities that were perfecting network transmission and packet switching technology. ARPA, however, had a greater goal: to develop a network of computers capable of surviving a major disaster — more specifically, a nuclear war – and sharing information with each other. Redundancy was a crucial factor in the design to ensure that vital information wasn't lost in a disaster. The idea was to establish a capability for the quick exchange of information from one computer to another. This Cold War-driven network became known as ARPANet.

The first packet switch was installed in 1969 by researchers at UCLA. Telephone lines then linked the UCLA system to a few other institutions, and ARPANet was off and running. More host computers were added on a regular basis, building a network that spanned the country. Soon, educational institutions and government agencies wanted access to this vast array of computers and their wealth of information, so these organizations began connecting to the ARPANet. However, there were no common protocols, so actual utilization of ARPANet, and navigating through it was difficult at best. A common protocol had to be developed to make ARPANet a viable tool.

In 1983, ARPANet's original protocol (called Network Control Protocol) was replaced with Transport Control Protocol/Internet Protocol (TCP/IP), which is what we all use today. The implementation of TCP/IP is what made the Internet a viable tool for information exchange.

The early Internet users were researchers, scientists, university students, and some government personnel. Their focus was on the exchange of information. ARPANet, even with the implementation of TCP/IP, handled text-based transmissions and little else. Graphics were never built into the design of ARPANet, so its users were restricted to sending and receiving emails and accessing simple files. Since most personal computers were now using graphical user interfaces (GUI), the Internet was behind the times.

In 1989, a campaign began to overlay the Internet with a GUI that would create the World Wide Web (WWW). By 1992, the campaign to encourage the development of web servers was underway in earnest. There are now over 16 million host computers acting as web servers with new ones coming on-line every day.

Although ARPANet was originally built for trusted users — not the general public — the combination of a new protocol and a graphical user interface made the Web accessible to any user. As it is today, anyone with a computer and modem can "surf" the Web, and find, retrieve, and exchange information in just a few keystrokes. Although the Internet is more than just the World Wide Web, it was the Web that made the Internet easy to use. Today, there are about seven million web sites and over one billion unique web pages on the World Wide Web. There are also over 600 million Internet users worldwide, and it is expected to double in two years.

The primary goal of the Internet was to establish an easy way for users to communicate and exchange data among themselves. Care was taken to ensure that the "net" was open and easy to navigate. The eventual implementation of the World Wide Web (WWW) allowed anyone with a computer and modem to connect to computers anywhere in the world at anytime of the day or night, making the Internet a useful commercial tool. The ultimate goal of the ubiquitous Web was to make things so easy that non-programmers could navigate and connect through the Internet in the comfort of their homes or offices. However, the Internet and e-commerce are not as compatible as most people think.

The Internet, which is used for the exchange of information, is built on the ability to easily find and retrieve information. E-commerce, on the other hand, requires a high level of secrecy. Bank account information, credit card numbers, business relationships, purchase/order information, and quite a bit of other proprietary information that is integral to e-commerce and business must be kept secure from unauthorized access.

The free and open exchange of information originally contemplated by the founders of the Internet runs completely contrary to the restrictive exchange of confidential data that forms the basis for e-commerce and business. In most companies, the one thing that gives them a competitive advantage is their proprietary information. Data and information dealing with trade secrets, personnel, pricing, clients, prospects, processes, marketing strategies, etc., are passed around on the Internet, stored on computers, and sent via email on a regular basis.

This need for strict security and restricted access is incongruous to a system whose fundamental concept is based upon openness and ease of access. This is particularly poignant to businesses that rely on an Internet presence that must be available to customers at all times, such as web sites, storefronts, and email.

The Internet has spawned problems for businesses, not only because of the lack of truly secure systems, but for the following reasons as well:

- Increased speed
- Email
- Anonymity
- Hacking
- Reproducibility
- Global reach
- Spamming
- Netiquette
- Pornography
- Wasted time
- Viruses
- Information theft

Each of these features, characteristics, or problems presents some kind of new ethical dilemma that business people did not have to deal with prior to the widespread use of the Internet. People can do things via the Internet that were heretofore impossible to accomplish. The problem is that many of these actions are unethical, and the anonymous and ubiquitous nature of the Internet provides people with capabilities that promote this unethical behavior. Described here in more detail are some of the ethical issues the Internet has created.

Increased Speed

Information can now travel anywhere in the world in nanoseconds. Communications that would have required slow mail or expensive international calling have been replaced with keystrokes and a "send" button. We can type a message and send it immediately to our desired recipient. Information about people can be requested or sent in a moment, without any formalities or second thoughts. If the information is erroneous, it can arrive and be used long before any error can be caught. In our fast-paced business world where we must move quickly to remain competitive, this can cause the wrong decisions to be made. In the past, the time lag between sending and receiving information was sufficient in many cases to allow errors to be caught and corrected before major decisions were made. Carelessness can be amplified through this speed, or unethical people can take advantage of it. Imagine someone sending time sensitive information that is false, knowing that it may take hours or days for the correct information to surface. This is particularly pernicious when financial transactions are involved.

This new increase in speed and the corresponding demand for it inhibits thoroughness and completeness. This allows costly errors to occur, or worse, it allows unscrupulous people to take advantage of it for their own gains.

Email

Email creates a whole series of ethical problems for businesses. Of course, there are always people who utilize email for personal correspondence, which may be in violation of company policies. This practice takes time away from productive business endeavors and utilizes corporate resources (computers, bandwidth, servers, etc.) for non-business purposes. But most companies tend to overlook this practice, and most employees feel entitled to it anyway…almost as if it were a fringe benefit. But this is not where the egregious problems occur.

Email has an inherent problem that many people fail to realize — its permanence. Unlike phone conversations that are fleeting (once the words have been spoken they are gone, usually with no details of the conversation), emails are permanent until someone actually makes the effort to delete them. So communications conducted via email (which has replaced the phone for many people), remain in the system until somebody actually goes to the effort to delete them. But that may not erase all of the copies. There is a copy with the sender, a copy with the recipient, and there could likely be many copies in between — on servers, in corporate archives and backups, or even archived at the Internet service provider (ISP). In fact, there is probably *always* a copy of an email somewhere. Furthermore, there could be forwarded copies as well. After all, once an email is sent, there is no way for the sender to know how many people may eventually see it. It can easily be forwarded to several individuals or to an entire address book with just a few keystrokes. It can also be forwarded in error by simply clicking on the wrong address in the list. Haven't you ever gotten someone else's email by mistake?

People fail to realize this possible unrestrained proliferation of their emails. Assuming some level of privacy, they say things in their emails that they would not want anyone else to know, yet fail to appreciate the fact that once sent, the information is no longer under their control. Many a corporate executive has regretted saying something in an email once it became public. Analysts with several brokerage firms have been investigated by various government agencies when their public "buy" recommendations for stocks conflicted dramatically with their internal emails calling the same stocks "a dog" with little chance of increasing in value. In fact, the SEC and other regulators now require brokerage firms and other financial organizations to retain and archive all of their emails. It is unlawful to delete them, and some organizations have been caught doing so.

One of the more recent Wall Street scandals where email was used to prove wrongdoing involved Merrill Lynch. In a settlement with the New York Attorney General's office, Merrill Lynch agreed to pay $100 million in fines and change the way its analysts do business. Evidence used by Eliott Spitzer, New York Attorney General, came from Merrill Lynch's own internal emails. Spitzer and his team of attorneys sifted through nearly 95,000 pages of Merrill Lynch's emails. Buried within this mountain of email were the specific emails that were able to demonstrate that Merrill Lynch's investment advice was tainted by conflicts of interest. For example, when the company was recommending to its clients that they should buy and accumulate a certain stock, its internal emails were calling the stock "a piece of crap." In another example, Merrill Lynch's analysts placed a stock on their "Favored 15" list and gave it their highest buy rating while simultaneously calling is a "piece of junk" and a "powder keg" in their own emails. The trail of these emails conclusively made the case for the State of New York.

Eventually, because of these emails, the Securities and Exchange Commission, the New York Attorney General's Office, the New York Stock Exchange, and the NASD announced the results of the most sweeping investigation of the top 10 Wall Street firms. Firms including Citigroup, Merrill Lynch, Bear Sterns, Lehman Brothers, and J.P. Morgan Chase was forced to pay $1.4 billion in fines. Two analysts, Jack Grubman of Citigroup's brokerage subsidiary, Salomon Smith Barney, and Henry Blodget of Merrill Lynch were required to pay a combined $19 million and accept a lifetime ban from the securities industry. All of this initially came to light through the review of emails.

Employees also fail to recognize that most employers "own" the email system and reserve the right to view any and all emails an employee may send or receive. What an employee believes to be private is actuality not private at all. Typically, when employees learn that their emails are not private, they feel violated and resentful. And of course, there is always the question of what someone should do if they receive an email sent to them in error that has private information that could be harmful to the company, to certain employees, or to shareholders. What is the correct protocol for such a situation? Sadly, most employees don't know.

Emails can prove costly for an organization too. Fourteen percent of companies surveyed by the ePolicy Institute have been ordered by courts to produce employee emails (up from nine percent in 2001). Yet only 34 percent of companies have a written email retention and deletion policy, the same percentage as 2001.[1] Here is an example of a real situation provided by the ePolicy Institute: A Fortune 500 company involved in a wrongful termination suit by a former employee was ordered by the court to turn over any emails that mentioned the name of the terminated employee. The company had no policy in place to purge old emails, so the company would have to search through over 20,000 back-up tapes that contained millions of emails messages. At a cost of $1,000 per tape, the search would cost the company $20 million.[2]

In another example, female employees won a sexual harassment suit against Chevron in 1995 because an email had been circulated by male employees titled: *25 Reasons Why Beer is Better Than Women.* Chevron paid the women $2.2 million to settle the suit.[3]

Anonymity

The Internet provides a level of anonymity that is unprecedented. Although we have had the ability for years to send anonymous letters or to make anonymous phone calls, nothing has magnified or extended that capability like the Internet has. In the time it takes to hammer a few keys on our keyboards, we can send messages to anyone in the world and never have to reveal exactly who we are, where we live, or what we look like. Many business people communicate regularly with other business people (clients, suppliers, colleagues, etc.) whom they have never met, seen, or spoken to. Although they "know" these people from their business dealing via the Internet and email, and may even feel that they have some rapport, they have still maintained a significant level of anonymity. They would not be recognized on a bus or in a meeting, nor identified by their voices in a conversation, either in person or on the phone. Neither their physical features nor the tone of their voice is readily apparent. For all practical purposes, they would be "indescribable" to others. So the anonymity is based on the lack of physical information we have about the other person. Anonymity also flows from the use of email addresses instead of actual names and real addresses. We can look at a person's name and use that to find or identify them. We can "look up" someone's address in the phone book or actually find the physical location the address represents. This gives us a sense of identity, even for people we do not know. The Internet, on the other hand, lacks this basic characteristic.

When I receive an email, as I often do, from someone calling themselves something like "hotdog221@yahoo. com"or "590act72@wng. net"or any of a million other indecipherable email addresses, I have no idea as to who is contacting me. Unless I have received email from these individuals in the past and memorized their email addresses, I cannot reasonably discern who they are. Not only is this frustrating, but it can be dangerous too.

But this is only one level of anonymity that the Internet fosters.

Pseudonymity

Another level of anonymity is created by the Internet's ability to foster pseudonymous communications. *Pseudonymity* is the ability to disguise oneself when communicating. Using false names, fake email addresses or domain names, or even bogus IP addresses, are several of the ways someone can maintain pseudonymity. A smart hacker can even assume someone else's identity. We often use the term anonymity when we really mean pseudonymity. The terms are somewhat interchangeable.

Anonymity and pseudonymity diminish the sense of accountability and responsibility that individuals would have otherwise experienced in telephonic or face-to-face communications. By being so cyber-distanced from the other participant, a feeling of anonymity ensues, reinforced by the reduced risk of being identified or seen. This anonymity emboldens some people to do unethical things. In some cases, this may be unethical behavior that they would never contemplate doing in a more personal setting. Cyberstalking, flaming, hacking, outrageous speech, pornography, threats, fraud, theft, and pernicious gossip are just some of the types of behavior that anonymity fosters.

I am reminded of an incident in a chat room where one participant so consistently used vulgar and obscene language (also known as *flaming*) that the other chat room members could no longer bear it. When he was finally confronted about his behavior and asked why he felt so compelled to use such crude and repulsive language, he replied that he did so because he could not "get away with it" elsewhere, but he could in the chat room. Since no one knew him in the chat room, he felt free to do as he pleased there without fear of embarrassment or punishment.

The Internet does indeed make unethical behavior easy. Although we can trace Internet communications through ISPs and back to certain IP addresses, servers, or computers, we still have to find the person who is responsible for the communications, which is a much harder task. According to Jonathan Wallace, "Today, one can set up an Internet account without one's full name being stored anywhere on the Internet; in fact, by setting up accounts on a private network attached to the Internet, users may gain use of the Net without placing their identities on file anywhere at all. Anonymity and pseudonymity are built into the architecture of the Net."[4] Enterprising hackers can also utilize phony IP addresses and other tricks to inhibit tracing and identification.

This anonymity and pseudonymity has so worried law enforcement officials, that they have actively been combating it at every turn. Their efforts, however, have met with little success, as the courts have consistently sided in favor of anonymity. Courts have linked anonymity to free speech and the ability to engage in political discourse without fear of retaliation. In fact, when Georgia implemented a law that criminalized anonymous and pseudonymous Internet communications, a federal district court issued a decision that invalidated the law.[5] The original law was H.B. 1630, an amendment to the Computer Systems Protection Act. This Georgia law made it a misdemeanor for anyone to "transmit any data through a computer network using any individual name…to falsely identify the person…transmitting such data."[6]

The ACLU and a group of plaintiffs filed suit challenging the constitutionality of the law. The court ruled that the act "prohibits such protected speech as the use of false identification to avoid social ostracism, to prevent discrimination and harassment, and to protect privacy."[7] Oddly enough, the very things that make Internet anonymity and pseudonymity dangerous also make them constitutional and protected.

Where previous generations of criminals maintained anonymity by hiding in shadows or using hoods or masks, today's cyber-criminals can achieve enhanced anonymity by simply using the electronic distancing so easily afforded to them by the Internet.

Hacking

Perhaps no other medium has been exploited for unethical purposes as effectively as the Internet.[8] The principal players in this destructive game are known as *hackers*. The term "hacker" was introduced by Steven Levy in his book titled: *Hackers*. He was referring to the original computer programmers that helped launch the computer movement that has since overtaken us. These people were creative, bright, and skilled programmers in an area where expertise was thin. They worshiped computers and thought they were doing something great by advancing technology. "Hacker" was a name they were proud of bestowing upon themselves. It was worn as a badge of honor. Today, sadly, that has changed. Although there are still "good guy" or "white hat" hackers, the term most typically refers to the "black hat" or "rogue" hackers that are destructive and malicious.

Anyone can become a hacker in today's world of "point and click" technology. Most of the programs utilized by hackers to breach security or launch denial-of-service attacks are readily available on the Internet from hacker web sites. Anyone with a computer can become a hacker by simply downloading the appropriate programs, following some simple instructions, and launching the program. The programs will do most of the work on their own, including finding the vulnerabilities they seek to exploit via the Internet.

There are professional hackers as well. These are people who hack for a living. They may steal trade secrets and sell them to competitors, lift credit card numbers for their own use or for sale, or hire themselves out for industrial espionage. They are usually more skilled and experienced than the typical hacker, but make use of the same tools and techniques. In many cases, they are capable of modifying or enhancing the programs they use to increase their capabilities.

Hackers, and the tools they utilize, are capable of delivering a full array of mayhem to an organization's computer systems. Typically, this is done by exploiting the existing weaknesses in the computer programs hosted by the target organization. Most software in use today is made up of millions of lines of complex code. Because of the size, complexity, and rush-to-market mentality intrinsic with most software, there are always flaws or "bugs" in most programs. In many cases, these bugs are not things that affect the operation of the program, so they typically go unnoticed by the user and remain a low priority with the developer. Hackers, on the other hand, depend upon these flaws in the programs to gain access to otherwise secure systems and do their damage. Most tools developed by hackers are focused simply on exploiting an existing weakness in a software program.

There are approximately 100,000 hackers worldwide. These hackers can be divided into three groups:

Amateurs — They are not very proficient from a technical standpoint and tend to get their kicks by simply proving that they can penetrate a system. They make up about 90% of all hackers.

Browsers — Browsers have more technical skills than amateurs and have the ability to gain access to proprietary files. They may steal information, but do little damage to systems. Browsers probably make up about 9% of all hackers.

Crackers — These individuals are true cyber criminals. They have sophisticated technical abilities, and they use these skills to steal information and corrupt or damage computer systems.

They can penetrate most secure systems, crack password files, and move undetected throughout a system. Crackers account for about 1% of all hackers worldwide.

To better understand the types of hacker attacks on a system, a more detailed explanation is provided here. Unauthorized intrusions into proprietary systems typically fall into four different categories. These are:

Vandalism — This type of security breach is often characterized as the work of a teenage sociopath with too much time on his/her hands. Breaking into a proprietary system simply amounts to a challenge. Defacing web pages and inserting pornographic pictures or graffiti are typical trademarks left behind to demonstrate that the system was breached. Some hackers consider this nothing more than a prank. Others, incredibly, believe they are doing you a favor by demonstrating the weaknesses in your system. Warped values are definitely at play here. This object lesson results in an organization spending significant amounts of time and money in repairing the damage done by these hackers.

Criminal Theft — Hackers in this category are typically professional cyber-thieves who attempt to gain access to credit card numbers, bank account records, and any other information that can be utilized to steal money. Since it is their profession, and this is how they make their living, these thieves are particularly skilled and persistent.

Industrial Espionage — Competitors that seek customer or prospect lists, new product information, proprietary data, formulas, or any other trade secret information that may be valuable in a competitive business environment fit this category. Additionally, disgruntled former employees or individuals that harbor grudges may seek to damage an organization by corrupting its data or debilitating its computer systems.

Military — The military is always subject to potential security breaches by known and unknown enemies that may range from an individual terrorist to entire nation-states. The purpose of military hacking, more commonly known as cyber-warfare, is twofold: to seek valuable intelligence and/or to disrupt command and control operations. The techniques are often the same as those used in industrial espionage but waged against military and political targets.

The types of attacks against systems can be better understood by outlining what tools and techniques hackers usually have in their bag of tricks. Listed here are some of the many ways in which hackers can breach security:

Sniffers — Hackers can insert packet-sniffing programs into remote network switches or host computers that listen to and read network traffic. Typically, by picking up the first 125 keystrokes of a connection, the hacker can identify passwords and user IDs that can be used to gain unauthorized entry into targeted systems. In most cases, the sniffer will be automated enough to extract the correct information, which may also include credit card numbers.

Remote Penetration — Hackers can use programs over the Internet that will allow them to take control of a system remotely. These programs can be attached to emails or inserted into systems via vulnerabilities in the Internet connection security. Programs that allow for remote control might also be disguised as a harmless shareware download from the Web, such as a screen saver or utility. These are typically called Trojan Horses.

Spoofing — Hackers can "spoof" or impersonate legitimate electronic messages or web sites to gain information. Sending phony emails with fake "from" lines in them requesting changes in domain names or IP addresses is one way of "high-jacking" a web site or IP address. Hackers can even set up a "shadow" web site (a copy of the target organization's web site) that sits in front of the legitimate web site, directing all of the information through the hacker's computer before routing it to the real web site. The hacker can pick up information such as passwords, user IDs, credit card information, or any other confidential information that was intended for the legitimate web site. The original web site owner and the customer have no idea that this is taking place.

Scanners — Internet scanning programs may be used by hackers that scan for vulnerabilities to certain types of attacks. Network scanning programs will map networks to determine which computers and programs are available to be attacked or exploited.

Password Cracking — Hackers have access to sophisticated tools from hacker web sites that are used to determine passwords in targeted systems. These tools are automated programs that systematically guess passwords, eliminating much of the work for the hacker. Some tools contain dictionaries of commonly used passwords; others use brute force techniques to compare all possible combinations of characters until a hit is found. Many hackers have dictionaries of commonly used passwords, such as common first names, sports terms, movie titles, industry terms, biblical references, and locations or characters from movies, cartoons, or TV shows. Studies have shown that between 25 and 30 percent of passwords can be cracked this way. Contrary to what is seen in most movies, password cracking is not the result of some genius or savant working at a keyboard. It is typically accomplished by programs that automate the process by using dictionaries, high-speed repetitive techniques, and the focused use of known approaches that exploit existing flaws in system security.

Sendmail — Hackers attach malicious code to an electronic message and send it to a networked machine. When Sendmail scans the message, it will execute the attacker's code. Since Sendmail executes at the system's root level, it has all of the system's privileges, so new passwords can be entered that will give the hacker access later along with complete system privileges, i.e. control of the system.

Denial-of-Service — This is an attack that attempts to take down the system, or impede the flow of information, often causing the system to come to a halt. Denial-of-service attacks can take many forms, and can be launched from a number of remote systems that serve as unsuspecting "zombies." Denial-of-service can be as low tech as flooding the email servers with spam or mailbombs, or as high tech as using tools that will cause buffer overflows, looped error messages, or overlapping IP fragments.

Viruses — Computer viruses are common today, and they are becoming more sophisticated. Viruses can be attached to other trusted programs or emails, or they can be inserted into systems via remote penetration of the system. Once in place, the virus replicates and attaches itself to other emails or programs, spreading quickly and doing great damage before it is detected.

War Dialing — Hackers utilize automated programs that dial a predetermined range of telephone numbers or a list of specific numbers searching for an answer from a computer modem. When the program finds an open modem, it will either record the number for later use or allow the hacker to enter the system immediately. Hackers use this technique to search for modems on PCs that are connected to the organization's network. They can then enter the network through this non-secure opening rather than trying to break through a more secure, firewalled, Internet connection.

Hackers have at their disposal, a wide range of tools and techniques that can be used to launch their attacks. The techniques that they use to penetrate systems or gain control of a system are described in more detail here:

Back Doors

Back doors (sometimes called "trap doors") are appropriately named because they allow an unauthorized intruder to gain access into a system in a way other than through legitimate means. Since hackers aren't authorized to enter through the front door of the system, they will enter through a back door instead.

Software developers often leave some back doors in programs they create so that they can gain access at a later date to make fixes or perform diagnostics without having to go through the systems administrator and the hassle of being assigned a user ID and password. Sometimes, hackers find out what these back doors are, and then exploit them. More typically, however, hackers insert their own back doors into programs that allow them to gain access at some later date. These back doors can be installed after an initial penetration has been accomplished, or they can come in as undetected code attached to an email message or code hidden within an otherwise legitimate program (a Trojan Horse).

The back door allows the hacker to circumvent the security controls that are in place on the system and bypass the normal procedures that trusted users go through to sign on to a system. Most back doors go undetected and allow hackers to enter systems at will.

Trojan Horses

Trojan Horses (or "Trojans") are programs that outwardly appear to be useful and legitimate programs but contain additional hidden code from a hacker. The additional code may allow the hacker to gain access to the system, exploit various software/system functions, destroy data, release viruses, or perform any function that the hacker intended. Trojan Horses are particularly nefarious since they can impersonate an innocent program. Employees can download games and screen savers from the Internet that contain these Trojans, yet appear to function properly and show no signs of the hidden code that lurks within. A Trojan Horse program might be embedded within a shareware program that appears to be a wonderful utility program, so copies of it are disseminated from employee to employee or from one organization to another, spreading the hidden code from system to system along the way.

Trojan Horses can also be picked up from unfamiliar web sites. Most of us are unaware that when we visit a web site, it visits us in return. Typically, the web site may implant a cookie in our system's cookie file. This is usually a harmless practice that helps the web site understand our browsing preferences. But the "cookie" might also be a Trojan Horse with other, more malicious intentions. For this reason, it is often best to refrain from visiting questionable web sites. Many a Trojan Horse has been brought into an organization's computer systems by employees visiting questionable web sites or downloading unauthorized programs.

Logic Bombs

A logic bomb is any program that is triggered by some event, or checks for some particular condition, and upon finding such a condition, executes. A logic bomb might destroy data, crash a system, release a virus, or perform some other unauthorized and malicious act. An easy to understand example of a logic bomb follows: An employee who believes he is about to be fired, installs a logic bomb within the Human Resource system that checks the payroll records for the absence of the employee's name. When the employee is eventually terminated, Human Resources removes his name from the active payroll. The hidden program he installed will detect this new condition and activate a data destruction program that wipes out all of the payroll records.

Other logic bombs can be triggered based on specific dates, specific events (additions or deletions to a database), or the presence of a certain condition. The ultimate actions of the logic bomb are only limited by the imagination and skill of the hacker.

Viruses

A virus is any program that contains malicious code and replicates itself by inserting copies of itself into other programs. It infects the host programs by substituting its code for some other code, or overriding instructions, causing the system to perform unwanted tasks. This could be deleting files, destroying the operating system, damaging documents, corrupting or changing important data, or sending out bogus emails under your name.

A truly malicious virus will not only wipe out the data in a system, but also wipe out any back-up copies. In some cases, the virus is also programmed to infect the back-up program. It will attach itself to the back-up program and execute a delete to the back-up data when there is an attempt to restore any previously deleted data to the system.

The only real purpose of a virus is to cause damage and to be able to spread the damage to as many systems as possible.

There are between 10,000 and 15,000 viruses at work today with more being developed by malicious hackers every day. No one knows the real number because there are so many variations and mutations of individual viruses and so many new ones coming out regularly. A report by *Computer Economics* revealed that all virus attacks cost organizations a worldwide total of $12.1 billion in 1999. Yet, in 2000, a single virus known as the "Love Virus," caused $8.75 billion in damages on its own. It is easy to see that viruses are getting more malicious and destructive.

It is estimated that the now infamous "Love Virus" affected over 45 million computers worldwide, including such notable systems as those of the Pentagon, the British Parliament, and the CIA.

On another note, the "Code Red" worm is estimated to have affected more than 360,000 servers in less than 14 hours.

Virus Hoaxes

Almost as damaging as a virus is a virus hoax. A number of virus hoaxes have occurred in recent years that were just as debilitating to organizations as a real virus. What happens in the hoax is that some new non-existent dangerous virus is announced, typically via email, with some kind of message that says "Please pass this on to others in your organization," or something to that effect.

Well-meaning employees, coworkers, and friends, who think they are doing something good, blast the message out to as many people as they can to warn them to protect themselves from this dangerous virus. Soon, the phony virus message is accepted as real and people begin to react. Perhaps they shut down their systems, or run special anti-virus programs, or stop sending emails. Some very large corporations, hit with virus hoaxes that were quickly spread by trusted employees, actually took their mail servers and other systems off-line as a precaution against the so-called viruses.

Even the news media has picked up on some hoaxes and reported them as real viruses.

Virus hoaxes are easy to start because you don't need to be a technically skilled hacker to do it. All you need is access to email. Once you start the hoax message, the phenomenon of the Internet takes over. Many people, who easily believe something sent to them by a friend, particularly when the message says, "I checked this with a contact of mine at Microsoft," will immediately send the message to everyone in their address book. After all, they believe that they are doing their friends a favor by warning them of this impending virus.

Denial-of-Service

The denial-of-service attack is utilized to cripple a system, typically by overwhelming it with bogus messages, excessive emails, erroneous data, or repetitive electronic signals. A hacker launches a denial-of-service attack to disrupt the operations of an organization or to impede its ability to process data. The denial-of-service attack is like declaring war on an organization.

Hacking has become one of the most widespread types of unethical behavior corporations face that can be linked directly to the proliferation of the Internet.

Reproducibility

Electronic information is easily copied. This is not just restricted to the Internet. Computers are the principal instruments of reproducibility, but the Internet has allowed them to reach their fullest potential. Electronic information can be copied without any loss of quality and without the knowledge that it has been copied. It can then be reproduced, over and over again, with all of the copies matching the original, bit-for-bit. Software programs can be copied and experience no difference in performance.

Electronic documents and electronic transactions flow through the Internet, often leaving copies of themselves in some nebulous archive as they pass through. And just like the previous discussion about the permanency of emails, electronic information that has not been deleted, can also endure forever. This electronic information can be reproduced at any time in the future. The ethical implications should be obvious. No matter how much we want to believe that our electronic information is secure and private, the Internet and its reproductive capabilities have left us open to potential losses of privacy, property, and control of our information.

Global Reach

The Internet has given us the ability to communicate on a global scale, both in geographic terms and in demographic terms. Information can be transmitted to any point in the world, at little cost, and immediately. Prior to the 1990s, this was unthinkable. Now, a person sitting in front of a PC, either at home or at work, in a small town in Nebraska, can send a message, or a document, or conclude a financial transaction with a person they have never met in Moscow, Milan, or Tokyo. But individual communication is only a small piece of the global picture. That same person can just as easily communicate with thousands of other people spread all over the world. This is the essence of the global reach provided by the Internet. In the past, this would have been a costly endeavor, requiring great logistics, and substantial effort. Mass mailings, publication of articles, and radio broadcasts were the only way to communicate on a mass scale. Any rational person can see the obvious limitations, logistical requirements, and costs involved in any of these approaches. The Internet frees people from these limitations.

This new form of global communications has given all of us a form of power we heretofore could not ever hope to obtain. Media personalities, heads of governments, owners of newspapers, magazines, radio, or television stations had a form of this power, but not on the scale given to us via the Internet. Whereas these individuals could leverage their positions and mediums to communicate on a broad scope, even they could not achieve the global reach of the Internet.

So the Internet has given to every person with access to a computer and an Internet connection, more communications power than any head of state, media mogul, or movie star had prior to 1990. Any individual can effectively compete with CNN, *Pravda*, or *USA Today* to get their message out. Even better, media communications are typically one-way. They can only deliver a message. The Internet allows us to be interactive, i.e., we can both send a message and receive a response instantly from any of the recipients.

This global reach provides a great benefit by allowing people who are separated by large geographical distances to exchange information. It also allows individuals to communicate on a mass scale, getting their message out to thousands, perhaps even millions of people. However, this power can be used for unethical purposes just as easily.

Unscrupulous hackers can proliferate deadly computer viruses rapidly and globally, affecting millions of people and thousands of businesses. Mischievous individuals can send out hoaxes to thousands of people that will in turn be forwarded to thousands more. This global reach has given birth to the Internet hoax phenomenon. It is amazing to see how many people will believe and forward a bogus article or message to all of their friends without ever checking its validity.

Spamming

Spam is nothing more than Internet junk mail. There isn't a single Internet user alive that has not been annoyed by unsolicited emails. In some cases, the spam has been so profuse that it overwhelmed the computer systems, disrupting operations and halting business for some period of time. Many ISPs and browser software vendors have tried to take steps to counter the effects of spam, but the spammers have always been able to find ways to continue their practices. The impact of spam, both in its annoying aspects and its disruptive effects, has prompted efforts by federal and various state governments to make it illegal. At this time, the practice has not been banned, and businesses must deal with it through expensive filtering programs. In fact, in a highly publicized case, the California Supreme Court ruled on June 30, 2003 that certain types of spam are protected free speech. In 1995, Kourosh Kenneth Hamidi was fired by Intel Corp. after a dispute over his disability leave. In retaliation, Hamidi blasted the company in a series of six caustic emails that were sent to as many as 35,000 employees. Intel filed a trespassing lawsuit, accusing Hamidi of assuming control of Intel's private property (its computers and servers) and wasting employees' paid work time by flooding them with emails that they took time to read. Intel initially won the suit, and lower courts agreed with Intel. However, the California Supreme Court threw out the ruling by a 4-3 decision, citing freedom of speech. Justice Kathryn Werdegar, writing for the majority, said that Hamidi's actions "no more invaded Intel's property than does a protester holding a sign or shouting through a bullhorn outside corporate headquarters, posting a letter through the mail, or telephoning to complain of a corporate practice."

After the ruling, Hamidi vowed to continue his relentless email campaign against Intel. According to the San Jose Mercury News, upon hearing that he could continue to blast the emails, Hamidi said, "I'm going to do it to the max."

Netiquette

Netiquette is a new word that was coined to express the concept of etiquette on the Internet. Going back to the examples of unethical behavior promoted by the anonymity of the Internet, netiquette deals with how we can communicate via the Internet using socially acceptable standards of behavior by encouraging civility. The basis behind netiquette is that we should communicate via the Internet as if we were having a face-to-face conversation. Netiquette is simply a set of rules for behaving properly when engaging in online communications. Bad online behavior, or the lack of netiquette, includes things like:

- Not respecting other people's bandwidth
- Using foul or offensive language
- Using ALL CAPS (which is considered yelling)
- Flooding chat rooms so no one else can comment
- Passing along chain letters
- Passing along virus hoaxes or other Internet hoaxes
- Using subject lines that are confusing or undecipherable
- Disguising your identity (a fifty year old man pretending to be a 16 year old girl)
- Flaming

Although netiquette is a positive term describing a set of rules for proper online behavior, the lack of netiquette, or the failure to follow these rules, is the unethical behavior that the Internet fosters. Not every instance of a netiquette violation is unethical, for example, using a confusing subject line or passing along a chain letter is not a breach of morality. These are just examples of not being courteous. But certain things like disguising your identity, flooding chat rooms, or flaming, are unethical.

Flaming is when someone who is communicating in a chat room or sending an email, uses insulting or offensive language. Since this language can often be inflammatory, the term *flaming* is appropriate.

Flaming often includes name-calling and cursing. The anonymity of the Internet has helped foster this kind of disruptive behavior.

When someone responds to a flame, a *flame war* is likely to ensue. A flame war involves two or more people sending each other flame messages, usually in an escalating manner. The war will continue until one of the parties involved gets tired of responding to the other, and simply chooses to ignore the other party's flames. The entire war is a waste of time and energy, and accomplishes nothing.

Pornography

The Internet allows individuals to send and receive pornographic material. Depending on the type of material, doing so may be completely legal in some states and in many countries, so the issue of unethical behavior is not whether the viewing of pornography is unethical, but whether downloading it while at work is unethical. Corporations have had to place strict limitations on Internet surfing and downloading to prevent employees from using corporate assets (their computers, Internet connections, bandwidth, servers, etc.) from being used to download pornographic material. Not only is this practice disruptive, but it uses corporate property for the wrong reasons. Employees who spend time downloading pornography also waste valuable time, causing losses in productivity. The pornographic material itself may prove distracting, and depending on where it is stored and viewed, it can easily offend other employees, subsequently causing lawsuits or sexual harassment complaints.

"The most commonly abused Web sites at work are porn," reports Dr. David Greenfield, the head of the Center for Internet Addiction. SexTracker, a service that monitors usage of porn sites, says that as much as 70% of traffic on porn sites takes place during work hours. Furthermore, SexTracker estimates that one in five white-collar male workers is accessing pornography at work.[9]

Wasted Time

The Internet opens new opportunities for employees to virtually leave their offices or cubicles while physically remaining there. Surfing the net, downloading programs and pictures, playing online games, participating in chat rooms, and sending personal emails all detract from productive work. In some organizations, this lost or wasted time can prove very costly. According to International Data Corp. (IDC), unauthorized Internet usage accounts for 30% to 40% of lost worker productivity. Websense Inc., a San Diego-based provider of employee monitoring software, estimates that the cost to corporations for all of this Internet diversion from work is $54 billion annually.[10]

Companies are taking steps to combat this loss of productivity. Approximately one-third of the companies that Websense polled, indicated that they had fired workers for inappropriate Internet usage, and two-thirds had to discipline some employees.

Here is a situation that was described in Business Week Online (2000):

> Consider what happened at public-relations firm Golin/Harris International in Chicago in mid-May. Barrett Buss, vice-president of information systems, was testing out the company's brand new software that tracks employees' Web usage when he noticed that 80% of the bandwidth at one of the branch offices was being chewed up by Napster Inc., the controversial site that allows users to download pirated songs for free. Turns out three Golin/Harris employees were ignoring work and downloading a virtual jukebox instead. Golin/Harris cracked down and banned the use of Napster at the office. "I thought there were definitely ethical problems here, and I don't like to see that stuff on my network," Buss says.[11]

Wasted time is only one of the many problems created by the improper Internet usage of employees. Here is a list of several of the problems that improper employee Internet usage can create:

- Loss of productivity — Employees spending significant amounts of time surfing the net.

- Bandwidth issues — Internet use by employees that is not related to business can eat up bandwidth and/or slow down the company's servers.
- Sexual harassment — Viewing pornographic material on the company's computers can offend someone enough to file sexual harassment charges.
- Legal issues - Downloading copyrighted software can make the company liable for software piracy claims.
- Earning outside income during company time — Some enterprising employees can actually run their own businesses via the Internet while sitting in their offices.
- Infecting company computer systems — Internet surfers that visit dubious web sites or download unauthorized programs can easily infect the company's computer systems with viruses or Trojan Horses.

Viruses

Employees who spend time sending and receiving personal emails, visiting non-business related web sites, or downloading unauthorized programs, will often inadvertently infect the company's systems with viruses or Trojan Horses that can have a deleterious effect on the company's systems.

Viruses can also be received through normal business correspondence when the sending party has an unknown virus in their system and fails to screen outgoing emails for viruses. Also, many viruses replicate by using the individual's address book to multiply. The virus itself, once it has infected a system, will send an email with copies of itself to everyone in the employee's address book. If an employee has an extensive address book, for example, all of her clients, customers, suppliers, and business contacts, the results can be disastrous.

Information Theft

The Internet has made information theft easier and the protection of trade secrets harder. In the past, it was difficult to steal information that was kept locked in offices and file cabinets in a building with secured access. A great deal of effort and stealth had to be used to accomplish a successful theft of some valuable proprietary information. In many cases, an insider had to be involved. The Internet changed this forever.

Since most proprietary information is now stored in electronic form, typically residing on a computer hard drive in some system, a crafty hacker or thief can surreptitiously copy or destroy the information without detection by entering the system via its Internet connection. Although corporations go to great lengths to secure their systems, the openness of the Internet has not made that task easy. Hackers always seem to be one step ahead of the security people by exploiting holes in systems before they can be plugged.

Failure to adequately protect information doesn't only result in the possible theft of trade secrets, but may also result in significant damage to clients and customers as well. If an electronic intruder can gain access to systems where customer data such as credit card information is stored, the results can be financially damaging to the customer. As an example, in December of 1999, when a hacker gained access to the confidential systems of CDUniverse, he stole approximately 300,000 credit card numbers. When CDUniverse refused his ransom demand for $100,000, the hacker published the credit card numbers, along with the respective cardholders' names and addresses, on a web site that anyone could access. Not only did this breach of security cause harm to the CDUniverse customers, but it also impacted the credit card companies that had to reissue all of the cards, and of course, it was a public relations nightmare for CDUniverse. Even more lasting is the damage this incident did to consumer confidence in the security of buying products on-line via the Internet. This and other incidents like it are reasons given by many Web surfers who, due to their security fears, still refuse to buy products on-line.[12]

Conclusion

Clearly, the Internet has created more opportunities for ethical abuses in business than any other technological development in the last

100 years. Corporations must be aware of the full range of ethical dilemmas posed by the Internet and how those situations can foster unethical behavior among employees.

Notes

[1] "2003 E-Mail Rules, Policies and Practices Survey," conducted by The ePolicy Institute, American Management Association, and Clearswift.

[2] www.epolicyinstitute.com/disaster/stories.html, July 10, 2003.

[3] www.epolicyinstitute.com/disaster/stories.html, July 10, 2003.

[4] Jonathan Wallace, "Nameless in Cyberspace, Anonymity on the Internet," Cato Institute Briefing Papers, No. 54 (December 8, 1999).

[5] *ACLU v. Miller*, 977 F. Supp. 1228 (N.D.GA) (1997)

[6] Act. No. 1029, GA Laws 1996

[7] *ACLU v. Miller*.

[8] This section is reprinted in part from the book: *Information Security: A Guide to Protecting Your Information and Computer Systems from Hackers*, Michael P. Harden (2003).

[9] Michell Conlin, "Workers Surf At Own Risk," *Business Week Online* (June 12, 2000).

[10] Conlin.

[11] Conlin.

[12] Harden, p. 6.

Michael P. Harden

Chapter Sixteen: Privacy

Privacy is one of the thorniest issues we must deal with in the business world. This stems from several areas: employee information, corporate information, and trade secrets. Businesses and business managers deal with privacy issues more often than they would like. That's because privacy concerns are ubiquitous in our society and therefore ever present in our workplace.

The Historical Perspective of Privacy

Contrary to popular belief, the U.S. Constitution does not guarantee the right to privacy. In fact, there is no mention of privacy in the Constitution or the Bill of Rights. Many of us believe that we have always had a right to privacy, that it is some natural law or granted by the government through various laws and regulations. Actually, the first real discussion of privacy didn't even take place until 1890 when the *Harvard Law Review* published an article by Samuel Warren and Louis Brandeis.[1] Both were young lawyers, and one of them, Brandeis, would go on to become a Supreme Court Justice. Their theory of privacy was not popular at the time and was slow to gain acceptance in most legal circles. In 1928, when Brandeis, as a Supreme Court Justice, offered his dissenting opinion in *Olmstead v. United States*, he declared that the right to privacy was the right to be left alone.[2] This was a dissenting opinion and did nothing to affirm the right to privacy, but it did set the stage for future decisions that would eventually affirm this right. It wasn't until 1965, when the Supreme Court decided the case of *Griswald v. Connecticut,*[3] that the right to privacy was declared to be a Constitutionally protected right. So basically, it was the Supreme Court that really gave us the right to privacy.

This Supreme Court decision was groundbreaking in that it promulgated a right that was not previously defined by the Constitution. In fact, no one could even cite a specific amendment that explicitly granted or protected this new right. At the time, many legal scholars pointed to the first and fourth amendments to the Constitution as laying some of the grounds for the right to privacy, and these scholars explained that the court ruling simply expanded upon those rights. In either case, the explicit or implied right to privacy in these amendments is a stretch.

The first amendment deals primarily with the right to a free press and freedom of speech. It reads as follows:

> Congress shall make no law respecting an establishment of religion, or prohibiting the free exercise thereof; or abridging the freedom of speech, or of the press, or the right of the people peaceably to assemble, and to petition the Government for a redress of grievances.

It is difficult to identify a right to privacy in these words, although they do deal with the right of the individual and the press to be free from government interference. Some people can interpret this to show a right of the individual to some level of privacy.

The fourth amendment deals with issues such as unreasonable searches and seizures of personal property. The amendment reads as follows:

> The right of the people to be secure in their persons, houses, papers, and effects, against unreasonable searches and seizures, shall not be violated, and no Warrants shall issue, but upon probable cause, supported by Oath or affirmation, and particularly describing the place to be searched and the persons or things to be seized.

One can make a better case that this particular amendment affirms some right to privacy...the privacy of not having our homes, our personal effects, our personal papers, or ourselves subject to unreasonable intrusiveness or seizure by the government.

In both of these amendments, it is difficult to truly identify a specific right to privacy, at least as we define it today. Moreover, these two amendments deal specifically with government invasiveness and do not address individual protection from the intrusiveness of other individuals. (Under law, corporations are treated as individuals and any such rights to privacy would therefore apply to corporations as well.)

So, although the Supreme Court was able to find a right to privacy in the Constitution where one did not previously exist, scholars and philosophers were careful not to immediately embrace the logic behind that decision. Instead, many believed that the right to privacy was a *natural law*, already granted to us by God or by nature. If this was the case, then our Founding Fathers did not see the need to draft provisions for the protection of something that was widely assumed to be a natural right of mankind at that time. They "overlooked" this right when drafting the Bill of Rights, simply because they did not see the need to create a right that they thought already existed without the consent of the government.

Natural rights are those rights we have by mere fact of our existence upon Earth and therefore cannot be granted to us by anyone or any government. We have these rights from the moment of our birth (or earlier as some would say). The concept of natural rights can be seen in the Declaration of Independence when Jefferson wrote "...that they are endowed by their Creator with certain unalienable rights, that among these are life, liberty and the pursuit of happiness."

Natural rights cannot be given to us by governments since we already have them from a higher source, but we can be deprived of them by unlawful actions, oppressive government regulations, or by unknowingly relinquishing them. This is why many people feel these rights need to be protected.

After the initial Supreme Court ruling, subsequent federal laws that affirmed and expanded the right to privacy were established. Some of these laws include the following:

- The Privacy Act (1974)
- The Family and Educational Privacy Act (1974)
- The Electronic Communications Privacy Act (1986)
- The Video Privacy Protection Act (1988)
- The Fair Credit Reporting Act (1992)
- The Driver's Privacy Protection Act (1994)
- The Telephone Customer's Protection Act (1994)

We must also be careful to not confuse liberty with privacy. As can be seen from the Declaration of Independence, we have a right to *liberty*. Many of the so-called privacy decisions of the earlier courts really dealt with the issue of liberty, not privacy. *Liberty* is the right to be able to do something, in essence, the freedom to make choices, for example, to own property, to smoke cigarettes, or to use birth control. *Privacy*, on the other hand, is the right to be able to do something without having to share the knowledge of such actions with others. These two rights are different, and as illogical as it sounds, in certain circumstances, we can have *liberty* without *privacy*, or *privacy* without *liberty*. Moreover, many arguments about privacy mistakenly deal with the issue of liberty or our freedom to choose and have nothing to do with privacy per se.

Privacy can be defined as our ability to control the amount of information we share with others. Yet, this is not a simple concept. Since certain information is a matter of public record, we cannot control that information. For example, corporate officers' salaries are typically disclosed in a 10k or an annual report. A criminal conviction is a matter of public record. Divorce decrees are accessible to the public at the county court house. Property deeds are on file for public examination. And the list goes on.

So the definition of privacy must have another element to further clarify it. It cannot just be the ability to control the amount of information we share with others. Obviously, there is a lot of information over which we have no control — the "public" information about each of us. Therefore, a more personal level of information must be a part of the definition.W.A. Parent, a professor of philosophy, defined this personal information in a 1983 article titled *Privacy, Morality, and the Law.*[4] Parent called it "undocumented personal knowledge." This kind of information is different from the publicly available information we typically consider to be non-private in nature. Parent is describing the kind of information that most of us do not wish to be known by others. The term "undocumented" means that this information is not recorded (or documented) as public records. For example, a criminal record is personal information we would not want generally known by others, yet it is documented and recorded as public information. When we go through a messy divorce, many of our personal problems and financial information become a part of the court records as well. Therefore, although much of this is personal information we do not want generally known by others, we have no control over its concealment or dissemination. We cannot make a claim to privacy for this "documented" information. But we can claim a right of privacy for the information we do not want made publicly known that isn't generally part of any public records — the "undocumented" information. Some examples might be our medical records, our personal mail, our bank account records, or our credit card numbers. We can also include here information that might be embarrassing to us if others knew about it.

Privacy can be a very complex issue since there are many philosophical aspects to it. Privacy is often confused with liberty, but it is also interwoven with other social issues. Intimacy, trust, loyalty, autonomy, and secrecy are just a few of the social issues that are intertwined with the concept of privacy. Because any or all of these issues may come into play, the right to privacy poses tremendous ethical dilemmas for us.

How Far We Have Come

In late 1914, Henry Ford initiated a bold plan to raise the wages of his workers. The plan was called the "five dollar day" program. In this program, Ford promised to pay eligible workers a rate equivalent to $5 per day. They would receive a base wage, and then share in the company's profits so that they would enjoy a total rate of $5 per day, which was quite a pay rate in those days.

There was a catch however. In order to participate in this program, workers had to demonstrate that they had the right character, as defined by Ford, to be able to use the additional money in a proper way. In Ford's mind, this meant that they had to demonstrate certain "values" in their personal lives. He expected his workers to practice sobriety, thriftiness, promptness, and good moral behavior. Ford believed that the way a worker lived his life outside of work, carried over into his job. The $5-a-day program was a way to impose Ford's values upon workers so that they would be more productive or efficient at work. To be eligible for the program, the workers had to meet certain requirements. Some of these were:

- Male employees over 22 years of age had to lead "clean, sober, and industrious" lives and demonstrate that they were thrifty. (Ford did not want them to waste the additional money he was paying them.)

- Married men, regardless of age, had to be living with their families and demonstrating sobriety, industry, and cleanliness.

- Men under the age of 22, who were the sole supporters of their widowed mothers, had to lead clean, sober, and industrious lives.

- Women employees who had some relative that was solely supported by them, could participate if they met the same standards as the men.

In order to make sure the program worked, Ford hired 150 investigators who would turn up at an employee's home to conduct an inspection and evaluate whether the standards were being met. Ford created a department called the "Sociological Department" under John R. Lee, to be responsible for inspections and enforcement of the program. Later, Lee was replaced by Ford's Pastor, Dr. Samuel Marquis. Marquis changed the department's name to something a little more politically correct. It was renamed the "Educational Department." Department investigators would spend time with employees, their families, and even their neighbors to determine if the employee was practicing good moral values. They looked for evidence of good moral character, sobriety, family values, and thriftiness. Thrift was important to Ford because it demonstrated self-control and responsibility. These were things he valued in a worker.

If the investigators thought that the workers were deficient, they would suggest to the workers ways in which they could improve their morals and values.

If workers didn't cooperate with the Sociological Department, or failed to meet the standards over a period of time, they would be put into special classes, not receive the additional money, and be given six months to get with the program. If, after six months, the employees failed to meet the standards, they were fired.

In most cases, the workers in this program were immigrants with little idea of what was going on. They reluctantly accepted the invasion of their privacy in order to make a good wage. There was significant debate among intellectuals as to whether these workers actually modified their behavior permanently, or simply complied during the program in order to enjoy its benefits. But no one could debate the success of the program from Ford's perspective. In 1915, the turnover rate dropped from 370% to 16%. Absenteeism went down while productivity went up. More workers owned their own homes, had savings accounts and life insurance, and stopped drinking.

Ford discontinued the program after a few years because it became too expensive to continue to pay workers both an increased salary to keep pace in the tight Detroit labor market and to provide the promised profit-sharing. Instead, Ford began to use informants and spies who would report on the behavior of workers and potential trouble-makers.

Imagine if you will, an employer today sending investigators out to an employee's home to ask questions of the employee, his family, and his neighbors about his personal behavior and habits. A deluge of lawsuits would be filed by close-of-business on the first day of the program. This kind of intrusive behavior by a corporation is not tolerated by our society today. This change in attitude clearly demonstrates the advances we have made in the notions of privacy in the workplace. During Ford's time, there was no right to privacy, and workers couldn't really expect one. On the other hand, Ford had a reasonable expectation that his employees should subscribe to his values if they wanted to work for him. Since Ford, like Aristotle, believed that values at work and values at home were the same, he expected to see his workers practicing his values while they were outside of the Ford Motor plant.

In order to make a better living, Ford's workers begrudgingly accepted the intrusiveness of the investigators and the humiliation of having someone else impose their values upon them. These workers were relegated to the roles of children being told how to behave by a paternalistic Ford. No one today would accept such an arrangement. In fact, our expectation of privacy is so well founded today that many people who read about Ford's program find it difficult to believe that it actually happened. But it did.

Why Privacy is Important

We can make all kinds of arguments about how privacy is a fundamental right, how it gives us security or autonomy, or that personal privacy keeps the government from being too powerful. All of these arguments in favor of privacy make sense, but they are not the reasons that privacy is important to us. Privacy has little intrinsic value. It is very much like the utilitarian concept (although a Kantian would disagree) where privacy is a means to an end. Privacy has no value unless it provides us with some consequence that is good and beneficial to us. And that consequence is *control*.

Privacy gives us control over the amount of information others know about us, and by controlling that information, we control our relationships. This is the value of privacy.

All of our relationships require that the other party has some level of knowledge about us. The amount of information we share with the other party varies with the kind of relationship we share with that party. Our spouses typically have intimate knowledge of us. Our best friends have intimate knowledge as well, but perhaps of a different type. Parents and siblings have knowledge about us too. Our employers know certain things about us, but not anywhere near the level of intimate knowledge that we share with our best friends. Our doctors know some important things about us, but our auto mechanics probably know a lot less. As you can see from this, each different relationship is maintained by our sharing a specific amount of information about ourselves. We would not tell our employer many of the things that we easily share with our best friends or spouses. As relationships grow, we share more information to nurture that growth. In all cases, however, we *control* the amount and type of information we share. And by controlling that information, we control how much we allow the relationship to grow.

The nature of our relationships is determined by the nature of the information we share with others. James Rachels[5] wrote in 1975 that people need a diversity of relationships, and that we maintain the diversity of these relationships through the different information we share with each party. Rachels argues that if everyone knows the same things about us, then all of our relationships would be the same. There would be no diversity. Our employers would know as much about us as our spouses, or our coworkers and neighbors would know as much about us as our best friends. So whenever we lose the ability to control the amount of information we share with someone, we lose our ability to control how others see us.

Think about this. On a first date, we only reveal a small amount of personal information about ourselves. We have no idea how the relationship will develop (if at all), and we are reluctant to say too many things about ourselves. If things go well and we have a second, third, or fourth date, we continue to share more about ourselves each time we go out together. If everything continues to go well, we can become quite intimate with each other. What we have done is to control the amount of information we share as we control the development of the relationship. We do the same thing with employers, coworkers, and neighbors. We control not only the amount, but also the type of information we reveal about ourselves. We would probably not tell our employers about problems we are having with our children, but we might easily share that information with a close friend or a counselor. We might tell our spouse about the results of a medical test but never even contemplate sharing that same information with our travel agent or accountant.

Insofar as we all have an interest in how others view us, we instinctively realize the importance of what they know about us. Some information might diminish us in the eyes of people we consider important to our careers; while other information might embarrass us to the people we love. So control of our personal information becomes very important…and that is what privacy is all about.

The moment we lose control of some bit of information about ourselves is the moment we lose control of our ability to shape how others perceive us. If we allow others, for example, the government, our employers, or our doctors, to gather and disseminate information that we would otherwise prefer to control on our own, then we have given away control of our identities. It is the way others perceive us that establishes who we are to them.

Since the information we share about ourselves influences the character of our relationships with others, it naturally follows that the same information will influence our relationships with organizations as well. We all have relationships with banks, mortgage companies, schools, credit card companies, employers, churches, clubs, charities, retail establishments, and many others. We also have relationships of which we are unaware, e.g. credit bureaus, government agencies, and marketing firms that maintain information about us, yet never communicate directly with us.

It is important that we understand how organizational relationships can be influenced by the information we provide them, and also how they can influence our other relationships if they share information about us with others. We may be turned down for a job or a loan if disparaging information about us is shared with a bank or a potential employer. On the other hand, if a bank or employer provides confidential financial information about us to our neighbors, we have lost some control of the nature of that relationship. When a club or magazine we subscribe to sells information about us to a marketing company, we may eventually find ourselves on a mailing list. When our bank or credit bureau provides information to a credit card company, we may find ourselves receiving a "pre-approved" credit card notification from a financial firm of which we have previously had no dealings. If we fill out one application or survey that asks us for our annual income, it is almost certain that other organizations will have that knowledge in a short period of time. They will then begin to formulate some kind of offering to us based on our annual income level. A credit card company may offer us a credit limit of $8,000 or $30,000, depending on the nature of the information they receive. Getting a loan from our local bank may be impossible if the credit bureau provides derogatory credit information about us. So information not only influences *who* we have relationships with, but also determines the *way* they deal with us.

Sadly, we have no control over information that moves from one organization to another. The information that is shared may or may not be correct, but we wouldn't know this, and that is why control of our information is crucial to shaping our relationships, not just with individuals, but with organizations as well.

Charles Fried argued that we value privacy because it gives us a "rational context" for those ends we cherish, such as love, trust, respect, and friendship. Fried rationalized that these were intimate relationships, and that these relationships were formed by the sharing of personal information that we would not share with others outside of the relationship.[6]

Fried's argument rings true. Love, trust, respect, and friendship are indeed elements of intimate relationships, and we control these relationships and who we have them with by controlling the amount and kind of information we share. Even in a work environment, trust and respect are key elements in our relationships with supervisors, subordinates, and coworkers. So these relationships have a level of intimacy as well. Therefore, we can control the level of intimacy of these relationships (the level of trust and/or respect we receive) by controlling the kind of information about ourselves that we share. If information we choose to keep secret is accidentally (or intentionally) revealed by someone, then the level of trust or respect others have for us can be diminished, thereby damaging our relationships.

Utilitarian and Kantian Arguments for Privacy

There are two arguments that express the need for a right to privacy. One is a utilitarian argument that deals with the consequences of privacy, and the other is a Kantian argument that deals with privacy in terms of respect for people.

Utilitarian Arguments for the Right to Privacy

We know that throughout our history people have been harmed by others who have revealed damaging information about them, or worse yet, many people may have been harmed by incorrect or erroneous information that was accidentally or purposely released. Few of us can say that at some time in our lives we haven't had something revealed about us that we would have preferred remained private.

Employers maintain information about employees. Depending on the type of job, the information in our personnel files might include background information, criminal record checks, financial history, counseling, results of polygraph tests, and even medical conditions. Typically, this information is supposed to remain private. Although some of the information might be very pertinent to our position with the company, it might be totally inappropriate for coworkers or others to have access to it. In most cases, we have no idea as to what information our employers gather and maintain about us. The information may not even be correct, and we would not know this. The fact that this information can harm us if it were revealed makes keeping it private imperative.

We accept the fact that employers must collect some level of information on their employees in order to operate effectively. This kind of information might typically include previous work history, resumes, family information, criminal background checks, and drug test results. If the company provides health insurance, then medical records and medical history could be included. But we also expect this information to remain secure and confidential. This is a basic social contract that we have with our employers. We understand the need for them to collect and maintain information about us in order for us to work for the company. This is the sacrifice we make as a trade-off to being able to earn a living. But because the same information, in the wrong hands, can harm us, we expect our employer to go to great lengths to keep it confidential and secure from others.

Although we realize that the possible release of this information can be harmful, we also realize that employers must have some information about their employees in order to be effective. Therefore, utilitarians view the collection of such information as a balancing act. They are concerned with the consequences of amassing personal information. Utilitarians ask themselves whether it is an invasion of privacy, and does it pose some level of harm to the employee. On one hand, the gathering of such information benefits the company and the employee, as both are well served by the employment of the worker. On the other hand, the maintenance of such personal information and the possible release of it have potentially harmful consequences.

Information would not be gathered on people if it didn't have some value. Otherwise, it would be a waste of time, energy, and money to go though the effort of collecting it. Companies and other organizations need information to function, but they also need it to make decisions about people. Companies need information to make hiring decisions. Banks need information to extend credit and make loans. Hospitals need information to ensure patients aren't allergic to drugs or have conditions that would interfere with a specific treatment. Landlords want credit history, previous addresses, and references before they will rent to someone. And the list goes on. This information, which may be different in each case, is essential for the organization to make informed decisions.

Businesses often collect information about their customers in order to better serve them, but more often to enhance the ability to target certain markets and maintain competitive advantages. This information might include the consumer's buying history, income levels, spending habits, personal preferences or tastes, and credit information. Marketers can more effectively direct special offers if they have sufficient information about their customers or potential customers.

When this tremendous need for information is weighed against the need for privacy, personal privacy is often the loser. Historically, the argument for not collecting this information has been difficult to make. As long as the information is kept confidential and not used for nefarious purposes, many people see no harm in organizations collecting it.

Utilitarians, who concern themselves with consequences, have not been able to make a defensible argument for more privacy. Weighing the benefits of information gathering against the desire for personal privacy and autonomy, utilitarians have not been able to show that the harm outweighs the benefits. The only harm seems to be when the information is misused or revealed without authorization. If this does not occur, then what harm is there? That is the question that has been difficult to answer.

Utilitarians may argue, albeit ineffectively, that privacy has its own intrinsic value, and by invading it through information gathering, we have created a situation where people feel uncomfortable about how much of their personal information they actually control, and therefore experience a loss of autonomy and/or identity. Some people may even feel fearful that embarrassing personal information is under the control of others. This is what utilitarians often claim is the harm caused by the organizational collection of personal information.

Kantian Arguments for the Right to Privacy

The Kantian argument for the right to privacy hinges upon the concept of respect — a stronger argument than those of the utilitarians. The Kantian argument is also much simpler. Since Kant's philosophy deals with maintaining respect for individuals, violating the privacy of an individual is the same as not respecting the individual. If we violate someone's privacy, we deprive them of the ability to control their own information. This results in a loss of identity and autonomy, because if a person cannot control who receives information and what type of information they receive, that person has lost the ability to control his relationships.

Under a Kantian theme, if someone has information about me that I cannot control, then I cannot control the nature of that relationship. Furthermore, if someone else, such as an employer, has personal information about me that can be revealed to others, I cannot control the relationships that may have access to that information. In either case, I have lost my autonomy and have been deprived of the ability to control my relationships.

Corporate Privacy Issues

Privacy in the workplace is one of the thorniest issues presented to both employers and employees. Workers value their privacy, but employers want to protect themselves by being able to monitor their employees' on-the-job behavior. This conflict creates problems for both sides. Typically, workplace privacy issues fall into three areas: email, employee surveillance, and employee records. Each of these will be covered here.

Email

Much has already been discussed in the previous chapter about email, however, this section will deal specifically with work-related email issues.

When we send someone a sealed letter through the U.S. mail we assume that it will be treated as private correspondence. Our expectation is that no one will open it and read it. Should someone do so, it would be a terrible breach of ethics, and under certain circumstances, against the law. When we send a sealed envelope through interoffice mail, we have the same reasonable expectation of privacy. After all, proprietary information is always flowing through interoffice mail. One would think that email, which is just an electronic version of mail, would have the same level of privacy accorded to it. Emails often contain proprietary information and confidential material that is not intended for anyone but the designated recipient. The assumption that email is private cannot be further from the truth.

Many employers believe that they have a right to read their employees' email. Employers contend that since the company owns the email system and provides the computers and networks necessary for email to operate, it has a right to monitor what goes on within its system. Managers assert that monitoring email is the only way they can assure that the system is not being abused. Their definition of abuse can be far-reaching and broad. For example, some companies may consider abuse to be using the system to send or view pornography, engage in illicit or illegal activities, or engage in sexual harassment.

On the other hand, some companies may consider abuse to be nothing more than engaging in idle chatter, gossiping, or sending personal emails during working hours.

Even though employees may believe that their emails are private, particularly if the company has not told them otherwise, their communications within the company and to others outside of the company may be monitored. When employees find out that their emails are being monitored, they are often outraged and become resentful. They certainly feel that a trust has been violated. This is one reason that many companies have a written policy that specifically states to employees that their emails are not private.

Employees who have been disciplined or fired because of email abuses have claimed that their right to privacy was violated and subsequently sued their employers. However, courts have sided consistently with the employer. Some cases that have been decided in favor of the employer are discussed here:

In the case of *Smyth v. Pillsbury*, an employee was terminated for transmitting over the company's email system comments that his employer deemed to be inappropriate and unprofessional, even though the employee had been assured repeatedly by the company that all email communications would remain confidential and privileged, and that *email communications could not be intercepted and used by the company against its employees as grounds for termination or reprimand.* After being terminated, the employee sued Pillsbury for wrongful discharge.

The case was dismissed based on the following:

"In the second instance, even if we found that an employee had a reasonable expectation of privacy in the contents of his email communications over the company email system, we do not find that a reasonable person would consider the defendant's interception of these communications to be a substantial and highly offensive invasion of his privacy. Again, we note that by intercepting such communications, the company is not, as in the case of urinalysis or personal property searches, requiring the employee to disclose any personal information about himself or invading the employee's person or personal effects. Moreover, the company's interest in preventing inappropriate and unprofessional comments or even illegal activity over its email system outweighs any privacy interest the employee may have in those comments."[7]

This case demonstrates that courts have upheld an employer's right to monitor email even when the employer has specifically informed employees that their emails were private and would not be used in any subsequent disciplinary actions.

In yet another case, *Bourke v. Nissan*, two employees were fired for sending personal messages, many of which were sexual in nature, over the company's email system. When several emails were accidentally discovered and read, Nissan decided to retrieve and review more of their emails. Based upon Nissan's actions in reviewing their email messages, the employees sued Nissan for common law invasion of privacy, violation of their constitutional right to privacy, and violation of the criminal wiretapping and eavesdropping statutes.

The case was dismissed on summary judgment. The court ruled that the employees had no reasonable expectation of privacy, and if there is no expectation of privacy, then there can be no violation of the right to privacy. Thus, the employees' causes of actions for common law invasion of privacy and violation of their constitutional right to privacy were dismissed.[8]

There are very few laws that specifically deal with email privacy, and it is generally accepted that regardless of any written or unwritten company policies, emails should not be considered as private correspondence.

A 2003 survey of 1,100 companies conducted by the ePolicy Institute found that 22 percent of companies had fired an employee over the improper use of email, up from 17 percent in 2001.[9] Even so, the number of companies that have a written email policy declined from 81 percent in 2001 to 75 percent in 2003.[10] The same survey also found that the average employee spends 25 percent of the workday on email, with eight percent devoting at least four hours a day to email. It is easy to see that email has become a staple of today's business environment.

Employee Surveillance

Another issue that creates ethical dilemmas for employers and employees is the issue of employee surveillance. Surveillance can take the form of video surveillance (cameras and two-way mirrors) audio surveillance (telephone monitoring) or electronic surveillance (computer monitoring). Companies seldom use the term "surveillance," which has a "big brother" connotation. The term "workplace monitoring," which has a more benign connotation, is the preferred term.

Workplace monitoring, which has exploded in recent years due to the advent of sophisticated technology, allows employers to observe and monitor their workers' behavior. This can include actual video cameras that allow managers to observe what their employees are doing during work hours in certain company locations. It might also include monitoring telephone conversations, identifying what numbers are being called, and reviewing the duration of the calls. Computer usage may also be monitored to determine the level of productivity of an employee (the number of keystrokes and/or time spent on the computer), which Internet sites are being viewed, and what content is being downloaded.

Out of 140 million workers in the U.S., approximately 40 million work online regularly (have Internet access and/or use email). 14 million, or 35% of the online workers are under continuous online surveillance.[11] The sales of employee-monitoring software are approximately $140 million each year. Since the company owns the computer system upon which the employee is working, then the company has the right to monitor what the employee does with the computer.

A survey was conducted by the American Management Association (AMA) in 1997. It found that 63% of the mid-sized and large U.S. companies surveyed engaged in one or more monitoring or surveillance activities. Of the 906 companies the AMA surveyed, more than one-third videotaped their employees, reviewed their computer files and emails, and recorded their phone calls or voicemail. A more recent survey (2002) of email and Internet monitoring recent survey (2002) of email and Internet monitoring conducted by the Center for Business Ethics at Bentley College, found that 92 percent of the surveyed companies monitored their employees' email and Internet usage at least some of the time. What was alarming about the survey was that 25 percent of the companies had no procedures in place to prevent abuse of the monitoring process itself.

Managers claim that workplace monitoring is necessary to ensure ethical conduct by employees, to enforce standards and policies, to provide a safe and crime-free environment, and to maintain productivity. Employers (who provide the workplace for their employees) claim a right to monitor what goes on in their offices and plants. They also claim a responsibility to ensure that their employees are safe, so providing a workplace that is free of hazards and free of crime is essential. This responsibility requires the use of some kind of workplace monitoring. A utilitarian argument that the benefit of workplace monitoring far outweighs the possible harm (invasion of privacy) is the basis for this philosophy.

Employees, of course, consider such tactics as violations of their privacy. When they make a personal phone call, they expect it to be private. This right has been upheld by federal courts. If employers are monitoring phone calls, and they realize that a call is personal, they must immediately stop monitoring the call and allow the employee to have some privacy. However, there is an exception. If employees have been *told* that they cannot make personal phone calls from their business phones, then those phone calls are subject to monitoring. Employers do have the right to review phone logs and registers that show what numbers have been dialed from an employee's phone.

Many employees who have sued over privacy issues with telephone monitoring have done so citing The Electronic Communications Privacy Act of 1986 ("EPA"), an amendment to Title III of the Omnibus Crime Control and Safe Streets Act of 1968. It is commonly known as the "wiretap law" and deals with third party eavesdropping on telephone (audio) communications. Most cases have been dismissed or decided in favor of the employer since the EPA was designed to govern third-party interceptions of electronic communications such as law enforcement agencies, not to govern an employers' right to monitor its workers' phone conversations.

Employees consider video monitoring one of the most invasive methods of surveillance that employers may use. Being "watched" by someone else seems to be the ultimate loss of privacy, but it also represents a more subtle psychological impact: the clear demonstration of a lack of trust.

Employers often set up cameras in areas where there are substantial opportunities for employee theft or other criminal activities such as drug dealing. Employers have also set up cameras in areas such as locker rooms, storage rooms, and break areas when they believed that sexual activities were going on in those locations. Typically, since the purpose of the surveillance is to catch someone in an illicit act, the cameras and other monitoring devices are hidden from view. This is very different from the cameras that may be jutting from the wall near the door or hanging from the ceiling in the center of the room. Knowing that you are being watched is quite different than being monitored without your knowledge. This is where some employers cross the line. Well-meaning employers, in their zeal to protect the company, may place cameras in areas that are not appropriate places for monitoring. When cameras are put in restrooms, locker rooms, or other places where employees have a reasonable expectation of privacy, employees are outraged and feel violated. Arguments from employers that they were simply trying to protect the company or the employees does not justify the harm created by the egregious violation of personal privacy. It does not take a genius to see that the employer's argument falls short under both the utilitarian principle and the Kantian principle. The harm far outweighs any possible benefit, and the principle of respect for individuals is certainly violated as well.

One of the conditions that determine if an action for invasion of privacy exists is whether or not the person had a "reasonable expectation of privacy." Courts have consistently found that no reasonable expectation of privacy exists with video or hidden surveillance if the actual physical space under video surveillance is an open or public space. But the courts have been divided on privacy issues when the area under surveillance is considered by the employees to be "private."

This would include areas such as locker rooms, changing areas, and rest rooms. Typically, when the courts have ruled in favor of the employee, the awards have been based on the emotional distress that the invasion of privacy caused.

Employers have found ways of conducting surveillance without the use of cameras or microphones. When employers are looking for fraud, drug use, and theft among employees, they can resort to hiring actors to pose as coworkers and spy on other employees. This practice is called "thespionage" for its use of actors (thespians) to perform corporate espionage activities.

The practice started back in the 1960s when employee drug use began to grow, which also resulted in increased employee theft. Employers were in desperate need of a way to ferret out drug users and thieves, so they began to hire private detectives to impersonate employees or to conduct spying activities. Eventually, employers began to use actors to pose as coworkers.

Activities that can be reported upon include more than drug use, such as theft of company property, theft of intellectual property and trade secrets, and safety violations. Actors simply act as coworkers and befriend other employees, hang out with them at work, and observe their conduct. Any information they pick up that may be helpful to management is reported. Employers can hire their own actors or outsource the activity to companies that specialize in *thespionage*.

One caveat that most employers who use actors as spies observe is to not let these spies socialize with employees outside of the workplace. To do so may create a violation of privacy that could result in litigation, so smart employers use *thespionage* only at work.

Employee Records

Organizations value information. We base many of our decisions on information we collect about people. Recruiting, hiring, promoting, and terminating employees is typically conducted based on some kind of information about the employee, such as resumes, time sheets, performance appraisals, background checks, counseling records, or training records. Businesses extend credit based on financial information.

Suppliers are selected based on proposals, specifications, price lists, references, etc. Information is crucial to helping businesses making sound decisions. So businesses amass information and keep it. Years ago, this was difficult and time consuming. Today, thanks in part to computers and the Internet, this task is much easier. Businesses can collect information quickly and store it in centralized computers and servers where many different managers and employees can access it. In most cases, the information is correct, although confidential in nature. Sometimes, however, so much information is gathered that we have no way of verifying its accuracy and veracity. In this case, we may be unknowingly collecting and keeping information that is incorrect.

Collecting and maintaining information brings with it an intrinsic ethical obligation to protect that information from unauthorized dissemination. Since the nature of our relationships is determined by the nature of the information we share with others, having banks of information about us available to others destroys our ability to control our relationships. Moreover, if the information can be easily accessed, then our control atrophies even more. Since many of us don't even know what kind of information about us exists in databases, we have no way of estimating the possible harm that could result from the release of that information. If the information is incorrect, the harm of releasing it can be greatly amplified.

Because, as the utilitarians argue, the amount of harm that could be caused by the information far outweighs the benefit of the information to the organization, we must be extremely careful in how we handle it. Moreover, duty theory tells us that because people have a *right* to control their own information and have a corresponding *right* to privacy, organizations that collect and maintain confidential information have a *duty* to protect it and use it carefully.

Notes

1 Samuel Warren and Louis Brandeis. "The Right to Privacy," *Harvard Law Review* 4 (1890): pp. 193-220.

2 *Olmstead v. United States,* 277 US 438 (1928). This case dealt with government wiretapping of telephones.

3 *Griswald v. Connecticut*, 381 US 479 (1965). The case involved the right of married people to be free from interference by the government in the use of contraceptives.

4 W.A. Parent, "Privacy, Morality, and the Law," *Philosophy and Public Affairs* (1983): p. 269.

5 James Rachels, "Why Privacy is Important," *Philosophical Dimensions of Privacy* (1975).

6 Charles F. Fried, *An Anatomy of Values* (Cambridge: Harvard University Press, 1970).

7 *Smyth v. Pillsbury*, C.A. NO. 95-5712, January 18, 1996.

8 *Bourke v. Nissan,* No. B068705, July 26, 1993.

9 "2003 E-Mail Rules, Policies and Practices Survey," The ePolicy Institute, American Management Association, and Clearswift.

10 2003 E-Mail Survey.

11 Andrew Schulman, "The Extent of Systematic Monitoring of Employee E-mail and Internet Use," *Workplace Surveillance Project*, The Privacy Foundation (July 9, 2001).

Michael P. Harden

Chapter Seventeen: Trade Secrets

One of the crucial ethical issues faced by organizations is how to protect their trade secrets. Trade secrets are an interesting and mysterious aspect of business. What is a trade secret? Why is it valuable? Why is it an ethical issue? These are all good questions because most of us don't really understand trade secrets and trade secret protection.

There is an interesting story about two friends who were hiking together in Yellowstone Park. One day they came over a hill and ran right into a giant grizzly bear. The bear rose up on his hind legs and let go with a terrifying growl. The two hikers froze in fear for a brief moment, and then one of them yelled, "Run for your life!"

The second hiker said, "What are you crazy? You can't outrun a grizzly bear."

And the first hiker yelled back as he ran off, "I don't have to outrun the bear. I only have to outrun you!"

Our trade secrets give us the ability to outrun our competition and leave them to be eaten by the bear. Without our trade secrets, we would be the ones left behind to deal with the grizzly. So what then is a trade secret?

Trade secrets are information that is proprietary to an organization, typically not known to others, and used to obtain an advantage over its competitors. This is a broad definition, and many scholars and business managers debate what information falls into this definition. Types of information that could be considered to be a trade secret might include: customer lists, software code, chemical formulas, mechanical or manufacturing processes, financial information, engineering designs, legal strategies, or marketing plans. Not all confidential information is a trade secret, and some information that is a trade secret is already protected by copyrights or patents.

The government has aided us in establishing a definition of trade secrets. The following is a reprint of the *Restatement of Torts* Section 757, comment b. (1939):

Definition of trade secret. A trade secret may consist of any formula, pattern, device or compilation of information which is used in one's business, and which gives him an opportunity to obtain an advantage over competitors who do not know or use it. It may be a formula for a chemical compound, a process of manufacturing, treating or preserving materials, a pattern for a machine or other device, or a list of customers. It differs from other secret information in a business (see Section 759) in that it is not simply information as to single or ephemeral events in the conduct of the business, as, for example, the amount or other terms of a secret bid for a contract or the salary of certain employees, or the security investments made or contemplated, or the date fixed for the announcement of a new policy or for bringing out a new model or the like. A trade secret is a process or device for continuous use in the operations of the business. Generally it relates to the production of goods, as, for example, a machine or formula for the production of an article. It may, however, relate to the sale of goods or to other operations in the business, such as a code for determining discounts, rebates or other concessions in the price list or catalogue, or a list if specialized customers, or a method of bookkeeping or other office management.

Secrecy. The subject matter of a trade secret must be secret. Matters of public knowledge or of general knowledge in an industry cannot be appropriated by one as his secret. Matters which are completely disclosed by the goods which one markets cannot be his secret. Substantially, a trade secret is known only in the particular business in which it is used. It is not requisite that only the proprietor of the business know it. He may, without losing his protection, communicate it to employees involved in its use. He may likewise communicate it to others pledged to secrecy. Others may also know of it independently, as, for example, when they have discovered the process or formula by independent invention and are keeping it secret. Nevertheless, a substantial element of secrecy must exist, so that, except by the use of improper means, there would be difficulty in acquiring the information. An exact definition of a trade secret is not possible. Some factors to be considered in determining whether given information is one's trade secret are:

1. the extent to which the information is known outside of his business;
2. the extent to which it is known by employees and others involved in his business;
3. the extent of measures taken by him to guard the secrecy of the information;
4. the value of the information to him and his competitors;
5. the amount of effort or money expended by him in developing the information;
6. the ease or difficulty with which the information could be properly acquired or duplicated by others.

Novelty and prior art. A trade secret may be a device or process which is patentable; but it need not be that. It may be a device or process which is clearly anticipated in the prior art or one which is merely a mechanical improvement that a good mechanic can make. Novelty and invention are not requisite for a trade secret as they are for patentability. These requirements are essential to patentability. These requirements are essential to patentability because a patent protects against unlicensed use of the patented device or process even by one who discovers it properly through independent research. The patent monopoly is a reward to the inventor. But such is not the case with a trade secret. Its protection is not based on a policy of rewarding or otherwise encouraging the development of secret processes or devices. The protection is merely against a breach of faith and reprehensible means of learning another's secret. For this limited protection it is not appropriate to require also the kind of novelty and invention which is a requisite of patentability. The nature of the secret is, however, an important factor in determining the kind of relief that is appropriate against one who acquires the secret wrongfully is ordinarily enjoined from further use of it and is required to account for the profits derived from his past use. If, on the other hand, the secret consists of mechanical improvements that a good mechanic can make without resort to the secret, the wrongdoer's liability may be limited to damages, and an injunction against future use of the improvements made with the aid of the secret may be inappropriate.

Although comment b. states, "An exact definition of a trade secret is not possible," it does list six factors that identify whether information falls into the category of trade secrets. We can use those six criteria to help us determine whether our proprietary information can be considered to be trade secret information.

Congress enacted the Economic Espionage Act (EEA) of 1996, making it a federal crime to steal an organization's trade secrets. Until 1996, only various state laws protected trade secrets. The EEA was originally written to prevent the theft of trade secrets by foreign governments or by parties intent on benefiting foreign governments. Theft of U.S. firms' trade secrets by foreign governments and their agents has cost U.S. firms upward of $24 billion each year. Many countries completely ignore U.S. copyrights and patents, and the EEA was passed to penalize those countries. However, the EEA also has a domestic aspect. It has a separate set of penalties for domestic trade secret theft, in essence, making it function as if it were two different laws. Foreign theft can land you a sentence of up to 15 years in jail and fines of up to $500,000. Prosecutors can further seize any property involved in committing the offense. Domestic jail sentences can reach 10 years with fines of up to $250,000.

Under this law, things that used to be unethical (but legal) are now strictly illegal. Since the EEA defines theft as the knowing misappropriation of a secret without its owner's consent, there are many behaviors than can be considered illegal. Alan Farnham (*Fortune*, 1997) gave the following three examples[1] of situations that could meet the test of criminal behavior under the EEA:

—You're on a plane. At takeoff, a report belonging to somebody a few rows up slides along the inclined floor, coming to rest against the toes of your well-waxed wingtips (or pumps, as the case may be). You pick it up, noting it's stamped CONFIDENTIAL. Hot diggity! It's a marketing report belonging to your archrivals at Nemesis Co. You gleefully digest its contents.

—Same airplane, different situation: Two guys seated next to you are blathering out loud about the sales presentation they'll be making when they land, ignorant of the fact that you're the enemy and that you'll be presenting against them. You soak up every detail.

—You're the head of Staples. (This example isn't hypothetical. It's taken from page 72 of Thomas G. Stemberg's 1996 exercise in braggadocio, *Staples for Success*.) You want to get the drop on Office Depot. So you have your wife, Dola, apply for a job at OD's delivery center in Atlanta. Dola, Stemberg writes, "had experience in telemarketing and in a soft, Southern accent, explained that she was anxious to move back 'home.' Staples did not offer delivery service at the time, so I wanted to investigate how Office Depot's delivery system worked, how many people were in the operation, and how it trained employees."…Thanks to Dola's dodge, Stemberg got his info.

Many of us do not know that these actions probably meet the definition of trade secret theft as promulgated by the EEA. It is almost as if, according to Farnham, we have to protect our competitors from their own stupidity. But there are loopholes that we must take into account. In the six factors listed in comment b. of Section 757 of the *Restatement of Torts*, to be a trade secret, we must show that we took measures to protect the information. If we leave confidential financial reports laying open on a public table in a restaurant, or we talk about our new chemical formula for turning water into gasoline while we are packed into a crowded elevator, or we fail to tell employees that the list of planned new products is confidential, we may be relinquishing our rights to claim this information as a trade secret. It may be easy for a competitor to make a case that since we didn't take adequate steps to protect it, we didn't treat it as a trade secret...And if we didn't treat it as a trade secret, then it must not be a trade secret.

The EEA goes beyond comment b. of Section 757 of the *Restatement of Torts* by explicitly describing the types of information that would be considered a trade secret:

> "All forms and types of financial, business, scientific, technical, economic, or engineering information, including patterns, plans, compilations, program devices, formulas, designs, prototypes, methods, techniques, processes, procedures, programs, or codes, whether tangible or intangible, and whether or how stored, compiled, or memorialized physically, electronically, graphically, photographically, or in writing if: (A) the owner thereof has taken reasonable measures to keep such information secret; and (B) the information derives independent economic value, actual or potential, from not being generally known to, and not being readily ascertainable through proper means by, the public."

Once again we see that the holder of the information must take "reasonable measures to keep such information secret" in order for it to be considered a trade secret.

The Importance of Trade Secrets

What most organizations fail to understand is that their proprietary information is often what makes them profitable and successful. Trade secrets, proprietary processes, competitive information, intellectual property, sales/marketing strategies, financial conditions, research and development efforts, pending patents, proprietary formulas, human resources, and client information are examples of just a few of the various types of information that corporations and other organizations utilize to make themselves successful.

Information is what makes an organization valuable. Keeping information confidential, yet ensuring that it can be shared with others in the organization who can maximize its value, are both high priorities that must be considered by management. Trusted employees (and contractors) must be able to easily access the organization's intrinsic knowledge base of information while keeping it out of the hands of competitors or criminals.

Management in many organizations fails to appreciate the value of its information. If an unauthorized person walked into your office and stole your laptop, briefcase, and coat, you would be outraged and would probably call the police. But when a competitor steals your valuable information by hiring a key employee away from you who has knowledge of your confidential manufacturing process, you may not even be aware that any information has been stolen.

It is also important to not lose sight of the fact that if information has value to you, it almost surely has value to someone else as well. Moreover, the information *belongs* to you, so it is your responsibility to protect it. Since information is developed, gathered, or created through someone's efforts, then information, to the extent that it is a valuable trade secret, is someone's property. This is compatible with the property rights theory of Locke. We own the fruits of our labor, which may include intangible property as well as tangible property. If we create, develop, or collect information as part of our jobs while we are employed, then we are exchanging that information for our wages. Our employer then owns the information that was created or collected by us.

However, information is different in one sense. Unlike other property that you own forever, information ceases to be your property once it becomes public. If everyone knows it, then it isn't a trade secret any longer, and you cannot make a legitimate claim to it. If others know the same information, then you cannot possibly claim to exclusively own it. This is another very good reason to prevent your proprietary information from becoming public. If a trade secret was published in a report, divulged in a conversation, or accidentally revealed by leaving reports or documents in the open, the right to trade secret status is lost.

Collecting Competitive Information

Organizations run into ethical issues with trade secrets in two ways:

1. The measures used to collect it.
2. The measures used to protect it.

Organizations must be careful about how they gather information. In certain instances, gathering competitive information, which may include trade secrets, can create ethical problems. Specifically, the methods used to collect competitive information can be unethical. Unethical methods of collection fall into the following commonly defined categories: theft, misrepresentation, surveillance, and improper influence.

Theft

Theft of proprietary information violates the property rights of the information's owner. Theft can occur by industrial espionage (hiring someone to steal the information), disgruntled employees (who may sell trade secrets to competitors), or theft by opportunity (a sales rep notices a competitor's confidential proposal on a prospect's desk and takes advantage of the opportunity to look through it for information).

Misrepresentation

Using false pretenses to gain access to information is unethical. Since we should treat others with respect, and we have a duty to be honest with others, misrepresenting ourselves violates these principles. Dola Stemberg getting a job with Office Depot to observe their operations is one example of this. Posing as a potential customer to get pricing and information from your competitor is another form of mis-representation.

Surveillance

Tapping phones, using eavesdropping devices, installing hidden cameras, or spying on competitor's employees to gather confidential information violates the right to privacy and the principle of respect for individuals.

Improper Influence

Improper influence usually takes one of three forms: bribery, inducements, or blackmail. Bribing an employee of a competitor to steal trade secrets is a form of improper influence. Inducing a competitor's employee to provide you with information by promising her a great job with your company is another form of improper influence. The most egregious form of improper influence is by blackmailing an employee of a competitor to steal and deliver secrets. This can be accomplished by threatening to reveal embarrassing information about the employee if they fail to comply.

Protecting Information

Organizations use several means to protect information. The most common are the non-compete agreement and the confidentiality agreement (or non-disclosure agreement).

Non-compete agreements

Employers often have their key employees (or employees who have access to trade secret information) sign a non-compete agreement as a condition of their employment. Basically, the non-compete agreement says that the employee will not leave the firm and join a competing firm within some specified period of time. These agree-ments are usually one-sided in that they favor the employer but offer little to the employee. Since these agreements are typically a condition of employment, most employees sign them as a matter of course. Usually, they give them little attention until they are seeking employment elsewhere.

Companies like these agreements because they prevent employees from leaving the firm and taking valuable information to their competitors. However, in some states, they are neither valid nor enforceable. And in states where non-compete agreements are valid, courts have been cautious in enforcing them. One of the reasons for this is that many companies require employees to sign these agreements as a standard hiring requirement even though these employees have no access to confidential information. These agreements really serve no legitimate purpose.

Another reason is that non-compete agreements may keep individuals from being able to make a living. If an individual has spent his entire adult life working in one industry that is made up of a few competitors and that is all he knows, prohibiting him from working for a competitor is tantamount to preventing him from being able to work at all. Courts are not keen on imposing such a hardship on a person. Everyone should be afforded the opportunity to make a living. In these situations, non-compete agreements are usually not enforced.

Some companies simply rely on the fear of legal action to prevent someone from joining the competition. Even though many employers know that their non-compete agreements are probably not enforceable, they rely on the employee's lack of this knowledge to keep the employee from seeking employment with a competitor.

Confidentiality or Non-disclosure Agreements

Since the release of confidential information can harm an organization, confidentiality agreements are often used to prevent unauthorized dissemination of confidential information and trade secrets. Agreements can be between the organization and its employees, contractors, consultants, and business partners. These contractual agreements are designed to ensure that parties who must have access to proprietary information in order to perform their jobs or fulfill their responsibilities can do so, but prohibit them from revealing this valuable information to others who do not have such a need. Organizations have a right to expect others that work for or with them to protect their information. Individuals also have a right to have their information protected. Inventors and entrepreneurs often have companies sign confidentiality agreements before presenting their ideas and business plans to them. This serves to protect them from having their ideas misappropriated by others.

Corporations and organizations must be constantly vigilant in protecting their trade secrets. In doing so, they must also be aware of the legal and ethical issues that surround trade secret protection. As a guideline, Section 757 of the *Restatement of Torts* provides us with a list of conditions under which we would be liable for disclosure of a trade secret. Generally, one who discloses or uses another's trade secret, without a privilege to do so, is liable to the other if:

(a) he discovered the secret by improper means, or
(b) his disclosure or use constitutes a breach of confidence reposed in him by the other in disclosing the secret to him, or
(c) he learned the secret from a third person with notice of the facts that it was a secret and that the third person discovered it by improper means or that the third person's disclosure of it was otherwise a breach of his duty to the other, or
(d) he learned the secret with notice of the facts that it was a secret and that its disclosure was made to him by mistake.

In other words, if you obtain a trade secret by improper means, learn it from somebody else who obtained it by improper means, disclose a trade secret to someone else, or use a trade secret that you learned by mistake (provided you knew it was a secret), you can be held liable.

As stated earlier, you must protect yourself from the stupidity of you competitors. By taking a common sense approach if you happen to accidentally obtain confidential information, you can avoid accusations of unethical behavior. Here is an example of a situation that happened to one company:

The company was involved in a heated legal battle with another company over patent infringement issues. Just a few days prior to the trial, its attorney, who I shall call "William," was sitting at his desk when a fax started to come through. As William glanced at the fax, he realized it was from the opposing counsel. As he began to read the fax, William realized that the fax contained the opposing counsel's complete strategy for its client's defense. William knew that the fax was obviously not intended for him! Somebody had probably keyed in the wrong phone number or hit the wrong speed dial number. The fax was supposed to go to another attorney in the opposing counsel's law firm. It was as if God had provided William with a wonderful gift — the entire legal strategy of his opposing counsel was being delivered into his hands by an obvious error. Many of us would pray for such a gift.

Not William. He immediately hit the stop button on the fax to prevent any more documentation from coming through. He then phoned the opposing attorney to inform him of what had happened. He also took the two sheets that had come through and immediately shredded them.

How many of us would have taken such an ethical action? Would we not take advantage of the stupidity of the opposing counsel and at least cop a quick glance at his strategy? Many people who respond affirmatively would liken this situation to when General George B. McClellan's soldiers found a copy of Robert E. Lee's orders that had been accidentally lost prior to the battle of Antietam (Sept. 1862). McClellan used this serendipitous information to obtain a strategic military advantage (he knew what Lee was planning to do). The course of the war might have gone differently had those orders not been found and McClellan not beaten back Lee's Army of Northern Virginia. Should McClellan have refused to read the orders and returned them to Lee? It is an interesting question, but ethical considerations in war don't always match those in business. War and business, although similar in many aspects, have very different ethical considerations. Like William, we must know what those ethical issues are and what the correct moral actions are as well. McClellan took the correct ethical action in his situation by using the documents to help win a major battle, and William took the correct ethical action in his situation by not using the documents to help win a legal battle.

Notes

[1] Alan Farnham, "How Safe Are Your Secrets?" *Fortune* (September 1997).

Chapter Eighteen: Termination

In 1884, the Tennessee Supreme Court ruled in the case *Paine v. Western*, that employers could dismiss their employees "at will…for good cause, no cause, or even for a cause morally wrong." Other court decisions in various states followed the same logic, and eventually, the U.S. Supreme Court did the same. Historically, the basis for our concept of *employment-at-will* has been established for well over one hundred years in this country.

If there are no employment contracts that detail specific conditions under which employment and termination may occur, then the doctrine of employment-at-will typically governs the dismissal of employees. This arrangement is reciprocal. Employers have the right to hire and fire employees "at will," without having to explain their reasons. On the other hand employees may refuse to accept a job or quit whenever they feel like it. Both parties — employer and employee — enter into a voluntary agreement to work together, under the working conditions provided by the employer, until either party decides to terminate the agreement. The employer can fire the employee, or the employee can quit, unless there have been certain conditions that were previously agreed upon, e.g., in an employment contract. Each has that right to terminate their relationship under their voluntary agreement.

Obviously, there have been many laws instituted over the years that govern working conditions (minimum wage laws, equal opportunity laws, and various labor laws), and employers are expected to follow those laws. As long as employers comply with these laws, the voluntary agreement of employment-at-will remains in effect.

The Utilitarian Argument

The utilitarian argument for employment-at-will expresses the principle that businesses must be able to enter into transactions that benefit the most people. In a business, this typically indicates cost-effectiveness and efficiency. For a business to be able to operate in the most efficient way, it must have the ability to determine who it employees without restrictions. Businesses must have the ability to hire whomever they want in order to increase their efficiency. To do this effectively, they must also have the ability to terminate whomever they choose as well.

Employees, on the other hand, have the ability to sell their services to the highest bidder. Experienced, skilled, and productive employees can seek employment from any employer who is willing and able to pay higher wages for their increased level of experience and skill. The employer who hires these kinds of employees gains significant benefits through increased efficiencies and productivity. In the end, customers and shareholders reap the benefits of this strategy.

The Property Rights Argument

The concept of employment-at-will is based on fundamental arguments such as the property rights argument.[1] Under Locke's labor theory of property, individuals have a right to the product of their labor, i.e., the right to the goods produced by their labor. If we work for someone else, the result of our labor is our property, except that we have chosen to exchange it for wages.

So an individual can choose to work in a factory, and in doing so, sell his or her labor to the factory owner for an hourly wage. The owner of the factory has the right to the profits that flow directly from the labor of his employees. He is entitled to whatever wealth his factory brings him even though he did not perform the labor himself. In this situation, a transaction or exchange takes place between the employer and the employee. Each party is free to accept the terms of the other. When they do, a voluntary agreement has taken place. Since it is voluntary, each party has the right to terminate the agreement at any time. Under the property rights argument, each party still owns their own property. The factory owner (employer) retains the ownership of the means of production, equipment, and facilities, while the employee retains the ownership of his own labor. Each party may seek a "better deal" somewhere else.

The employer can terminate the employee and hire others in his place, or the employee can seek employment with another factory owner elsewhere. Under the property rights argument, neither the employer nor the employee has violated any rights of the other when they terminate the agreement.

Freedom of Contract Argument

Immanuel Kant's argument that we should treat others with respect forms the basis for the *freedom of contract* argument. "Respect" means that we allow others to make their own decisions and to live by their decisions. Kant's argument of respect grants to others a measure of autonomy. People with autonomy have the right to enter into their own agreements or contracts without interference by others. These contracts can be *implicit*, as are most employment arrangements where no written contract exists, or they can be *explicit*, where a written employment agreement is provided that details various circumstances and conditions of employment.

If we place restrictions on the freedom to enter into contracts of our choice, we then begin to force employers and employees to enter into or remain in employment agreements that they would otherwise choose to terminate. This makes the agreement no longer voluntary. Restricting the types of conditions or terms under which agreements can be made, for example, through laws or regulations, could mean that employers would have to keep workers they do not want, and employees would have to work for employers they do not like. If we restrict the types of agreements that employees and employers can enter into, then we violate the right to autonomy. In the case *Adair v. United States*, Supreme Court Justice John M. Harlan delivered this majority opinion:

> "It is a part of every man's civil rights that he be left at liberty to refuse business relations with any person whomsoever, whether the refusal rests upon reason, or is the result of whim, caprice, prejudice or malice. With his reasons neither the public nor third persons have any legal concern. It is also his right to have business relations with anyone with whom he can make contracts, and if he is wrongfully deprived of this right by oth-

ers, he is entitled to redress...While, as already suggested, the rights of liberty and property guaranteed by the Constitution against deprivation without due process of law are subject to such reasonable restraints as the common good or the general welfare may require, it is not within the functions of government — at least in the absence of contract between the parties — to compel any person, in the course of his business and against his will, to accept or retain the personal services of another, or to compel any person, against his will, to perform personal services for another. The right of a person to sell his labor upon such terms as he deems proper is, in its essence, the same as the right of the purchaser of labor to prescribe the conditions upon which he will accept such labor from the person offering to sell it. So the right of the employee to quit the service of the employer...for whatever reason, is the same as the right of the employer, for whatever reason, to dispense with the services of such employee."[2]

Subsequent court decisions have modified the freedom of contract argument somewhat by asserting that there are certain conditions which can limit who can enter into a contractual agreement, for example, children, people under duress, and mentally incompetent people. Also, certain conditions may invalidate a contract, such as contracts entered into under fraudulent conditions.

Legal vs. Ethical Concepts

Almost three-quarters of the employees in the United States operate in an employment-at-will environment. Union contracts and written employment contracts typically govern the remaining one-quarter of employees. In essence, the vast majority of employees in the United States can be terminated at any time, for any reason, or for no reason at all.

Organizations should keep in mind that the employment-at-will doctrine is a legal argument that does not take into account many of the ethical and moral arguments related to employment. Ethical concepts such as justice and fairness, duty and rights, respect for individuals, and other moral arguments must be taken into consideration when employee termination actions are being contemplated. Since termination decisions often have tremendous impacts on the lives of the people involved, they must be arrived at in an ethical manner, weighing carefully the amount of harm and benefit caused by these actions. Simply following the law is not always sufficient in ethical decision-making since ethics must often go beyond what the law establishes as a minimum. A reasonable person would understand what Michael Josephson (quoted in Bill Moyers" *World of Ideas*) meant when he said: "An ethical person ought to do more than he's required to do and less than he's allowed to do."

Notes

[1] John Locke, *Second Treatise Concerning Civil Government* Chapter V: (1690).
[2] *Adair v. United States,* 208 U.S. 161 (1908) (USSC+), October 29, 30, 1907.

Chapter Nineteen: Discrimination

Discrimination, for whatever reasons (sex, race, nationality, religion, etc.) is a basic violation of the principle of justice and fairness. Discrimination can take place in areas such as housing, employment, group/organization membership, lending, medical care, access to services, and education. In a business environment, discrimination can happen in areas such as hiring, firing, promotions, wages, and benefits.

Favoritism and discrimination are not the same thing, although both behaviors violate the principle of justice. Favoritism is when an employer provides some advantage to an employee because she favors that employee. Discrimination, on the other hand, is when an employer *withholds* something from an employee, treating him unequally from the other employees. Typically, this takes the form of withholding promotions, raises, or better job assignments. On a larger scale, it can involve the hiring and/or firing of people. In any case, the discrimination usually results in the unequal treatment of people based on a difference that is not relevant to the job. Unequal treatment may be based on sex, age, race, disability, or some other prejudice of the employer.

The word "discriminate" has not always had a negative connotation. Historically, to discriminate meant to use good judgment or to draw a distinction between one thing and another. We often discriminate in this sense. We chose one option over another because it is better. We married our spouses because we made a discriminating decision — we chose them over the other single people that we had dated. We made a discriminating decision when we picked a college to attend or a supermarket in which to shop. Discriminating decisions are made regularly in the course of our day-to-day behavior.

Discrimination becomes morally wrong when we make discriminating decisions that adversely affect others, and those decisions are based on their membership in some group or class rather than their own individual merit or capability.

Usually, there are three elements present in an unethical decision to discriminate:

1. The decision has a negative impact on the employment conditions of the person, such as personnel decisions, e.g., hiring, promotions, pay, and benefits.

2. The decision is based on group membership rather than individual merit, such as experience, previous job performance, or education.

3. The decision results from some morally unjustified attitude or prejudice, such as sexual or racial stereotypes.

Discrimination within an organization can take on two forms. It can be either individual or institutionalized:

Individual — An individual, perhaps a department manager, discriminates based on his or her personal stereotypical beliefs or prejudices.

Institutional — Members of an organization routinely practice discriminatory behavior because it has become part of the corporate culture or organizational attitude.

Legal Aspects of Discrimination

There is a legal definition of discrimination that we can use to more fully understand what discrimination means in a business environment. Section 703(a) of Title VII of the Civil Rights Act of 1964 states:

It shall be an unlawful employment practice for an employer -

(1) to fail or refuse to hire or to discharge any individual, or otherwise to discriminate against any individual with respect to his compensation, terms, conditions, or privileges of

employment, because of such individual's race, color, religion, sex, or national origin; or

(2) to limit, segregate, or classify his employees or applicants for employment in any way which would deprive or tend to deprive any individual of employment opportunities or otherwise adversely affect his status as an employee, because of such individual's race, color, religion, sex, or national origin.[1]

Subsequent laws were enacted to outlaw other forms of discrimination. The Age Discrimination in Employment Act of 1967 states the following:

It shall be unlawful for an employer -

(1) to fail or refuse to hire or to discharge any individual or otherwise discriminate against any individual with respect to his compensation, terms, conditions, or privileges of employment, because of such individual's age;

(2) to limit, segregate, or classify his employees in any way which would deprive or tend to deprive any individual of employment opportunities or otherwise adversely affect his status as an employee, because of such individual's age; or

(3) to reduce the wage rate of any employee in order to comply with this chapter.[2]

Other laws were enacted to protect other classes or groups as well. Some of these laws are:

- The Rehabilitation Act of 1973
- The Pregnancy Discrimination Act of 1978
- The Americans with Disabilities Act of 1990

When a group falls under one of the various anti-discrimination laws, it is considered a *protected class*.

Exceptions

Even if a person fits into a protected class, there are certain circumstances where an exception to the law may be made. Title VII of The Civil Rights Act specifies that "…it shall not be an unlawful employment practice for an employer to hire and employ employees…on the basis of his religion, sex, or national origin in those certain instances where religion, sex, or national origin is a bona fide occupational qualification reasonably necessary to the normal operation of that particular business or enterprise…"

This exception, which allows employers to hire specifically based on religion, sex, or national origin is know as the BFOQ (bona fide occupational qualification) exception. The test for such a BFOQ is very tough and only in a few instances have courts upheld this exception to The Civil Rights Act. In *Dothard v. Rawlinson,* 433 U.S. 321 (1977), the Supreme Court ruled that the BFOQ exception is extremely narrow. In fact, based on the courts' reluctance to establish any BFOQ exceptions based on sex, the only real BFOQ exceptions that are likely to be allowed on the basis of sex would be either sperm donor (which *requires* a male) or egg donor (which *requires* a female). There is <u>no</u> BFOQ exception that allows for employment decisions based on race. No one has yet been able to prove there is a job with a bona fide occupational qualification based on race.

An employer must be able to make a case that the BFOQ is absolutely essential to the performance of the job. Simply claiming that the BFOQ may contribute to the conduct of the business, or that it is a customer preference, is not sufficient to establish the exception.

Ethical Arguments Against Discrimination

Utilitarians argue that discrimination is wrong because it is inefficient for businesses to engage in it. When companies hire and promote people based on merit, then the most productive and efficient people are working for the organization. This makes the entire company more efficient and productive. Discrimination keeps organizations from utilizing these productive resources and thereby harms the organization. Under the utilitarian principle, more people are harmed by, rather than benefited by discrimination in hiring and promotions.

Since race, sex, and religion typically have nothing to do with job performance, they are irrelevant to productivity. On the other hand, experience, skills, previous job performance, aptitude, knowledge, and prior training, are valid reasons for hiring and promotions. Managers who practice discrimination inadvertently hurt their own companies and business units by artificially reducing the pool of qualified labor and by failing to hire based on merit. Utilitarians would say that everyone loses — the company and the individuals suffering the discrimination.

Kantians would argue that discrimination is wrong because it violates the basic rights of people to be treated with dignity and respect — to be treated as an end, not as a means. In discrimination, people are a means because they are being used to satisfy some prejudicial ends, for example "keeping Asians out," or "keeping women in their place."

Kantians also consider discrimination wrong under the concept of universalization. In essence, if *everyone* practiced discrimination *all of the time*, what would the world be like? Would we want to be treated in such a way?

The principle of justice has a strong hand in determining that discrimination is wrong. The principle of justice and fairness tells us that *differences in what someone receives should be justified by differences that are relevant to the basis for the distribution.* If race, sex, religion, age, and other factors are not relevant, then the principle of justice is violated.

Thomas Jefferson once wrote: "Equal rights for all, special privileges for none." This is one of the first times in U.S. history that the principle of justice was used as a statement against discrimination. Jefferson was merely restating in a more relevant way, Aristotle's original notion that "equals should be treated equally and unequals unequally." Discrimination and favoritism violate this concept. Historically, discrimination has been practiced for thousands of years, but there has also been a corresponding belief in justice that has consistently opposed this practice. Justice and fairness have been the age-old nemesis of discrimination and favoritism as well as one of the strongest arguments against this conduct.

It should be noted that the same arguments we use against discrimination (utilitarianism, Kantian, and justice) are also the same arguments we use for proclaiming that *affirmative action* is wrong.

Regardless of our beliefs about repairing past injustices and providing opportunities for the less privileged among us, we cannot use our arguments against discrimination in one situation and then claim they are not relevant in another. Ethical principles have a universality about them that does not allow them to be used in one situation and tossed aside in another. If it is wrong to discriminate based on race, sex, or other reasons, then it is *always* wrong to discriminate for these reasons. The individual against whom the discrimination is being directed, whether white or black, male or female, does not suffer any less if the motives for the discrimination are supposed to achieve a different objective. In affirmative action, organizations still deprive themselves of the most qualified employees by not utilizing merit as their criterion for making personnel decisions, thereby harming the organization and its various stakeholders. A valid argument can be made that "reverse" discrimination does just as much harm as "real" discrimination since there is no such thing as "reverse" discrimination, only discrimination against a different class of people.

The only true way of creating a society (and business) that is free from discrimination is to ensure that *no* discrimination takes place. Opening the door to any type of discrimination requires that someone be harmed. This is unfair under any circumstances. We must follow the underlying principle that if there are no relevant differences between individuals, then there should be no differences in the equality of distribution. If an employer discriminates against someone, regardless of the reasons, they are depriving that person of something without basing that decision on a relevant difference. Morally, this is wrong.

There are some logical arguments against affirmative action. The first argument is that affirmative action means that organizations will hire and promote less qualified people. Some proponents of affirmative action claim this is not necessarily true, since many people who are the likely beneficiaries of affirmative action are also well qualified. This fails to take into account the *quality argument.* The quality argument expresses the logical notion that the most qualified person for a position doesn't *need* any special consideration. If they are the most qualified, they have earned the job or promotion on the basis of merit. Therefore, a person who is given preference on the basis of race or sex *cannot* be the most qualified person and *cannot* perform as well in the job as someone who is more qualified. If individuals must rely upon affirmative action to get their jobs, then this is the strongest indicator that they are not the most qualified. Having less qualified people as employees lowers the quality of the workforce.[3] This is a strong utilitarian argument against affirmative action since more people will suffer than benefit when the organization becomes less efficient and quality drops.

A second argument against affirmative action is that it increases or heightens race consciousness. Affirmative action actually promotes more discrimination and causes others to develop more prejudicial behavior. If we truly believe that people are not basically different and should therefore not suffer discrimination, we contradict this by using affirmative action, which increases everyone's awareness of the differences we claim do not exist. Obviously, if we proclaim that all people are equal and should be treated equally, but then declare that certain people should be given special consideration in order to be equal, we have made a clear statement that some people are not equal after all. Affirmative action causes us to highlight differences rather than eliminate them.[4]

The third argument against affirmative action is that it demeans the recipients of its preferential treatment. Self-esteem is diminished for those employees who are hired or promoted through affirmative action because they, as well as their coworkers, know their hiring or promotions are not the results of their merit. In fact, it builds upon the first argument that says that they *cannot* be the most qualified person for the job. This is a good Kantian argument against affirmative action. Preferential treatment violates the Kantian principle of respect. By promoting people under an affirmative action program, an organization has made a very strong expression that these people are not as qualified as other people, and in fact, could not have succeeded without preferential treatment. It also hurts women and minorities who have succeeded on their own merits by creating a lingering question in the minds of others as to whether the success of these people is based on their own efforts or preferential treatment. As long as affirmative action is practiced, people will always be skeptical of the qualifications or capabilities of any successful woman or minority. The unasked question will be: "Did they do it on their own, or was it handed to them?"

Comparable Worth

Wage discrimination often occurs when people are paid different wages for basically the same job. This is most likely to occur in situations where women and men perform similar work, but the women are paid at a lower wage. Any smart employer would pay his employees based on the productivity of those employees. Under the free market system and the labor theory of property, more productive workers are able to sell their services to the highest bidder. Experienced, skilled, and productive employees can seek employment from any employer who is willing and able to pay higher wages for their increased level of experience and skill. On the other hand, the employer who hires these kinds of employees gains significant benefits through increased efficiencies and productivity. The ultimate beneficiaries are the customers and shareholders who reap the benefits of this strategy. So logic tells us that successful businesses pay their workers based on productivity.

However, artificial factors have come into play that interfere with this natural process. Those factors are based more on psychological notions rather than sound business principles. Wage discrimination almost always occurs against women. Our history of treating women unequally with men has been hard to shake loose, and we continue to practice this unequal treatment today.

It has been forty years since President John Kennedy signed the Equal Pay Act. In 1963, women earned only 58 cents for every dollar men earned. Forty years later, women earn, on average, about 75 cents for every dollar men earn. Although this has been a 29 percent increase, it is still far below equality. Part of the problem is that the Equal Pay Act of 1963 only dealt with pay for identical jobs, not similar jobs. This has been the big loophole in getting wages equal across the board.

According to a 1999 study by the Institute for Women's Policy Research and the AFL-CIO based on U.S. Census Bureau and Bureau of Labor statistics, women who work full time earn 26 percent less than men. On average, that equals $148 less each week, or $7,696 a year. Minority women who work full time are paid even less, only 64 cents for every dollar men earn, or about $210 less per week and $11,440 less per year than men.

There are now over 64 million women in the workforce. So unequal pay hurts the majority of American families. Families lose $200 billion in income annually to the wage gap — an average loss of more than $4,000 for each working family. Additionally, wage discrimination lowers total lifetime earnings, thereby reducing women's benefits from Social Security and pension plans.[5]

One reason for the wage disparity between men and women is due to occupational segregation. There are many jobs that could be performed equally as well by men or women, but society and stereotypes have created this occupational segregation. There are occupations that are traditionally male-dominated and others that are traditionally female-dominated. For example, nurses tend to be female while doctors tend to be male. Engineers tend to be male while dieticians tend to be female. Secretaries tend to be female while mechanics tend to be male. However, even allowing for such occupational segregation, studies have found that women earn on average about ten percent less than men, even in comparable jobs where education, experience, and training are equal.

This phenomenon is also present when we compare black males with white males. Although occupational segregation is less common for race than it is for gender, black males with similar education and experience in comparable jobs will earn about ten percent less than their white counterparts.

To counter these discrepancies and inequalities in wages, the principle of comparable worth can be practiced. The principle of comparable worth argues that even jobs that are not similar can still be compared based on certain features. Jobs that hold similar features should be paid the same. By analyzing a job's content or the type of work performed, we can determine if two jobs are comparable. If the jobs are comparable, then they should be paid the same wages.

Notes

[1] Title VII of the Civil Rights Act of 1964 (Pub. L. 88-352) (Title VII), as amended, as it appears in volume 42 of the United States Code, beginning at section 2000e, Unlawful Employment Practices, SEC 2000e-2. [*Section 703*]

[2] Age Discrimination in Employment Act of 1967 (Pub. L. 90-202) (ADEA), as amended, as it appears in volume 29 of the United States Code, Prohibition of Age Discrimination, SEC. 623. [*Section 4*]

[3] John R. Boatright, *Ethics and the Conduct of Business.* 3d Edition (Upper Saddle River, New Jersey: Prentice Hall, 2000) p. 208.

[4] Boatright, p. 209.

[5] Obtained from the American Association of University Women (AAUW)

Michael P. Harden

Chapter Twenty: Sexual Harassment

Sexual harassment has become a problem in the workplace for a variety of reasons, and sexual harassment claims have increased dramatically since the 1980s. However, many business managers do not feel that the amount of sexual harassment has really increased over the years, just that it is more widely reported. Moreover, incidents that were not considered as harassment in the past now fall under an expanded definition or heightened awareness. Whereas, twenty years ago a boss could ask an employee to go out with him without any thought of this being an improper act, today few managers would risk doing the same thing in fear of an accusation of harassment. Either our concept of harassment has changed, or our sensitivity to it has increased.

The Equal Employment Opportunity Commission (EEOC) provides the following definition of sexual harassment:

"Unwelcome sexual advances, requests for sexual favors, and other verbal or physical conduct of a sexual nature constitutes sexual harassment when submission to or rejection of this conduct explicitly or implicitly affects an individual's employment, unreasonably interferes with an individual's work performance or creates an intimidating, hostile or offensive work environment."

The EEOC states that sexual harassment is a violation of Title VII of the Civil Rights Act of 1964. Originally, this was not true since there is no reference to sexual harassment in the Civil Rights Act of 1964. However, subsequent court rulings have concluded that sexual harassment is a form of discrimination based on sex, and therefore does indeed violate the Civil Rights Act.

Sexual harassment can occur in a variety of circumstances, including but not limited to the following[1]:

- The victim as well as the harasser may be a woman or a man. The victim does not have to be of the opposite sex.
- The harasser can be the victim's supervisor, an agent of the employer, a supervisor in another area, a coworker, or a non-employee.
- The victim does not have to be the person harassed but could be anyone affected by the offensive conduct.
- Unlawful sexual harassment may occur without economic injury to the victim or discharge of the victim.
- The harasser's conduct must be unwelcome.

Examining the definition and the circumstances, we must closely interpret what some of the key elements mean. For example, how does someone making a sexual advance know whether that sexual advance is "unwelcome" until after the advance has been made? What makes a specific action "unwelcome" to one person but innocuous to another? If a person makes a casual but off-color joke while gabbing around the office water cooler and five of the six people present laugh while one is offended, has harassment taken place? If a supervisor asks an employee out for dinner, is that harassment? What if a coworker asks out a fellow coworker? The only way to answer these questions is to say it "depends."

It depends on how it is done and how it is interpreted. Sexual harassment is in the eye of the beholder. The definition also states that conduct "constitutes sexual harassment when submission to or rejection of this conduct explicitly or implicitly affects an individual's employment, unreasonably interferes with an individual's work performance or creates an intimidating, hostile or offensive work environment." What does this mean? One person can feel intimidated while another just shrugs it off. If a person willingly accepts a sexual proposition in order to gain some job advancement, is that person experiencing harassment? It would seem that the advance is more *welcome* than *unwelcome* in this situation.

What we see in these questions is the ambiguity of sexual harassment definitions and interpretations. This is precisely why so many companies end up with sexual harassment complaints. Typically, the offending party didn't think they were doing anything wrong. While the offender thought the overture was welcome, the recipient felt it was unwelcome. While the offender thought asking someone out on a date was not a sexual advance, the recipient thought it was. And even if the recipient of the conduct didn't feel that harassment had taken place, a third party might be affected or offended by the conduct. Note that the EEOC guidelines state: "The victim does not have to be the person harassed but could be anyone affected by the offensive conduct." In many cases, a simple remark, a funny comment, or a gesture may be enough to create a sexual harassment claim.

In the case of *Mackenzie v. Miller Brewing Company*, we see how easily a case of harassment can develop and what it means to all the parties involved.

Jerold Mackenzie, a male manager at Miller Brewing Company, told Patricia Best, a female coworker, about an episode he had seen on the TV sitcom *Seinfeld*. In the episode, Jerry Seinfeld forgot the name of his date. He remembered that her name rhymed with a female body part. Finally, he recalled that her name was Dolores. Best could not figure out what female body part rhymed with Dolores, so Mackenzie found an anatomically correct dictionary and pointed out the respective body part to her in the book. Best complained to management and Mackenzie was subsequently fired from his $95,000 a year job. Mackenzie then filed suit against the company claiming wrongful termination along with fraudulent misrepresentation against Best, alleging that she wasn't really offended by what he had said. A jury, which included ten women, found in his favor and awarded Mackenzie $27 million in damages from the company, his supervisor, and Best (for tortious interference with his employment relationship).

Later, on appeal, the case was reversed by the Wisconsin Court of Appeals.[2] The Court rejected Mackenzie's argument that Miller Brewing did not have the right to terminate him based on allegations of sexual harassment unless Miller could prove that those allegations were true. Mackenzie's position was hurt because the court noted that in 1989 his secretary had filed a sexual harassment case against him. In that case, Miller Brewing had settled the claim with Mackenzie's secretary, and Mackenzie's supervisor had warned him that any repetition of such conduct would lead to his termination.

The State Supreme Court upheld the appeals court ruling. However, prior to the Supreme Court hearing, Miller offered Mackenzie $3 million to settle. Allegedly, under advice of his counsel, Mackenzie declined the $3 million. Ironically, after the state Supreme Court ruling, Mackenzie declared bankruptcy and sued his former attorneys for malpractice.

Although Miller Brewing eventually won, its legal fees were no small amount. In harassment battles, particularly when appealed, companies can pay out millions in attorney's fees, even if they are not found to be liable.

Three key points can be derived from this case[3]:

1. Employees who make honest reports of sexual harassment are protected from liability.
2. Employers are entitled to take appropriate discipline against employees accused of harassment.
3. These cases consume years of time, energy, and resources for all concerned.

Types of Harassment

Sexual harassment can occur whenever an employee is treated unfairly because of their gender. Most sexual harassment cases are based on one of two types of sexual harassment:

Quid pro quo **harassment** — This occurs when an employee's salary, promotions, benefits, or performance evaluations are tied to some kind of sexual activity. If a supervisor offers to promote an employee or give a raise to an employee in exchange for sexual favors, then that would be an example of *quid pro quo* sexual harassment, where something is given in return for sexual favors. *Quid pro quo* harassment is much less prevalent than hostile working environment harassment.

Hostile working environment harassment — This type of harassment occurs when employees are uncomfortable in their workplace because of its sexually charged environment. Behavior such as making unwelcome sexual advances, treating women differently from men, making sexually derogatory comments or jokes, or displaying sexually-oriented pictures in the area (even in "private" cubicles or offices), contribute to a hostile environment.

Responsibility

Sexual harassment claims can be lodged over egregious violations or over what appears to many to be innocuous behavior or remarks. This ambiguity and lack of certainty is what makes any kind of behavior that can be remotely construed as sexual in nature, perilous. This is particularly true since the employer is often held accountable for the behavior of its employees. Court rulings have consistently upheld that even if the employer is not aware of the sexual harassment, the employer is still responsible. The reasoning behind this argument flows from the belief that businesses must provide workplace environments that are free of sexual harassment. Since harassment can occur through the actions of a supervisor, a coworker, a customer, or even a vendor, management must be constantly vigilant in order to provide a non-hostile working environment. Courts have ruled that companies must show that they exercised "reasonable care" to ensure that harassing behavior was prevented or corrected.

It is difficult to control the thoughts and actions of employees who may like to engage in sexual activities at work. An August 2002 "office sex" survey of over 10,000 people conducted by *Playboy* magazine found some startling statistics.[4] Of the survey respondents, 86% of males said they flirted at work, while 81% of the females said they flirted. 75% of the males said they joked about sex at work, while 67% of the females said they joked about sex. Additionally, 32% of the males said that they send risqué emails at work and 36% of the females said they sent risqué emails.

The survey also asked more specific questions about sex in the workplace. Of the respondents, 18% of male employees said they had sex with their boss, while 48% of the females said they had sex with their boss. 26% of the males said they had sex with a subordinate, and 22% of females claimed to have had sex with a subordinate.

When asked specifically about harassment, the respondents answered as follows:

- Only 26% of the men and 21% of the women thought that a boss asking out a subordinate was sexual harassment.

- Only 22% of the men and 17% of the women thought that telling a woman that she looks "hot" was actionable.

- Only 30% of the men and 24% of the women thought that telling dirty jokes in mixed company was out of line.

- Only 15% of the men and 18% of the women objected to a coworker touching their arm or back while talking.

Although this survey is not statistically accurate, it does demonstrate that sexual activity, whether flirting or actual sex, is occurring in the workplace, opening up the possibility of sexual harassment suits to employers. If the survey results reflect, even anecdotally, the amount of sexual activity that is taking place in the workplace today, then employers are going to have a very difficult time creating an environment that is free from sexual harassment.

Notes

1 Obtained from The Equal Employment Opportunity Commission.
2 *Mackenzie v. Miller Brewing Company*, No. 97-3542, Wisc. Ct. App. 2/22/00.
3 Ann Kiernan, "Seinfeld case reversed on appeal; management upheld on all counts," *Fair Measures* (February 1, 2000).
4 Playboy Magazine, January 2003, from a survey conducted on www.playboy.com. This survey of over 10,000 men and women cannot be considered as representative of the workplace in general since the respondents were "volunteers" who visited the Playboy website and participated in the online survey. No randomization or demographic factors were taken into account. It is interesting to compare the percentages from the male answers vs. the percentages from the female answers in the survey results. We should also consider the number of respondents (10,000) in the six-week period the survey was available on the site. The average age of male respondents was 29, with 26 for females. The ratio of men to women was 9 to 1 (which may reflect the readership of *Playboy* magazine and/or the reluctance of females to visit the *Playboy* website).

Michael P. Harden

Chapter Twenty-One: Software

Since it first came into common usage, software has consistently created many ethical issues for businesses. This stems originally from the problem that software was a brand new creation that had never before existed. No one really understood how it fit into current ethical and legal practices. It took many years for software to reach its current status as a form of legally protected property.

Without trying to define the distinctions between source code and object code here, attention should be focused on the property rights issues of software. Software, like any other product of someone's labor, belongs to the person who created it. Any software developer who has spent long days and nights isolated in a cubicle writing code understands this principle. If the developer works for a company, then the company will likely own the software (which the developer exchanged for wages). In hindsight, it seems strange that the idea of owning software was not always so well understood.

In the early days of computing, business managers, attorneys, and intellectual property experts had a difficult time determining exactly what software really was. It wasn't a printed document, a work of literature, or a recording, so it didn't seem to fit under copyright laws. In fact, since its most basic component was nothing more than a series of binary bits (1's and 0's), the pressing question was what exactly was there to copyright?

The idea of patent protection didn't seem to make much sense either. If software is nothing more than a set of processes (formulas and algorithms), can it really be patented? The reason for a patent is to protect an invention so that the inventors can hold a monopoly of sorts, at least for some period of time, on their inventions. This allows the inventors to reap the rewards of their efforts in creating their new invention. But patents are typically not granted for things that already exist in nature (like natural laws, principles of physics, etc.), for "mental" processes, or for mathematical calculations and formulas (such as algorithms). So software, which is based on all of these — mathematical calculations (algorithms), natural or physical laws (electronic representations through 1's and 0's), and mental processes (some set of instructions to perform a function) — didn't seem to be an appropriate candidate for a patent. No one wanted to consider patenting mathematical calculations, natural laws, or mental processes. To do so would inhibit future inventions that might rely on the same basic principles. If someone were to patent a mental process, such as a set of commands or instructions on how to do a certain thing, no one else would ever be able to utilize the same or similar processes without infringing on a patent. What if someone could patent the formula for calculating the average of the sum of multiple numbers or the formula for determining the circumference of a circle? This is the dilemma that software created.

Eventually, various interpretations of the nature of software led to a firm determination of its status. By applying analogies that made sense, we were finally able to ascertain that software is indeed like a literary work; that it is a form or property; that it is the result of someone's labor, albeit mental labor rather than physical labor; and that it is more than a set of mental processes, formulas, and algorithms.

Today, software is typically protected under copyright laws, through patents, and as trade secrets. Yet, because of the esoteric nature of software — its intangibility — along with its easy reproduction and portability, many people have a difficult time accepting the idea of it being protected property. This creates an ethical minefield for many organizations.

Ethical and legal issues surrounding software almost exclusively fall into the area of theft, which is often referred to as "pirating." Software is easily pirated. Pirating can occur in two different ways:

1. Employees can pass around a single copy of some application, for example, MS Word, and allow others in the office to install and use it without obtaining a proper license.

2. Vendors can pirate software code from other companies in order to utilize it to enhance or speed-up their own development efforts on similar products.

In both cases, the offending parties disregard the notion that the software is property and rightly belongs to someone else just like a car, house, or personal belongings. When we pirate software, we deprive the creators of the software from obtaining their equitable remuneration for their labor, effort, and investment. We violate the principle of property rights.

From a utilitarian perspective, one could easily make the argument that software should not be owned by anyone so that it could be available to all and thereby benefit everyone. This would be for the greater good (all of us) at the expense of just a few (the software creators). What this argument ignores is the logical idea that if we make all software freely available to everyone and deprive software developers of their ability to enjoy the rewards of their labor, they will cease to produce software. If that were to happen and no one but a few altruistic people developed software applications, all of us would suffer greatly as computer technology grinds to a halt. Few, if any people would benefit from this system, and the consequences of not having software would negatively impact us all. Therefore, the utilitarian argument really favors the concept of software as protected property.

Another ethical issue that deals with software comes from the practice of selling software that has not been thoroughly tested. Whether done intentionally or by accident, organizations must be careful to observe ethical standards in delivering software that may not be "ready to go."

Sometimes, competitive pressure forces a company to rush its software to market without thoroughly testing it. The philosophy is to get the product out the door and then provide the appropriate fixes later. Although this may give the company an advantage for some period of time, there are ethical issues that come into play. Most of us can relate to this situation. How often have we purchased some application software or computer operating system only to have to repeatedly download upgrades and service packs to plug holes in the product? This is both annoying and time-consuming. If the flaw is a security hole, we may be open to unauthorized intrusions and theft of our data until it is fixed.

If we are the provider of the software, we have to explore this situation from the perspective of the customer. From a utilitarian argument, are we creating more good than harm by selling software that is seriously flawed in order to get a jump on our competition? From a Kantian perspective, are we showing respect for our customers? If everyone were to sell flawed software, what would the world be like? And from a rights and duties perspective, we know that our customers have a right to the best quality software we can provide, fully tested and ready to go; and we have a duty to provide it. If we can't do it, we should at least make sure that customers are aware of the problem before they buy the product.

Another instance where a company may sell software prematurely is when a customer has placed an order that requires delivery by a certain date. Failure to make the delivery date could cost the company the contract. So, when the company finds that it cannot make the delivery date with a fully tested product, it delivers an inferior, flawed product with the expectation of fixing it later. The company is trying to buy itself time at the expense of its customer. After the installation, the customer begins to experience severe operating problems, which the company promises to address. The company made the sale, kept the contract, and probably got some kind of payment, but its customer experienced problems caused by the flawed product. The ethical issues in this situation scream at us. Once again we must look to our ethical theories and arguments. If we were in a similar situation, we would have to ask ourselves several questions:

- Who is being harmed and who benefits (utilitarian)?
- Are we respecting the rights of our customer (Kantian)?
- What if everybody did the same thing (Kantian)?
- Are we fulfilling our duties (duty theory)?
- Were our actions fair to our customer (justice and fairness)?

The answers to these questions will help us determine the morality of our actions.

Chapter Twenty-Two: Conflicts of Interest

Managers and employees have an obligation to avoid conflicts of interest. Typically a person has a conflict of interest when that person must exercise some official duty, i.e., a duty related to his position or profession, but also has some other interest or obligation that will either interfere with his ability to exercise proper judgment or influence the performance of his duties. Conflicts usually arise from private or personal interests which are typically financial, although personal interests can be any situation where an advantage is gained, for instance, social status, prestige, favors for family members, or non-monetary benefits.

In some situations where a conflict exists, simply disclosing the conflict is sufficient to remove any ethical conflicts. As an example, if a stock analyst makes a "buy" recommendation on a company's stock but discloses that he owns shares in that company, this will typically allow him to continue to own the stock while making the recommendation to others to buy the stock. A conflict obviously exists, but the conflict has been made public so that everyone is aware of it. Any potential investors who may act on the analyst's recommendations are informed of his possible biased judgment and can take that into consideration in evaluating his recommendations.

In many situations, we *allow* people to have a conflict of interest as long as they make us aware of it. This is a matter of necessity since placing the burden of *avoiding* conflicts on certain professions or positions may be too burdensome for the individuals involved. Therefore, *disclosing* the conflict is sufficient. For example, if a stock analyst has done extensive research on a company and believes that it is a good investment, preventing him from owning shares in the company because he has made a "buy" recommendation on it may effectively prevent him from having the same opportunity as the rest of us to make profitable investments.

Conflicts can occur in any of these three areas of official duty:

Employees — Managers and employees of a company who are obligated to serve the interests of their employer.

Public officials — People that hold elected or appointed positions in the government, or those who work for government agencies, and are obligated to serve the public interests.

Professionals — Attorneys, accountants, doctors, engineers, and other professionals who typically have a responsibility and an obligation to provide an objective professional judgment.

In some cases, these official duties may overlap. For example, an accountant employed by a firm has a professional responsibility as an accountant and a responsibility to the company as one of its employees. A doctor who works for the Department of Health and Human Services has a duty as a professional (doctor) and as a public official.

We typically view conflicts as having to do with personal interests, but there are cases where private or personal interests are not involved in the conflict. For instance, lawyers cannot represent a client if that representation may be limited by the lawyer's responsibility to another client. Obviously, a conflict would exist if an attorney could represent both the plaintiff and the defendant in a legal action, but this conflict is neither personal nor private insofar as the personal interests of the attorney are concerned.

There are distinctions between *actual* conflicts of interest, *apparent* conflicts of interest, and *potential* conflicts of interest. These distinctions are important because they govern the way we look at conflicts and how individuals should treat them.

Actual conflicts of interest — For a conflict to be real, there must exist a private interest that is known by the employee or official and can interfere or influence the exercise of that person's official duties.

Apparent conflicts of interest — A conflict is apparent when a reasonable person can have an apprehension that a conflict exists.

Potential conflict of interest — A potential conflict exists when a reasonable person can foresee that a possible private or personal interest exists that is sufficient to influence his judgment. Even if he believes it will *not* influence his judgment, as long as it is *sufficient* to influence his judgment, a potential conflict exists.

Classifications

Conflicts can take place in several different areas. These areas can be classified into eight categories according to Ken Kernaghan and John Langford (*The Responsible Public Servant*).[1] Listed here are the eight categories of conflicts of interest:

1. **Self-dealing** — This refers to a situation where someone takes an action in their official capacity that involves conferring a private or personal benefit on themselves. For example, a purchasing manager awards a contract to a vendor in return for the vendor hiring the contract manager's son.

2. **Accepting benefits** — This refers to instances where someone accepts a gift or an outright bribe. For example, a vendor seeking to win a contract with your company sends you a box of expensive cigars or treats you to a weekend at one of their resorts.

3. **Influence peddling** — This refers to someone soliciting some form of benefit (monetary or otherwise) in exchange for using their influence on behalf of another party.

4. **Using your employer's property for personal gains** — This could be stealing property from your employer that

you can use for yourself. It may take the form of using telephones, copiers, and faxes for personal use, using a company car for personal travel, or stealing office supplies that can be used at home.

5. **Using confidential information** — This category deals with using information that is not known to the public to achieve a private gain. For example, you find out that your company is proposing to acquire another company. You have your relatives buy stock in the other company in anticipation of its stock price rising with the announcement of the acquisition. Insider trading falls into this category.

6. **Outside employment** — Often called moonlighting, this refers to outside employment that conflicts with (or appears to conflict with) your current employment or official duties. For example, a systems engineer sets up her own consulting business and actively seeks work from her employer's clients. Another example is an accountant with a large accounting firm who sets up his own practice in direct competition with his employer.

7. **Post employment** — Usually, this occurs when someone leaves their job or public office and then goes into the same line of business or tries to take improper advantage of their previous position. We see this often when a government employee leaves her government position to join the private sector and uses her prior position, knowledge, and contacts to gain an advantage for her new employer.

8. **Personal conduct** — A conflict of interest can occur based on personal conduct when that conduct makes the person vulnerable to pressure to use her official position improperly, or when the conduct of the individual brings discredit to her employer and adversely affects the company. There are many examples of personal conduct that can reflect

back on the company (drug addiction, lewd conduct, criminal conduct, even drunken or obnoxious behavior). On a larger scale, we can look at examples such as Martha Stewart. Her personal conduct in the ImClone scandal, which was not related to her company, created a backlash that cost her company and its shareholders billions in lost value. So a conflict of her personal interests and her company's interests existed in that sense.

How do we know when a conflict exists? Sometimes the answer is very obvious and at other times it may be very subtle. Much of our judgment about conflicts comes from what seems to be a conflict to a reasonable person. Basically, it comes down to whether there is a violation of trust. We must ask ourselves whether our actions violate the trust of the people we work for, or who work for us. Do our actions violate the trust of our shareholders or other stakeholders in the company? Avoiding conflicts is the smartest thing we can do, so following some simple guidelines will be helpful. Here are six rules we can use to help avoid conflicts of interest:

1. Employees should not seek personal gain by giving preferential treatment to anyone.

2. Employees should not solicit anything of value from people they are dealing with in their official capacity.

3. Employees should not seek personal gain by using confidential information that they acquired in their official capacity.

4. Employees should not engage in any business or have a personal interest that is incompatible with their official capacity.

5. Employees should refrain from using employer-owned property for activities that are not directly related to their official duties.

6. Employees should not engage in any personal conduct that would discredit their employer or adversely affect their employer.

It is interesting to note that Enron had a set of rules covering conflicts of interest. The board of directors waived the rules twice to allow Andrew Fastow, the CFO, to set up the private partnerships that would end up doing business with Enron and eventually bringing the company down.

Loyalty

A natural follow-on to personal conflicts of interest (those that have some personal gain) are those conflicts that are based on a person's professional or civic responsibilities. These conflicts draw themselves from the various competing loyalties that people often face in their employment.

Everyone experiences some feelings of loyalty. It may be stronger in some people than others, but any reasonable person would say that a moral person practices the virtue of loyalty along with other desirable virtues. In fact, loyalty is a strong and valued virtue in our society. Loyalty can be felt toward your employer, your direct supervisor, your coworkers, or your profession. All of these have to do with your workplace and employment. However, there are several other loyalties that people experience. Listed here are the main loyalties that can be associated with a person's position in an organization:

Loyalty to their employer — Employees often feel a sense of loyalty to the company or organization they work for. This loyalty can also manifest itself in loyalty to their direct supervisor, their coworkers, or their division.

Loyalty to their profession — Many people who are in professions such as accounting, medicine, and law, find that they have a loyalty to their profession as well as their jobs. They feel strong ties to their professional positions; for example, doctors have a strong feeling of loyalty to their profession of medicine and all of its ethical standards and practices as well as loyalty to their position in the hospital (chief surgeon, pathologist, resident, etc.). Lawyers, accountants, and engineers often feel a strong loyalty to their professions as well. This is outside of their actual position within their organization (chief accountant, legal counsel, senior engineer).

Loyalty to their customers — Employees who work with customers often have feelings of loyalty to their clients. They develop relationships with customers, and develop strong concerns for treating their customers fairly and with respect for their needs. These relationships can become very close when the employee works exclusively for a customer, for example, a consultant assigned to a client's site for six months may begin to feel a strong sense of loyalty to that client.

Loyalty to their community — Employees also feel a sense of loyalty to their community. This can include the local community, or it can also be a loyalty to the public in general. This is particularly true with people who work for the public interests, such as people in the professions of healthcare, public policy, law enforcement, or community service.

Problems develop when these loyalties compete with each other. This happens when two or more entities have competing needs and the employee finds herself in a situation where her loyalties to competing entities create a conflict of interest. There are many instances where this occurs. Listed here are a few examples to demonstrate how easily a conflict can develop:

Example One: Loyalty to Employer vs. Loyalty to Customer

An engineer must deliver a new production management software product to a customer with which he has a close relationship. The company hasn't fully tested the product and is aware that there may be some bugs that could cause the client problems. But it has a deadline to meet if it wants to be paid, so it decides to ship the product and install it on schedule, and fix the problems later. The engineer, who is responsible for the client implementation, knows there is a problem with the software, knows there is a deadline to meet, and knows that the client is unaware of the potential problems. The engineer feels a conflict between his loyalty to his employer (to get the product installed before the deadline in order to get paid) and his loyalty to his customer (not to create problems with their production management system which could hurt their operations). The engineer is faced with an obvious moral dilemma.

Example Two: Loyalty to Profession vs. Loyalty to Employer

A doctor who works for a private for-profit hospital is told to use an inexpensive, and probably inferior, prosthesis on his patients. Clearly, the hospital will save money, but the patient will likely experience problems with the prosthetic device that will prolong her recovery and cause her unnecessary pain and discomfort. The doctor feels a conflict between his position as a resident physician at the hospital and his Hippocratic oath to "do no harm" which obligates him to provide his patients with the best possible care. He is faced with an ethical dilemma between his two competing loyalties.

Example Three: Loyalty to Employer vs. Loyalty to Community

A manager is told that he must install a new line of equipment that will increase the productivity of the company's manufacturing by 25% through process improvements, thereby increasing profits substantially. However, the new equipment is not as environmentally friendly as he would like. Although it meets minimum pollution standards, the equipment is likely to create more pollution than the previous process created. More pollutants will be dumped into the local water supply, which may cause long-term health problems for the community. He is uneasy with managing the installation of the new manufacturing process because he is experiencing a conflict between his loyalty to his company and his loyalty to his community.

Example Four: Loyalty to Profession vs. Loyalty to Employer vs. Loyalty to Customer vs. Loyalty to the Community

An accountant in an auditing firm is reviewing the books of one of the firm's best clients. During the audit, she notices that many transactions that would normally be classified as debt are being placed in "subsidiaries" which are shell companies, taking the debt off of the corporate balance sheets. The result is a balance sheet for the corporation that reflects much less debt than it should show. She also notices that two of the corporation's divisions are reporting their sales as revenue even though the products have not yet been shipped to the customer. She knows that both of these practices are unethical and are helping to artificially inflate the value of the company and drive up its stock price. She feels mixed loyalties to her client (who would experience a tremendous financial setback if these practices were reported), her employer (who considers this customer its best client and cannot afford to upset it), her profession (a professional accountant and auditor who is supposed to be impartial and independent), and the community (all of the stockholders who are being lied to and who would experience a loss if the company's deceptive accounting practices were made public).

These are just four examples of the various types of conflicts of interest that people may experience due to the competing interests of their four possible loyalties — employer, customer, profession, and community. Each individual must decide how to resolve the moral dilemmas that these conflicting loyalties create. Since loyalty can have strong emotional ties, it is often difficult to determine which loyalty "wins" in a particular moral dilemma. People often make emotional decisions that are unethical in order to satisfy their ties to various loyalties.

There is another form of loyalty that causes conflicts of interest. It is the loyalty that professionals feel for other members of their profession. We see this often when we witness doctors who are unwilling to criticize other doctors, even when they know that their colleagues may have made crucial errors or acted unethically. Physicians seem to go to great lengths to protect other physicians, but they are not alone in this practice. Lawyers are typically unwilling to criticize other attorneys. Architects and engineers are also reluctant to say anything publicly that might be critical about another member of their profession. It seems that professionals do not like to publicly criticize other members of their profession since it reflects on the profession in general. Professionals will often go to great lengths to protect the image and reputation of their profession in the misguided notion that anything that hurts the image of their profession ultimately reflects on them as well. By protecting other members of their profession, they believe they are protecting the profession itself and that results in the protection of their own self-interests. This conflict in loyalty is why so many people are skeptical of professional organizations that claim to be able to "police" themselves. We have seen instances where "bad" doctors have been protected from prosecution or civil liability by other doctors, even when these "bad" physicians were hurting their patients. We have seen Catholic priests who were obvious pedophiles being hidden and protected by their bishops in order to protect the image of the church. If you are not yet convinced of this "circle the wagons" mentality, try filing a complaint against a doctor with the AMA, or an attorney with the ABA, and see how many other members of their professions support you and how many fight you.

This kind of conflict of interest is a harsh assault on our moral principles. The professionals that go to such great lengths to protect their colleagues are actually hurting their professions in the long run. When "bad" professionals are protected by their colleagues and their actions are allowed to continue, the public is eventually harmed and its level of trust for the profession is ultimately diminished. Covering up or protecting unethical behavior is just as unethical as the behavior itself. What professionals fail to understand is that their loyalty to their profession really means ensuring that its professional standards are upheld by *all* of the profession's members. This requires not protecting bad apples in a misguided attempt to protect the profession, but rather, vigorously imposing sanctions on those that do not uphold its professional standards. By doing this, the profession enforces its standards, ensures that its members behave ethically, promotes the trust of the public, and enhances its reputation and image.

Notes

[1] Ken Kernaghan and John Langford. *The Responsible Public Servant* IRPP/IPAC: 1990 (fourth printing 1995) pp. 142-153.

Chapter Twenty-Three: Whistle-Blowing

As children we are taught not to be "tattletales." We are told not to "air our dirty laundry" in front of others and to "keep our mouths shut." As we grow up, we learn to use words such as "snitch," "fink," "rat," "squealer," "stool pigeon," "weasel," "blabbermouth," and "informer" to describe anyone who informs or "tells" on another person. To describe what these people do, we say that they "named names," "put the finger on him," "dropped a dime on her," "sold him down the river," "shot his mouth off," "let the cat out of the bag," or "blew the whistle on him." None of these terms are positive and all have a decidedly derogatory and demeaning characterization that reflects how our society feels about people who "tell" on others.

Yet we encourage "whistle-blowing," a behavior that is in complete contrast to everything we have ever learned about keeping silent and not informing on others. The whistle-blower must fight conflicting emotions in order to come forward, and the people he must deal with have to overcome their disdain for "squealers" to treat the whistle-blower fairly and without retribution. As a society, we have spent thousands of years upholding a notion of honor — an ideal that teaches us that it is dishonorable and disloyal to be a "snitch." In fact, our feelings about this are so strong that we willingly ostracize and retaliate against people who take it upon themselves to report the unethical conduct of others even though it may be in our best interests to have this unethical behavior reported and punished. This is the sad dilemma of whistle-blowers. They are performing a moral good, yet due of our conflicting ideals of loyalty and fidelity, they are viewed almost universally as despicable and unworthy of our trust. Even if they keep their jobs, coworkers and managers treat them as *persona non grata*.

To better understand whistle-blowing, we must first look at what whistle-blowing really is. The term "whistle-blowing" can be traced back to 1934 and the phrase "blow the whistle." It is a metaphor for a sports official calling a foul, in essence, blowing the whistle to signify that a foul has been committed. The actual term "whistleblower" only dates back to 1970 and was used initially to refer to a civil servant (government employee) who publicly denounced illegal or wasteful practices.[1] The term has since come to represent any member or former member of an organization, public or private, who publicly reveals mismanagement, corruption, or waste.

However, this definition is not sufficient to fully define whistle-blowing in its truest sense. John Boatright, Professor of Business Ethics at Loyola University Chicago, lists six points[2] that he believes must be present for whistle-blowing to occur:

1. Only a member of an organization can blow the whistle on it. It is not whistle-blowing if someone from outside the organization observes improper behavior and reports it to the authorities. Since an employee or member of an organization is expected to maintain an obligation of confidentiality, going public with information that may hurt the organization is a breach of this obligation and trust. This obligation does not apply to an outsider.

2. There must be information to report. Simply disagreeing with management is not the same as whistle-blowing. A dissenter who is taking a position against the organization is not "blowing the whistle" because there is no release of information that was heretofore nonpublic.

3. The information must be evidence of some form of significant misconduct on the part of the organization or its members. There needs to be some kind of serious wrong that could be averted or rectified by the release of the information.

4. The information must be released outside of the normal channels of communications. Organizations typically have channels to report abuses, waste, or misconduct. Following the proper chain of command is not whistle-blowing. Whistle-blowing is when someone goes around the chain of command or bypasses other mechanisms that are in place to

report wrongdoings. Whistle-blowing can be either internal or external. A whistle-blower can either go "public" with the information by reporting it to regulatory officials or to the press, or a whistle-blower can keep the information internal, but report it outside of the normal chain, for example, going directly to the board of directors to report managers or supervisors who are creating bogus revenue figures. The information must be revealed in such a way that there is an expectation that some kind of change will occur. The whistle-blower must provide the information to some individual or organization that has the ability to utilize the information to change things. Simply telling a coworker who has no authority to act on the information, is not whistle-blowing.

5. The release of the information must be voluntary. Revealing incriminating information because they have been subpoenaed, threatened with prosecution, or offered a plea bargain, is not whistle-blowing. Although many whistle-blowers are obligated under certain laws to reveal the information, it is their *voluntary* revelation of the information, without being legally forced to do so, that makes them whistle-blowers.

6. Whistle-blowing must take place as a moral protest. To be a whistle-blower, the motive must be to right a wrong, not to seek revenge, personal advancement, or monetary rewards. Trying to make a name for oneself, getting a rival fired, or claiming a reward, are not factors that constitute true whistle-blowing.

Using these six points, Boatright constructs a more concise definition that provides a realistic and comprehensive description in one sentence of what we should consider to be the characteristics of whistle-blowing:

"Whistle-blowing is the voluntary release of nonpublic information, as a moral protest, by a member or former member of an organization outside of the normal channels of communication to an appropriate audience about illegal and/or immoral conduct in the organization or conduct in the organization that is opposed in some significant way to the public interest."[3]

People who become whistle-blowers must often overcome their fear of retaliation by management, of being ostracized by their co-workers, of losing of their job, and of the constant humiliation of being labeled a "snitch" or "informer." They must also deal with their own emotional conflict of loyalty to their company and their moral obligation to right a wrong. Deciding to become a whistle-blower, particularly when there is no expectation of reward, and in light of all of the negative implications, is not something most people are willing to do. This is why true whistle-blowers demonstrate real moral courage. Yet, for a society that places such great value on courage, we seem all too willing to condemn whistle-blowers. The irony is obvious. We value courage, morality, and the triumph of good over evil, yet we treat the people who demonstrate those very characteristics as pariahs rather than heroes.

In a recent Time/CNN poll, 73% of the respondents said that they would become whistle-blowers if they saw serious wrongdoing at work. 59% said they thought whistle-blowers were heroes. But 18% actually said they thought whistle-blowers were traitors, and 14% said they were not sure. When asked if they thought whistle-blowers faced negative consequences at work, such as being treated poorly or being fired, only 8% said they thought it didn't happen very often. 87% thought it happened most of the time or some of the time.[4] What is interesting to note is that although 73% of the respondents said they would become whistle-blowers, the real life statistics are very different. The Government Accountability Project, a non-profit group dedicated to protecting whistle-blowers since 1977, said that only 30% of the people who see something wrong actually do anything about it. The other 70% "…don't want to be made into martyrs or commit career suicide," said Louis Clark, the organization's executive director.[5]

In a different survey conducted by the non-profit group, the National Whistleblower Center in Washington, DC, about half of the whistle-blowers who responded said they were fired after reporting unlawful conduct. Many said they faced harassment in the workplace or unfair discipline.[6]

In a study conducted by the Occupational Safety and Health Administration (OSHA), the organization found that 67% of the workers who blew the whistle on unsafe working conditions were fired.

Legal Aspects of Whistle-Blowing

The federal law that established the concept of the whistle-blower was the False Claims Act of 1863. It was originally created to combat rampant fraud committed by suppliers to the federal government and the Union Army during the Civil War. Contractors were supplying the army with rancid food, rifles that wouldn't fire, gunpowder that wouldn't explode, and shoes that fell apart after only a few days of wear. President Abraham Lincoln was a strong proponent of the law, and it soon came to be known as the "Lincoln Law." Congress passed the statute on March 2, 1863. The Act contained *qui tam* provisions that allowed private citizens to file suit, on behalf of the government, against companies or individuals that were defrauding the government. *Qui tam* is a shortened version of the Latin phrase *qui tam pro domino rege quam pro se ipso in hac parte sequitur*, which means "he who brings an action for the king as well as for himself."

The False Claims Act of 1863 allowed those individuals who brought suit to receive fifty percent of the amount the government recovered as a result of their cases. Congress, which seems to always have a propensity to fix things that aren't broken, decided in 1943 to alter the statute's *qui tam* provisions, substantially cutting the rewards. With the cut in rewards, there was less of an incentive for people to file claims. Also, a new provision established that no claim could be filed if the government already had some knowledge of the possible fraud, even if it wasn't being investigated. So, if a person provided information to the government, they could no longer sue under the *qui tam* provisions. These two changes effectively made the law useless.

Then in the mid-1980s, widespread fraud was occurring in the Defense Department as contractors were over-billing and defrauding the government. During that period, nine of the top ten defense contractors were under investigation for fraud. Congress decided that it had to do something, so it dusted off the False Claims Act and revised it to promote more whistle-blowing. The newly amended False Claims Act provided that whistleblowers are entitled to 15 to 30 percent of the government's recovery for any suit they successfully brought. Additionally, companies that defraud the government are liable for treble damages. Moreover, whistle-blowers who also provided information to the government could once again sue under the *qui tam* provisions. On October 27, 1986, President Reagan signed the bill into law.

There were also other fronts on which whistle-blowing was being strengthened. In 1978, federal legislation was enacted that barred reprisals against anyone who exposed government corruption. Subsequently, the revelation of widespread waste and fraud in defense contracting and the associated harassment and dismissal of whistle-blowers led Congress to strengthen the protection of whistle-blowers in 1989. There are also many different state laws that protect whistle-blowers. But there were also a number of states that offered no protection. In fact, it was the memo from Enron's attorneys that provided some of the impetus for the whistle-blower protection in the federal *Corporate and Criminal Fraud Accountability Act of 2002*. Documents subpoenaed by Congress turned up an email from Enron's attorneys on how to handle Sherron Watkins after she reported the company's accounting irregularities to Ken Lay, Enron's CEO. It read: "Texas law does not currently protect corporate whistle-blowers. The Supreme Court has twice declined to create a cause of action for whistle-blowers who are discharged." Clearly, Lay was contemplating firing the person who had reported the "bad news" to him. In contrast, it is reasonable to assume that a concerned CEO with no culpability would have welcomed the information.

However, it was not until the passing of H.R. 3763, otherwise known as the Sarbanes-Oxley Act of 2002 (also known as the *Corporate and Criminal Fraud Accountability Act of 2002*, the *Public Company Accounting Reform and Investor Protection Act of 2002*, and the

White Collar Crime Penalty Enhancement Act of 2002)[7] that solid protection for whistle-blowers was finally established. Much of the stimulus for this comes in the wake of the egregious corporate scandals that took place in the last two years.

The Act has two sections that deal explicitly with whistle-blowers. Sections 806 and 1107 provide protection for whistle-blowers and remedies for retaliation against whistle-blowers. Here is the text of the relevant provisions:

SEC. 806. PROTECTION FOR EMPLOYEES OF PUBLICLY TRADED COMPANIES WHO PROVIDE EVIDENCE OF FRAUD.

(a) IN GENERAL- Chapter 73 of title 18, United States Code, is amended by inserting after section 1514 the following:

"§ Sec. 1514A. Civil action to protect against retaliation in fraud cases

"(a) WHISTLEBLOWER PROTECTION FOR EMPLOYEES OF PUBLICLY TRADED COMPANIES- No company with a class of securities registered under section 12 of the Securities Exchange Act of 1934 (15 U.S.C. 78l), or that is required to file reports under section 15(d) of the Securities Exchange Act of 1934 (15 U.S.C. 78o(d)), or any officer, employee, contractor, subcontractor, or agent of such company, may discharge, demote, suspend, threaten, harass, or in any other manner discriminate against an employee in the terms and conditions of employment because of any lawful act done by the employee—

"(1) to provide information, cause information to be provided, or otherwise assist in an investigation regarding any conduct which the employee reasonably believes constitutes a violation of section 1341, 1343, 1344, or 1348, any rule or regulation of the Securities and Exchange Commission, or any provision of Federal law relating to fraud against shareholders, when the information or assistance is provided to or the investigation is conducted by—

"(A) a Federal regulatory or law enforcement agency;

"(B) any Member of Congress or any committee of Congress; or

"(C) a person with supervisory authority over the employee (or such other person working for the employer who has the authority to investigate, discover, or terminate misconduct); or

"(2) to file, cause to be filed, testify, participate in, or otherwise assist in a proceeding filed or about to be filed (with any knowledge of the employer) relating to an alleged violation of section 1341, 1343, 1344, or 1348, any rule or regulation of the Securities and Exchange Commission, or any provision of Federal law relating to fraud against shareholders.

"(b) ENFORCEMENT ACTION-

"(1) IN GENERAL- A person who alleges discharge or other discrimination by any person in violation of subsection (a) may seek relief under subsection (c), by—

"(A) filing a complaint with the Secretary of Labor; or

"(B) if the Secretary has not issued a final decision within 180 days of the filing of the complaint and there is no showing that such delay is due to the bad faith of the claimant, bringing an action at law or equity for de novo review in the appropriate district court of the United States, which shall have jurisdiction over such an action without regard to the amount in controversy.

"(2) PROCEDURE-

"(A) IN GENERAL- An action under paragraph (1)(A) shall be governed under the rules and procedures set forth in section 42121(b) of title 49, United States Code.

"(B) EXCEPTION- Notification made under section 42121(b)(1) of title 49, United States Code, shall be made to the person named in the complaint and to the employer.

"(C) BURDENS OF PROOF- An action brought under paragraph (1)(B) shall be governed by the legal burdens of proof set forth in section 42121(b) of title 49, United States Code.

"(D) STATUTE OF LIMITATIONS- An action under paragraph (1) shall be commenced not later than 90 days after the date on which the violation occurs.

"(c) REMEDIES-

"(1) IN GENERAL- An employee prevailing in any action under subsection (b)(1) shall be entitled to all relief necessary to make the employee whole.

"(2) COMPENSATORY DAMAGES- Relief for any action under paragraph (1) shall include—

"(A) reinstatement with the same seniority status that the employee would have had, but for the discrimination;

"(B) the amount of back pay, with interest; and

"(C) compensation for any special damages sustained as a result of the discrimination, including litigation costs, expert witness fees, and reasonable attorney fees.

"(d) RIGHTS RETAINED BY EMPLOYEE- Nothing in this section shall be deemed to diminish the rights, privileges, or remedies of any employee under any Federal or State law, or under any collective bargaining agreement.".

(b) CLERICAL AMENDMENT- The table of sections at the beginning of chapter 73 of title 18, United States Code, is amended by inserting after the item relating to section 1514 the following new item:

"1514A. Civil action to protect against retaliation in fraud cases.".

SEC. 1107. RETALIATION AGAINST INFORMANTS.

(a) IN GENERAL- Section 1513 of title 18, United States Code, is amended by adding at the end the following:

"(e) Whoever knowingly, with the intent to retaliate, takes any action harmful to any person, including interference with the lawful employment or livelihood of any person, for providing to a law enforcement officer any truthful information relating to the commission or possible commission of any Federal offense, shall be fined under this title or imprisoned not more than 10 years, or both.".

It should be noted that this Act provides protection only for whistle-blowing that takes place in publicly traded companies. There are no provisions for private firms, not-for-profit organizations, or government agencies. However, for those organizations that are covered under the Securities Exchange Act of 1934, these provisions offer excellent protection for whistle-blowers, and managers will have to be careful not to violate any of the protections since the penalties are rather steep to both the corporation and the individual manager. This law establishes the first-ever criminal penalties for retaliation against whistle-blowers.

There are also other protections afforded whistle-blowers under their First Amendment right to free speech. Although few people think of whistle-blowing in these terms, there have been many court cases that have upheld this right, particularly with government employees. The First Amendment does not explicitly protect whistle-blowing, but it does however, grant citizens the right to exercise their free speech without fear of retaliation. In 1968, the Supreme Court ruled in *Pickering v. Board of Education*, that a teacher who wrote a letter critical of the school board (and was subsequently fired) had the right to engage in free speech under the First Amendment, even though he was a government employee. The Supreme Court ruled that "a teacher's exercise of his right to speak on issues of public importance may not furnish the basis for his dismissal from public employment."[8] Subsequent rulings followed that established the same rights for government contractors. Then in 1983, the Supreme Court further defined its *Pickering* decision in *Connick v. Myers*. Part of the opinion read: "For at least 15 years, it has been settled that a State cannot condition public employment on a basis that infringes the employee's constitutionally protected interest in freedom of expression. Our task, as we defined it in *Pickering*, is to seek a balance between the interests of the [employee], as a citizen, in commenting upon matters of public concern and the interest of the State, as an employer, in promoting the efficiency of the public services it performs through its employees." The Court upheld the dismissal of the employee because the speech that prompted the termination did not involve matters of public concern.[9] "We hold only that when a public employee speaks not as a citizen upon matters of public concern, but instead as an employee upon matters only of personal interest, absent the most unusual circumstances, a federal court is not the appropriate forum in which to review the wisdom of a personnel decision taken by a public agency allegedly in reaction to the employee's behavior. Our responsibility is to ensure that citizens are not deprived of fundamental rights by virtue of working for the government; this does not require a grant of immunity for employee grievances not afforded by the First Amendment to those who do not work for the State."[10]

Basically, the Court ruled that a First Amendment free speech violation cannot occur if the speech that caused the dismissal does not involve issues of public concern and interferes with the efficient operations of the government office. This is the "balance" that the Court was referring to.

Emotional Aspects of Whistle-Blowing

If whistle-blowing is really a metaphor for a legitimately appointed referee or a sports official who blows his whistle to signal that a foul has been committed, then why do we have such disdain for the whistle-blower? Perhaps because a whistle-blower isn't really like the official, who by his position, is *supposed* to identify and call fouls. A whistle-blower is like having one of our teammates calling the foul on our own team. No sports team would ever stand for having its own teammates calling fouls on themselves. Could you imagine a quarterback stopping the play of the game to declare that he had an ineligible receiver downfield and then request a penalty for it? He would be yanked from the game immediately and replaced with the backup quarterback. Fans would wonder out loud whether he was crazy. People would claim he was trying to throw the game. This is the situation that confronts the whistle-blower. We simply haven't been able to see the whistle-blower outside of his role as a member of our team. When he calls a foul on his teammates, he becomes a traitor.

This is the psychological or emotional aspect of whistle-blowing. Both the whistle-blower, and those around him, view him as a traitor. This goes back to the notion of loyalty to the company, in essence, loyalty to the team. Revealing problems to outsiders or going outside of the chain of command is a betrayal of trust. The mentality that governs this reaction is similar to that found in close-knit organizations such as police departments. In a police department, officers who report unethical or criminal behavior are often ostracized by their fellow officers and labeled as a "snitch" or "rat." Their peers treat them far worse than they treat the officers who are actually guilty of the misconduct. This irony should not go unnoticed. In an organization dedicated to upholding the law, one would think that there would be little tolerance of misconduct and admiration for those who report it. However, the contrary is true. Misconduct is tolerated, and anyone who exposes it has betrayed a trust. Yet, isn't it really the corrupt cop who betrays the trust of his fellow officers? This is logical to any reasonable person, yet the stigma of snitching on another cop is so deeply-rooted that this logic doesn't matter. The result is that it is worse to report a dishonest cop than to actually be a dishonest cop.

The same phenomenon happens in the business world. Sometimes it is the corporate culture that creates this environment. Other times it is peer pressure or the social environment of the workplace. But in any case, the whistle-blower, who is really performing a good deed by exposing corruption or waste, becomes a pariah, while the workers who are engaging in the misconduct are tolerated and even protected. Looking back in hindsight, there are probably many people at Enron who wish there had been more people with the moral courage to come forward and expose the corruption before in took its toll. Yet, while the company was flying high, people who outwardly expressed doubts or thought something was "fishy" were chastised by their peers and pressured to "get with the program." This is the paradox faced by the whistle-blower. We all want to be protected from debacles like Enron, but we also don't want anyone to rock the boat. We admire virtues such as honor and integrity, but we also value loyalty and being a team player. We want to live in a world free of fraud and corruption, yet we don't want to hear about it if its revelation jeopardizes our jobs, income, or security.

What corporations fail to understand is that the whistle-blower is the true protector of the corporation. People who can muster sufficient moral courage to risk losing their jobs and spawning the disdain and contempt of their coworkers in order to expose corruption, fraud, waste, mismanagement, or unsafe working conditions, are remarkable corporate assets. Many corporations spend hundreds of thousands of dollars each year to pay ethics officers, to fund waste prevention programs, to manage employee hotlines, and to implement employee ethics training classes, yet a voluntary whistle-blower doesn't cost them a dime. This has got to be the deal of the century. Then why does management treat whistle-blowers so badly?

On a psychological level, people dislike anybody who "goes around" them. Few people enjoy the prospect of having someone "snitch" on them. And even fewer relish the prospect of being told that there is something wrong within their area of responsibility. These factors create barriers to the acceptance of whistle-blowers by managers. Often, competing values are at play. Managers value loyalty and teamwork, but they also realize that corruption and waste are harmful to their company. This is the dichotomy faced by employers.

The Arguments for Whistle-Blowing

There are several arguments in favor of whistle-blowing. The first is that loyal employees have a moral obligation or *duty* to bring corrupt or wasteful practices to the attention of management. By doing so, the whistle-blower is performing a service to her employer. Whenever any employee, supplier, contractor, manager, executive, or board member acts in a way that does not serve the best interests of the company, that person's actions should be reported to whoever has the authority to rectify the situation. Employees who possess this information are morally obligated to report it. True loyalty to an employer means notifying that employer of any situation, conduct, or behavior that has the potential to harm the employer.

The second argument is from the employer's perspective. Employers have a *right* to expect their employees to act in the company's best interests. If an employee has information about detrimental situations such as fraud, abuse, waste, mismanagement, or hazardous conditions, management should be encouraging them to come forward. If we look at the tremendous amount of harm that was caused by the scandals at WorldCom, Enron, and so many others, we can see that these companies would have been better served if everyone with knowledge of the misconduct had come forward and alerted the company to the pending calamities. In the Challenger Space Shuttle disaster, engineers at Morton Thiokol warned against launching in the freezing temperatures. Two engineers were so concerned that they tried to delay the launch by making several phone calls outside of their chain of command the night before the launch. They were overruled by Morton Thiokol management that wanted the launch to go ahead as planned. After all, NASA was their biggest customer. As a result, seven astronauts lost their lives and billions of dollars were lost. Had Morton Thiokol executives listened to their engineers, this terrible catastrophe would have been averted. Instead, Thiokol ignored their concerns and later demoted the engineers.

The third argument is that employees have an obligation to their coworkers. At just three companies, Enron, WorldCom, and Arthur Andersen, 28,500 workers lost their jobs and nearly $2 billion in their retirement savings. Would it not have been to their advantage to have their coworkers who were aware of the misconduct, cooked books, and corruption to come forward and expose it before it took such a devastating toll? Certainly, if we were to ask these unfortunate former employees today if they would have appreciated someone blowing the whistle, they would all respond affirmatively. Even though, at the time they were still employed and "riding high," they may have treated the whistle-blower badly, their hindsight now shows them the true value of the whistle-blower. If they were now able to relive the years preceding the companies' debacles, these employees would probably be very supportive of anyone who stepped up and exposed the corruption. Of course, that is the problem with hindsight. But the concept involved remains unchanged. Employees have a *duty* to their coworkers to expose potential threats to their wellbeing, and their coworkers have a *right* to expect it. But those coworkers have a reciprocal *duty* or moral obligation to support the whistle-blower as well.

Reviewing these three arguments, we see that the employer has a right to expect its employees to come forward when they know of misconduct. The employee has an obligation to report such misconduct. The employee's coworkers also have a right to expect him to come forward with knowledge of misconduct. But this is a reciprocal arrangement. If individuals step forward to do a great service for their company and their coworkers, then they should have a reasonable expectation that those they are helping will support them in fulfilling their moral obligation.

The Arguments Against Whistle-Blowing

Whistle-blowing has some very powerful positive arguments, however, one cannot fully understand the ramifications of whistle-blowing without understanding the negative factors as well. Alan F. Westin[11] provides the following factors for consideration:

- Not all whistle-blowers are correct, and not all whistle-blowers have the correct facts. Determining the accuracy of a whistle-blower's allegations can be difficult. There is no guarantee that a whistle-blower knows all of the facts. There are also unclear legal definitions of what is a safe product or what constitutes misconduct.

- There is an inherent danger that an incompetent or poorly performing employee will use the whistle-blower protections against dismissal or retribution to avoid justified personnel actions. As an example, an employee who is aware that he may be terminated for poor performance, may blow the whistle on some alleged misconduct in order to prevent the termination from occurring. Westin calls this "antidismissal insurance" because it prevents the company from taking justified personnel actions against employees simply because they were clever enough to lodge a whistle-blowing complaint.

- Employees might choose to use disruptive means to blow the whistle, which might not be necessary to expose the problems, for example, going to the newspapers when internal channels would have been sufficient to take care of the problems.

- Employees' whistle-blowing actions may be protests of corporate social policies with which the employees disagree rather than an attempt at exposing real issues of misconduct, waste, or safety.

- The efficiency of the organization and the ability of management to run the company as it sees fit could be hampered by creating a system where employees can dissent easily and then bring in the courts to handle what would typically be routine personnel matters.

Justification for Whistle-Blowing

Because of the ramifications to the individual whistle-blower and the organization, anyone contemplating blowing the whistle must consider several points. Potential whistle-blowers must ask themselves whether their actions are justified. Justification is based on factors such as the motives for the whistle-blowing, the manner in which the information is disclosed, and whether the release of the information does more good than harm. Richard T. De George[12] and Gene G. James[13] are just two of the many people who have proposed guidelines for the justification of whistle-blowing. I have combined and edited their separate lists of justification to create one comprehensive list that covers the various factors in the justification of whistle-blowing. Anyone who may be in a position to blow the whistle on some wrong-doing should follow the following guidelines:

1. **Is there harm to others?** Any conduct or circumstances to be exposed must pose a risk of serious harm to the general public or the members of the organization. Disagreements with management policies, conflicts with issues of social responsibility, or general dissatisfaction with personnel policies are not issues that require or justify whistle-blowing.

2. **Are your motives noble?** Whistle-blowers must act out of conscience and a sense of moral obligation, not in an attempt to become famous, reap financial rewards, or prevent possible negative personnel actions against themselves.

3. **Will exposing the problem result in change?** The whistle-blower should have good reason to believe that some positive change will come from blowing the whistle before undertaking such a risky endeavor.

4. **Is the information verifiable and documented?** Any information that is being brought to the attention of others in a whistle-blowing situation must be well documented and able to convince an impartial observer.

5. **Should the release of information be internal or external?** Whistle-blowers must follow the proper channels before going outside the organization. The first step is their immediate supervisor, then follow the management chain upward until all internal channels have been exhausted. If the organization has guidelines, they should be followed. If there are hotlines or ethics officers responsible for whistle-blowing, they should be used. Only when there appears to be no resolution to the wrongdoing from internal sources,

should the whistle-blower go external. And even then, there should be a good reason to believe that going outside of the organization will be effective.

6. **Should the whistle-blower be open or anonymous?** Potential whistle-blowers must decide whether they wish to remain anonymous (by using hotlines or anonymous letters) or whether they are willing to put themselves under the spotlight. In some case, only by coming forward publicly (for testimony or to put a face on the issue) can the whistle-blower really effect change.

7. **Are you willing to risk retaliation?** A whistle-blower should not enter into this undertaking without fully evaluating the possible retaliation that can occur. This may include peer pressure, social banishment, ridicule, labeling, or overtly hostile actions. There are also actions from management such as demotion or termination. If you are not willing to accept these possible outcomes, then you may not be able to follow-though on your whistle-blowing complaint when placed under such pressure.

There are other considerations that whistle-blowers must appreciate. Here are a few:

- Make certain the disclosure will result in more good than harm.
- Avoid hurting innocent people or organizations.
- Do not drag unwilling coworkers into the mess with you.
- Do not personalize the issue or act out of revenge.
- Make the disclosures in a responsible and dignified manner.
- Do not exaggerate the facts.
- Be willing to document and fight retaliation.

Whistle-Blowing Policies

Organizations that undertake the development of whistle-blowing policies must consider all of these arguments, both for and against whistle-blowing, in their policies. Since any company can be affected by misconduct or corruption, having a whistle-blowing policy makes good business sense. Any organization should have in place a mechanism that would allow for the exposure of practices that harm or have the potential to harm the organization. Although employees do not need a written policy to blow the whistle, it helps to have a policy in place that encourages whistle-blowing within a framework that the organization can effectively manage internally. An effective whistle-blowing policy should have the following characteristics:

1. A code of conduct that explains the employee's obligation to report wrongdoing, safety concerns, and misconduct. This should be accompanied by a statement of management's obligation to take action on those allegations.

2. A definition and/or description that clarifies the types of actions that employees should report to management. Employees should know what are legitimate complaints vs. issues that are personnel actions or social responsibilities.

3. A formal process that can be understood and followed by the employees. Everyone should understand how to file a complaint and what investigative process the complaint will follow.

4. A guarantee that there will be no retaliation against the employee. If management wants employees to come forward, it must ensure that they believe they will not be mistreated for their actions.

Organizations must recognize the amount of moral courage that is needed to step forward and blow the whistle. Moreover, whistle-blowers must be viewed as assets to the organization and encouraged to come forward. In 1994, Gary Brown was working in the marketing department of Abbey National, a British bank. Brown noticed that something was wrong and reported it to the bank's management. Subsequently, a person who was suspected of theft was suspended, but Brown was so mistreated by the organization that he eventually left. Then, in 1997, the thief was convicted of stealing $3.3 million and sentenced to eight years in prison. Brown received a commendation from the judge and over $40,000 from the bank. He was also asked to come back to his former job at the bank, and within a few years, he had been promoted three times. After considering the amount of money Brown probably saved the bank by exposing the thief, Abbey National now encourages its employees to blow the whistle and gives them guidance on how to do it. More businesses should experience the same epiphany as Abbey National.

Notes

[1] From www.wordorigins.org

[2] John R. Boatright, *Ethics and the Conduct of Business.* 3rd Edition (Prentice Hall, 2000) pp 107-109.

[3] Boatright, p.109

[4] Telephone poll of 1,006 adult Americans taken for Time/CNN Poll by Harris Interactive, December 17-18, 2002.

[5] Julie Dunn, "Helping Workers Who Spill the Beans," *New York Times* January 19, 2003, p. 3.2

[6] "Whistle-Blowers Being Punished, A Survey Shows," *New York Times* September 3, 2002, p. A14.

[7] The different names come from the various amendments that were added to the legislation, each covering different areas of corporate fraud. The Act was signed by President Bush on July 30, 2002.

[8] *Pickering v. Board of Education*, No. 510, Supreme Court of the United States, 391 U.S. 563, June 3, 1968.

[9] *Connick v. Myers*, Supreme Court of the Untied States, 461 U.S. 138, April 20, 1983.

[10] *Connick v. Myers.*

[11] Alan F. Westin, editor *Whistle Blowing: Loyalty and Dissent in the Corporation* (New York: McGraw-Hill, 1981).

[12] Richard T. De George, *Business Ethics.* 2nd Edition (New York: Macmillan, 1986).

[13] Gene G. James, "Whistle Blowing: Its Moral Justification," reprinted in *Markets, Ethics and Law*, 8th Edition (New York: Pearson, 2001).

Chapter Twenty-Four: Executive Compensation

Perceptions mean a great deal to a corporation's image, and today, many people are upset and resentful of the seven, eight, and nine-figure compensation paid to many CEOs and senior executives of our big corporations. With all of the recent corporate scandals in the headlines, many critics of business are harping on the "exorbitant" or "obscene" salaries of our corporations' top executives. Even the public has joined the fashionable trend to rage about the inequitable situation of top managers being paid so much more than the "rest of us." Is there an ethical dilemma arising from this inequality that needs to be addressed? Are huge executive salaries and bonuses unethical? Perhaps, but let's look at the entire set of circumstances before we decide.

When these well-meaning but misguided critics see a headline stating that the CEO of such-and-such company is being paid $10 million a year, they squeal in protest. Yet these same people have no problem with a professional athlete being paid $40 million to throw or hit a baseball, to shoot baskets and run the court, or to sack an opposing quarterback. These people also see no problem with a movie star being paid $60 million for four months of work shooting a film. Yet what do the athlete and movie star give us for the monumental amounts of money they collect in compensation? They give us entertainment. Certainly entertainment is important in our lives, but except for the few hours of enjoyment we get from it (or the excitement of living our lives vicariously through the athlete or movie star), what is the lasting contribution of a baseball game or a movie? Did the entertainment create the same wealth that corporations create? Did it create new jobs, new technologies, new medicines, new houses, new buildings, higher standards of living, new modes of transportation and communications, or new ways to grow more food and feed the world. No. These are things that only corporations can do.

Corporations create things. They conduct research and development to give us new and useful products. Appliances that make our lives easier, pharmaceuticals that save our lives, products that make us safer, devices that allow us to communicate around the world in seconds, and vehicles that transport us to almost anyplace we need to go are all the results of corporations investing time and money. In essence, corporations create things or provide services that we need to make our lives better. And these corporations would not be able to do these wonderful things without someone at their helm making sure it all happens. Shouldn't someone who can run a complex multinational corporation that creates wealth, useful products and services, and makes our lives better be paid at least as much as someone who entertains us?

People fail to fully appreciate the skill, training, intuition, foresight, and stamina it takes to run a major corporation. Very few people can do it successfully, and those that can do it, have spent all of their adult lives learning how. Surely, an outstanding CEO is worth what the market will bear. In both Adam Smith's free market system and John Locke's labor theory, laborers who seek higher wages must typically produce more or contribute more to their employer. This contributes to the efficiency and productivity of the business, which in turn results in a benefit to consumers and society. These rules apply to CEOs and senior executives as well as any other employee. A CEO that can turn a poor company around or deliver high value to its shareholders is worth a lot to a corporation and all of its various stakeholders (shareholders, employees, business partners, and many others). In a free market system, corporations will pay whatever it takes for the right CEO or other competent senior-level executives, just like the New York Yankees will pay whatever it takes to get a star homerun hitter. If we are going to pay Tom Cruise millions for starring in a movie or pay Michael Jordan millions to shoot baskets, then why would we begrudge a corporation for paying millions to a CEO that can increase its profits and market value?

When an executive is really good, the results to shareholders can be truly wonderful. One such highly paid CEO was Jack Welch of General Electric (GE); someone who definitely deserved to be highly paid. He turned GE into the most valuable company in the world. Considering what Welch did for GE, few of GE's shareholders should ever complain about Jack Welch's income. During a period when other corporations were facing disaster or sharp declines in earnings,

Welch took GE from one profitable year to another, increasing earnings to record levels along the way.

No other CEO has ever created the shareholder value that Jack Welch did. In 1981, when Welch took over the reins of GE, the company was little more than a light bulb manufacturer with revenues of $28 billion, earnings of $1.6 billion, and a market value of $12 billion. In 2000, Welch's last year as CEO, GE was a diversified, complex, global company with revenues of almost $130 billion, earnings of $12.7 billion, 313,000 employees, and a market value of $532 billion. Welch did this through his leadership and strategy. In the first few years after he took over as CEO, Welch divested the company of 117 business units and eliminated about 100,000 jobs, earning him the nickname of "Neutron Jack," referring to the neutron bomb, which kills people but leaves the buildings intact. But Welch also acquired over 600 companies during his 20 years as CEO, moved the company into diverse lines of business, and created a company unlike any other in the world. During the time that Welch ran GE, the S&P 500 had a compounded annual growth rate of 15%. If you bought GE stock when Welch took over, you would have experienced a compounded annual growth rate of 23% over the 20-year period. Try finding that kind of return somewhere else.

Jack Welch received total compensation of nearly $107 million during his last year as CEO. Considering that he delivered earnings of nearly $13 billion that same year, it would appear that GE's shareholders got a terrific deal with Welch.

Of course, there are also CEOs like Ken Lay and Jeffrey Skilling at Enron. While they were driving their company headlong toward disaster, Lay collected $168 million in total compensation and Skilling received $139 million. And there was Bernie Ebbers at WorldCom, Dennis Koslowski at Tyco, John Rigas at Adelphia, and Gary Winnick at Global Crossing; all of whom collected outrageous compensation while they were sucking the life out of their companies and making their shareholder value disappear faster than a bag of bananas in a monkey house. In fact, from 1999 to 2001, CEOs at 23 companies under investigation by the SEC for improper accounting, collectively took in $1.4 billion (or about $62 million each). While they were collecting the big bucks, their companies were losing $530 billion in value (about 73% of their total value), and laying-off 162,000 employees. A prime example is Dennis Koslowski of Tyco. From 1999 to 2001, Tyco paid Koslowski $331 million and gave him another $135 million for luxury living. During that time, he succeeded in driving down his company's value by nearly 60% and laid-off 18,400 employees.[1]

Ironically, the executives of these 23 companies earned 70% more than their counterparts at other publicly traded corporations that were not under investigation.

If we take a close look at highly compensated executive officers, we can see that pay has not always matched performance. Although most boards explain that they link pay to performance, the truth is that much of this never goes beyond lip service. Boards often justify the high salaries and stock option packages they give to top executives by claiming that these executives are worth it because they generate value for the shareholders. However, the facts dispute this. In a 2001 report by United For A Fair Economy[2] that examined the performance of the top ten highest paid corporate executives (from 1993 through 1999), the following information was presented:

- In six out of the seven one-year periods following an executive's pay bonanza, at least half of the companies underperformed the S&P 500.
- In 40% of the cases, the variance was substantial. 27 of 67 of the companies trailed the S&P 500 by more than 15 percentage points.
- Looking at 3-year performance, 39% (16 of 41) of the companies trailed the S&P 500 by 40% over that period.

Some notable examples are given here:

Michael Eisner, Disney's CEO, is one of the highest paid executives in the country (he topped the Business Week list of highest paid executives in 1993, the first year of the report, with $203 million in pay). Yet, from 1993 through 2001, Disney's stock returned just 128.3%. This is far less than the S&P 500 return of 204.2% for the same period, and less than the S&P Entertainment Index return of 163.3%. In light of the poor results from Eisner, the board actually voted to get rid of the pay-for-performance targets of Eisner's compensation plan, now basing his bonuses on the board's discretion.[3] In fact, the board gave Eisner a salary increase, two million stock options valued at $37.7 million, and an $11.5 million bonus after three years in which the company's net income fell by almost $1 billion.[4]

In 1999, Charles Wang of Computer Associates (and two other executives) shared in $1.1 billion in company stock after achieving their performance goals. Less than two months after receiving this enormous payout, the company announced that its sales forecasts would not be met, and the stock took a precipitous drop, losing one-third of its value. After a shareholder suit challenged the size of the bonuses/options, Wang and the other executives had to return $558 million to the company.[5]

In 2000, when Compaq Computer's shares fell in value by more than 50%, the company actually agreed to forgive a $5 million loan to Michael D. Capellas.[6]

Sometimes the egregious compensation comes as a severance package for a failed CEO. For example, after a period of failing to meet several performance targets, Jill Barad of Mattel resigned as CEO. She was awarded severance payments of nearly $50 million. Although some of this package was earned throughout her twenty years as an employee of Mattel, other aspects are questionable. A loan of $3 million that was used to purchase her home was forgiven. A $4.2 million loan to pay taxes on vested stock options was also forgiven. And finally, she was given $3.3 million to cover the taxes on the forgiven loans.[7]

No reasonable person can say that paying a CEO what he's worth is wrong. If a good CEO delivers sustained value to his shareholders, then paying for that sustained value is a good investment. The CEO's value to the company determines his compensation in a free market. However, it is when boards of directors pay bad CEOs who are responsible for decreased earnings, unethical conduct, or diminished shareholder value the same large salaries as good CEOs, that we create the perception of overpaid "fat cat" executives and incur the resentment and scorn of the public. If there is an ethical issue with executive compensation, it isn't with the concept of value paid for value received — most people will accept this philosophy. The problem is when we disregard this concept, insofar as we pay bad executives huge amounts while they kill the very companies they are supposed to safeguard, protect, and grow. Individuals responsible for corporate governance must be keenly attuned to this ethical issue. If we employ the principles of justice and fairness, then "equals should be treated equally and unequals unequally." Therefore, paying failing CEOs and executives who do not deliver shareholder value the same or more compensation than executives who do deliver increased value is neither equitable nor fair. Shareholders and the public are not imperceptive to seeing the injustice of this situation.

Directors can easily justify large compensation packages to senior executives that create value, but how can they explain paying millions to CEOs that drive their companies into bankruptcy? This is the ethical dilemma that must be resolved.

Notes

[1] Scott Klinger, Sarah Anderson, Chris Hartman, John Cavanagh, and Holly Sklar. "Executive Excess 2002: CEOs Cook the Books, Skewer the Rest of Us," *Ninth Annual CEO Pay Study* Institute for Policy Studies and United For A Fair Economy.

[2] Scott Klinger, "The Bigger They Come, The Harder They Fall: High CEO pay and the effect on long-term stock prices," United For A Fair Economy (April 6, 2001).

[3] Klinger.

[4] Louis Lavell with Frederick F. Jespersen. "Special Report: Executive Pay," *BusinessWeek Online* (April 16, 2001).

[5] Klinger, Executive Excess 2002.

[6] Lavell.

[7] Carl R. Weinberg and Mandi Mazza. "CEO Compensation: How Much Is Enough?" 2000 Annual CEO Compensation Review, *Chief Executive*.

Michael P. Harden

Section Three: Ethical Decision Making

Understanding ethical theories and knowing what types of dilemmas are common in the workplace are not enough to solve the underlying problems that businesses face with unethical behavior. It isn't rational to believe that unethical people can go through some forced metamorphosis and become ethical beings. Ethical people behave ethically, and conversely, unethical people behave unethically. It is their nature to do so. We understand this concept from the theory of virtue ethics. So, we must acquiesce to the fact that we cannot change an adult who is already immoral, into one that is moral. But we can do one thing. We can teach people, regardless of their current moral deficiencies, how to make moral and ethical decisions. We can provide people with the tools they need to make ethically defensible decisions. Whenever we make an ethical judgment, we must ensure that our decision is based upon well-grounded ethical principles and carefully thought-out arguments.

Since many ethical situations are ambiguous — where right vs. right is more common that right vs. wrong — trying to figure out the correct moral answer is tough. The first problem with which an individual is faced is actually determining whether an ethical dilemma really exists. If an ethical dilemma does exist, then the individual must be able to make an ethical decision and defend that decision using generally accepted ethical principles. There is a reason for this. Since any two people can look at the same ethical question and come up with completely different answers, the chances are that one answer is better than the other. To ensure that we always reach the best answer to a moral dilemma, we can teach people to go through a process, using the ethical principles in this book, to arrive at a solution that can be defended against other possible alternatives as the best, or most ethical solution.

This section will cover various ethical "tests" and ways in which we can apply the ethical theories covered previously in this book so that we can utilize what we have learned in order to:

1. Determine if an ethical dilemma exists, and
2. Arrive at the best defensible ethical decision.

To accomplish this, we apply three sets of ethical standards or ethical tests. These are: the law, professional or organizational standards, and traditional ethical theories.

The Law

Our laws and regulations are created specifically to let us know what is acceptable behavior and what is prohibited behavior. We can look at the law as the bare minimum because many actions that are lawful are not ethical. If it is against the law, we do not need to analyze whether an ethical issue exists. However, the law may be unclear or may not go far enough. If that is the case, we need to analyze the ethical issues further.

Professional Standards

When the law isn't clear about an action, or when we are unsure that a lawful act is ethical, we can always refer to written standards of behavior such as codes of conduct or organizational policies. Many professions, such as lawyers, accountants, and physicians, have written guidelines for ethical behavior. Organizations, employers, and government agencies often have written codes of conduct for their members and employees. We can refer to these to give us guidance on ethical decision-making.

Ethical Theories

When all else fails, we can apply the traditional ethical principles we have studied in this book to help us identify ethical dilemmas and guide us to the best ethical decision.

Chapter Twenty-Five: Ethics and The Law

Laws are written to provide us with rules to govern our behavior in a wide range of situations. Laws typically are a society's way of taking the ethical principles that society, as a whole, considers valid, and then formalizing them into "rules" that can be enforced. We create laws for several reasons. As human beings, we realize that not every person will follow the ethical principles we consider important for a well-functioning society. So we use these principles as the basis for our laws. We codify our ethical principles so we can impose them on everyone, and by doing so, force people to follow the principles we, as a society, believe to be valuable. People who violate these principles can be punished, and in order to do so, we establish penalties for those that fail to uphold our collective ethical standards.

Laws derive from ethical principles that history has shown us to be beneficial to our society. Although politicians and proponents of the separation of church and state[1] do not like to admit it, many of our laws derive from religious rules, which were the original means for formalizing ethical principles. The Ten Commandments, typically banned from display in public or government buildings, permeate our laws. Which came first: "Thou shall not kill," or our laws against murder? How about: "Thou shall not steal," or our laws against theft, burglary, embezzlement, and shoplifting? Obviously, our current laws, just like Hammurabi's laws, are nothing more than the formalization of what we already knew to be right and wrong. The Uniform Commercial Code (UCC), which deals primarily with financial and business transactions, is a modern formalization of what we believe to be ethical in our business dealings. Laws simply make the criteria for determining offenses clearer (and more specific), and provide appropriate punishments for offenders so these ethical principles can be enforced.

As a society, we have a sense of what is right and what is wrong. We admire certain virtues, and we try to uphold ethical principles. By doing so, we make our society function better, we are able to operate in an environment of trust, and we apply pressure on individuals who do not follow our moral ideals. But the law takes it to another level. Laws make people accountable for their unethical behavior by establishing criminal or civil penalties for violators. Laws are basically utilitarian in nature as they specifically tell us that a certain behavior by an individual is harmful to our society and that we should prohibit and punish that behavior for the benefit of our society. In a broader sense, the law signifies that our society, through our lawmakers, has determined that the actions prohibited by the law hurt our society, or the actions permitted by the law benefit our society.

Because laws are founded on ethical principles and are representations of our moral beliefs, checking with the law is a good first step in determining whether an ethical dilemma exists. If an action is against the law, it is an easy supposition that the behavior is unethical. However, there are many people who will say that not all laws are ethical. This is true. There are some laws that ethical and moral people will disagree with on the basis that the law is bad or goes against a moral principle. In fact, people throughout history have disobeyed certain laws as an ethical protest. Laws that once enforced racial segregation are an example. We are now in the midst of many debates on the ethicality of certain laws. Abortion opponents believe that the current laws that allow abortions are immoral. Environmentalists believe that certain laws that allow logging, oil drilling, pollution, and toxic waste dumping are unethical. There will always be disagreements on some laws based on differing ethical beliefs.

Even though some laws may not be grounded in socially accepted ethical principles, a general assumption that laws represent our collective ethical beliefs *most of the time* would not be out of line. So using the law as a first step in determining whether an ethical dilemma exists is a sound policy. When we are presented with a moral decision and are uncertain of the correct action, we can investigate what the law says about it. Looking at the legal interpretation, by referring to the law, allows us to identify a course of action quickly. In most cases, the law will give us a clear direction for coming to an ethical decision. The bottom line is that if the action is against the law, we should make an assumption that the action is unethical. If we believe that the law is a bad law, then we will have to go through many other steps to determine the morality of the action. But in most cases, the law will adequately reflect our societal notions of right and wrong.

Nevertheless, not every unethical action is against the law. There are not enough laws on the books to cover every possible situation and its potential ethical outcomes. So although the law is a good place to start, it will not always give us the direction we need. For example, there is no law that says I must contribute as much effort as my teammates on a project we are working on for our company. There are always social loafers who sit back and watch their teammates carry the workload. Is it unethical for some team member to loaf and force their fellow workers to carry the extra load? Many people would say that is unethical behavior, however, it isn't against any law that I am aware of. So there will be times when the law offers no direction for us. In those cases, we must follow other approaches to make an ethical decision.

We cannot rely entirely on the law in all cases. Jennifer Wagner[2] listed four possible states that exist between ethics and the law. These states depend upon whether a specific action is ethical or not ethical, and legal or not legal. Those four states are shown in the following table:

	Legal	Not Legal
Ethical	I	II
Not Ethical	III	IV

I = An act that is ethical and legal
II = An act that is ethical but not legal
III = An act that is not ethical but is legal
IV = An act that is not ethical and not legal

Since an action or behavior may fit into any of these four categories, we cannot rely one hundred percent on using the law as a final determinant. However, if the law is clear and the act appears to be in either I or IV (ethical and legal or not ethical and not legal), then the dilemma can be considered resolved and we need not go through any further analysis. If, on the other hand, the law is not clear and the act appears to fall into categories II and III, the situation needs to be examined in more depth to determine the likely resolution of the dilemma. There is still ambiguity as to whether the action is either ethical or legal, so further analysis is necessary.

Notes

[1] This concept comes from the First Amendment to the Constitution. Ironically, the amendment reads: "Congress shall make no law respecting an establishment of religion…" yet almost all of our laws are ways in which we enforce ethical principles, most of which have been basic tenets of Judeo-Christian religious beliefs long before these laws were ever written.

[2] Jennifer Wagner, "Using a taxonomy of ethical situations in MIS," *Journal/Proceedings Information Systems and Quantitative Management,* Midwest Business Administration Association (1991): pp 112-118.

Michael P. Harden

Chapter Twenty-Six: Casual Tests

Before delving deeply into ethical analysis, anyone pondering whether an ethical dilemma exists can do a few real quick tests. These quick tests are called *casual* because they are not based on many of the ethical principles we have reviewed earlier in this book, nor are they written into some code of conduct or professional standards, but they are simply questions we can ask ourselves in an easy way that gives us an idea of the general ethical direction of an action. There are several casual tests that can be used to determine whether an action may or may not be ethical.[1] These are:

The "Mom" test. This is where we can ask ourselves the question: Would I tell my Mother about what I did? Or turned the other way, how would I feel if my Mother did what I did? The "Mom" test is a way of determining quickly whether you would be ashamed of your actions. Would you want to hide it from her? It also can show whether you would be proud of what you did. Would you want to brag about your actions to her? Of course, the result of feeling either shame or pride from these questions is a personal reaction based on a completely personal emotional response.

The "Shush" test. If somebody says, "I just did something, but if I tell you, you can't tell anyone else," then there is a high probability that something isn't ethical. People who do this are called "shushers." It's like putting your index finger to your lips and whispering "shush." Typically, these people will pull you aside, lower their voices, and say, "Make sure that Mary doesn't find out, but…" You have to ask yourself: if the situation or action is ethical, then what is the reason for all the secrecy?

The "Media" test. This test asks the question: How would I feel if what I did was reported on TV or in the newspaper? Would I want millions of people to know my situation? Would I feel proud or embarrassed if my actions were made public in such a ubiquitous way?

This question causes you to think about the reaction of millions of people to your action and how you would feel dealing with their knowledge of it.

The "Promotion" test. This test asks a very simple question of any business person: "Would telling prospective customers about what I did promote my business or cause them to not do business with me?" The basis behind this informal guideline is the reaction by potential customers to your business's practices. Do your actions provide a positive or negative image of your business? Would knowledge of your actions promote your business or hurt it? Would people want to do business with your firm after hearing about its behavior?

The "Golden Rule" test. This test simply asks the question: How would I feel if someone did the same thing to me? If the shoe was on the other foot, how would I like being treated in this manner? Would I feel good or bad, happy or sad, or would I feel that I was being treated fairly or being cheated? The "Golden Rule" test is a quick way of seeing things from the other person's perspective, and this enhances your ability to determine if the action is ethical. The "Golden Rule" has been with us since Confucius first coined it around 500 BC. It has been paraphrased in many ways, but basically goes like this: "What you do not want done to you by others, do not do to them," and has also been turned into a more positive statement: "Do unto others as you would have them do unto you."

The "Smell" test. This is one we hear about often. Its basic assumption is: Does this action or situation "smell" right? Although there may be no outward reason to suspect that something may be unethical, does it not feel right to you? Is there something that just sticks in the pit of your stomach that tells you that it isn't right? If so, then the action or issue doesn't pass the "smell" test.

The "Kid" test. With this test, we simply ask ourselves whether we would teach our kids to behave this way. Since we all want our children to grow up to be responsible adults that can be respected by others, we can easily look at a behavior and determine whether it is something we would be proud to see in our children.

Using these tests as a warning alarm for unethical conduct is a good way to determine if an ethical issue is present. Although none of these tests, alone or together, can ultimately determine the morality of an action or behavior, they are excellent tests to determine whether a need exists to analyze things further. They can help us determine that an ethical dilemma exists.

Notes

[1] Several of these tests can also be found in *Ethical Decision Making and Information Technology*, 2nd Edition, Ernest Kallman and John Grillo, Irwin/McGraw Hill, 1996, where they are listed as "informal guidelines."

Chapter Twenty-Seven: Formal Guidelines

Anyone who believes that an ethical dilemma might exist in a certain situation can always refer to various *formal* guidelines that exist in the business community. Formal guidelines, unlike *casual* guidelines, give us written rules that we can use to judge the morality of a certain action. By applying these guidelines, we can typically figure out if an ethical dilemma exists, and in many cases, what we should do about it.

The two major formal guidelines are professional codes of conduct and organizational policies:

Professional codes of conduct. In many instances, professions (such as attorneys, doctors, accountants, and engineers) have formal, written codes of conduct that are specific to their profession. These codes of conduct are used to establish standards for the profession that govern the behavior of its members. Having written guidelines in the form of a code of conduct makes it easy for anyone to reference. A written code also helps to make members of the profession aware of ethical problems. Codes of conduct are also used to ensure that new members coming into the profession are aware of the expectations and standards of the profession. Codes of conduct also have a self-serving purpose. Professions can use their code of conduct as a form of public relations, demonstrating to the public that the profession follows ethical standards. Having a formal code of conduct also helps to keep external regulators at bay. If professions can show that they have a code of conduct that they enforce on their members, regulators are more likely to allow them to self-police their membership. This is why you typically see the American Bar Association and the American Medical Association handle most matters relating to the professional conduct of their members.

Corporations and organizations often have codes of conducts as well. These guidelines are not based on standards that deal with specific professions, but on standards that govern the behavior of its members in their general actions as they relate to the organization. Many organizations have written codes of conduct that are part of the new employee orientation, are included in the employee handbook, and may be framed and posted throughout the facility for all to see. These codes serve the same purposes as the professional codes of conduct.

Using a professional or corporate code of conduct as a guideline for ethical behavior is a good idea. But we must make certain that the code is actually used. Copies of the Enron code of conduct can occasionally be found offered for sale on eBay as a somewhat ironic souvenir or novelty item.

Organizational policies. There are numerous policies in any organization that specifically tell its members or employees how to behave and what to do in certain situations. In some organizations, the policies may be more like mottos such as "Treat all employees with respect," or "The customer is always right." They can also be very specific with guidelines about things like giving gifts to clients, how to report suspected misconduct, or rules about drug use in the workplace. These policies are all designed to provide guidance on how to behave ethically as an employee or member of the organization. Since many of these policies are specific to an organization, they are a good source of guidance on making ethical decisions about issues that might be found in the organization.

Chapter Twenty-Eight: The Dialectic

In 300 BC, Socrates actively taught his students (one of which was Plato) through a technique of asking questions that caused his students to engage in a series of arguments that would result in a reformulation of their original claim. Socrates often feigned ignorance, forcing his students to more thoroughly and clearly express their arguments to him. His technique became known as the Socratic or dialectic method.

Plato refined this technique and used it frequently. The dialogical or dialectic method requires questions and answers as a form of arguing for a claim. Continued questioning of an argument helps to expose gaps in that argument. In the "give-and-take" of questioning an argument, exposing gaps in the argument, and then reformulating the argument to close the gaps, one can eventually arrive at an argument that has a strong and solid footing to defend the original claim, or result in a modification of the original claim. This is a form of philosophical analysis that forces us to thoroughly evaluate our claims.

The dialectic techniques works this way:

You put forth a claim and an argument for why that claim is correct. Another person may then ask a critical question that exposes a hole in your argument. You respond by revising your argument to close the hole or modify your original claim. The process can continue until the original claim is either fully defended or the original claim is modified.

This is an example of how it might actually work:

Let us assume that you make a claim that killing is wrong. You further state that the basis (or argument) for your claim is that life is precious, and only God has the right to take a life. I may then ask you: What about self-defense? Is it wrong to kill someone if they are about to kill you? In response, you might hold fast to your original argument and say that it is *always* wrong to kill, even in self-defense. Or you might modify your argument to say that it is wrong to kill, *except* in self-defense. I might then ask you whether it is wrong to kill if we are at war and you are in a heated battle with the enemy. Or I might ask you whether it is wrong to kill a convicted murderer (capital punishment) who has killed several innocent people. In both cases, you will need to critically evaluate your argument and determine whether it remains unchanged or whether it should be modified. This can go on for some time as arguments become more refined and defensible. Finally, an argument is reached that, although it may not be definitive, is the best argument that can be presented for the claim. You might eventually make the claim and argument that killing is wrong, except in cases of self-defense, war, and legally sanctioned capital punishment. This is a distinctly different argument than was originally presented by you. The dialectic has caused you to reformulate your argument or claim to better state your *true* belief. It also helps you to understand your true belief.

As you can see, this technique can be done for just about any moral claim. It can be used to better understand our beliefs on ethical issues such as abortion, killing, capital punishment, euthanasia, off-balance sheet partnerships, gun control, corporate social responsibility, cloning, stem cell research, adultery, and many others.

We can use the dialectic technique on our own without requiring others to question us. We can simply question ourselves. We can make our claim, state our argument, and then begin the process of asking questions that force us to evaluate our arguments. We can modify our arguments and then question them again until we better understand our own beliefs. In the process, we might find that we reject some of the aspects of our original argument in light of the questioning that has taken place. The dialectic helps us to clarify our positions and beliefs so that we can better articulate our arguments.

The dialectic method is particularly useful in situations where we face an ethical dilemma and need to clarify our position, either to ourselves or to others, through arguments that support our claim. The dialectic also provides us with a tool to determine if other people's arguments actually support their claims. Through careful and thoughtful questioning we can determine if someone's arguments support their ethical claim. Conversely, by asking probing questions that make them rethink and refine their arguments, we may get them to modify their original claim.

Chapter Twenty-Nine: Identifying the Stakeholders

Ethical issues are always about people, although organizations and corporations can represent people. To cheat a corporation is equivalent to cheating the corporation's employees and shareholders, so people are always involved one way or another. Therefore, ethical decisions are usually based on trying to benefit as many people as possible while harming as few people as possible. To fully determine the benefits and harm that might occur from an action or decision, we must first understand who the parties are that might be affected. Anyone who has an interest in the outcome of an action is a *stakeholder*. They have a *stake* in what happens. Further defined, a stakeholder is any person or entity that can be affected by your actions, or conversely, any person or entity that can affect your actions.

In a business environment, there can be a large number of different stakeholders, each with competing interests. Here is a list of some of the possible stakeholders:

Employees
Managers
Stockholders
Suppliers
Creditors
Business Partners
Bankers/lenders
Customers
Competitors
Government
Community

It is easy to see from this list how competing interests can come into play. Decisions that enhance or benefit stockholders (by reducing costs and increasing the value of the corporation) may do so at the expense of the employees (due to salary freezes, layoffs, and reduced benefits). If a corporation decides to move its facility to another country to take advantage of tax breaks, cheaper materials, and lower wages; the current employees, the local community, the government, and suppliers may suffer from the move through lost jobs, taxes, and sales. On the other hand, the stockholders, creditors, customers, and the new host country will likely benefit from the move. In the process of making such a crucial decision, the board of directors and the corporate executives must identify which stakeholders will be impacted by the proposed move and how they will be impacted. They do this by considering which stakeholders are benefited and which are harmed, and to what extent, and then weighing the outcomes.

Subconsciously, we do this all the time in our personal lives. We constantly make decisions by weighing the pros and cons, and weighing who will benefit and who will be harmed. In business, however, the ramifications can be significant. For example, closing a plant or restructuring a division might affect thousands of employees and hundreds of thousands of stockholders.

Stakeholders do not have to be entire classes of people such as customers or employees. An ethical decision can affect only one or two people. In fact, many ethical decisions in business involve only a small number of stakeholders. As an example, a sexual harassment incident may involve only two people: the accuser and the alleged perpetrator of the harassment. These are the two principal stakeholders. As management, we could expand this by evaluating whether other coworkers will be affected by any actions we take, but generally, the benefits and harm from any decision or action will most likely be limited to the two stakeholders we have identified.

Since any ethical decision will involve stakeholders, we must be fully aware of who the stakeholders are before we can appreciate the benefits and harm that may occur. Therefore, identifying the stakeholders is a logical and necessary first step in ethical decision-making. Here is an example of how various stakeholders may be involved in an ethical dilemma:

In March 2003, Electronic Data Systems (EDS) ousted its Chairman and CEO, Dick Brown, due to the company's poor performance and drop in its stock price. The company also came under investigation by the Securities and Exchange Commission (SEC). It suffered steep earnings declines and a revenue shortfall in the second half of 2002, and also announced plans for layoffs. As part of his 1998 employment contact, Brown was to receive a severance package of $35 million in cash, monthly payments, and stock. To cover his severance, the company took a one-time charge against earnings of six cents per share. The EDS board of directors negotiated the employment contract that allowed for this exorbitant payout for a chief executive that failed to deliver. The package was guaranteed by Brown's contract, so shareholders couldn't fight it without having EDS face possible legal liabilities.

There are many ethical issues involved in this situation. In this ethical dilemma, who are the stakeholders? Obviously, Dick Brown is a stakeholder. There are also shareholders who suffered financially with the decline of the company's performance and who are now being asked to take a one-time charge to cover Brown's severance. There is the board of directors, who negotiated the employment contract, and who now must answer to the shareholders. There are also employees, particularly the ones being laid-off. Sometimes, not all of the stakeholders are apparent at first glance. Are there any others you can think of? How about the SEC?

It is also easy to see how there are competing interests among these various stakeholders. That is why we must identify the stakeholders early in the process if we are to fully understand the different ethical dilemmas that exist.

Here is another recent example of different stakeholders being involved in an ethical dilemma:

During March and April of 2003, American Airlines was faced with the possibility of filing for bankruptcy protection. In order to avoid this drastic measure, the CEO, Don Carty, asked the airline's various labor unions (pilots, mechanics, and flight attendants) to take pay cuts equal to $10 billion spread over six years. However, while Mr. Carty was asking the employees to make substantial concessions, he hid from the employees and their unions the fact that executives would receive lucrative bonuses ($1.1 million for Carty himself) and that the executives' pension plans of $41 million would be kept in place and insulated from any possible bankruptcy. Employees were outraged when this came to light. To placate the employees and gain their concessions, Carty resigned.

In this ethical dilemma, who are the stakeholders? Don Carty and the employees are obvious stakeholders but what about the labor unions, the other executives, the shareholders, the airline's customers, and its creditors? Had Carty so outraged the employees that they refused to take the cuts and forced the airline into bankruptcy, think about who would have been harmed?

So stakeholders can be just about any party with an interest in the outcome of an action. They can be relatively few or number in the thousands, perhaps even millions. Many people may also argue that certain shareholders have *more* interest than others. For example, local merchants might have only a nominal interest if a small plant relocates out of their area, but the employees who are laid-off and facing long-term unemployment have a significant interest in the decision to move the plant. If we look at things from the perspective of Milton Friedman we can see an inevitable clash between the interests of the employees and the interests of the shareholders. Friedman believes that the self-interests of employees in retaining their jobs conflicts with the interests of the shareholders who are more concerned with the efficient use of capital. Since shareholders have none of the contractual protection typically enjoyed by employees (collective bargaining agreements, employment contracts, severance policies, etc.), the shareholders bear the risk when the company fails. According to Friedman, "You want control…in the hands of those who are the residual recipients because they are the ones with the direct interest in using the capital of the firm efficiently."[1] This concept would compel us to value the interests of the shareholders more so than the interests of the employees. Control, i.e., decision making, should rest in the hands of the stakeholders who have taken the greatest risk and have a greater concern for efficiency. There is some validity to this notion, but it cannot be considered in a vacuum. It must be evaluated with other factors and the interests of other stakeholders. For example, should shareholders be allowed to operate a plant that produces toxic chemicals that are polluting a city's water supply, even if it is the most efficient use of capital?

Thus, when we analyze the interests of stakeholders, we are compelled to evaluate their interests and the ultimate weight of those interests. But to do so, we must know who the stakeholders are.

Michael P. Harden

Notes

[1] Quoting Milton Friedman in an article by Simon London. "Lunch with FT: Milton Friedman." *Financial Times* (www.ft.com) June 6, 2003.

Chapter Thirty: Determining the Relevant Facts

Once we have identified those people who have a stake in the situation, we must also ensure that we understand all of the relevant facts. Bad ethical decisions are often made because not all of the relevant facts are known to the decision-maker. If we are cognizant of all of the various facts involved in the ethical dilemma, we are much better prepared to apply the appropriate ethical principles without missing an important point or failing to consider an aspect that would impact our decision.

Just as we have gone through quickly and identified all of the various stakeholders, we must do the same with the relevant facts. To demonstrate how this works, we can review the following case:

John is the systems administrator for a company that has fifty employees, many of whom work at home by remotely dialing into the company's system. It is part of John's responsibility to assign passwords and user accounts, upgrade software, and monitor the system. One day, John is approached by his boss, Allen, with a request. Allen is responsible for the MIS function as well as human resources and administration. Allen tells John that he suspects that some employees are "goofing-off" and not working the number of hours they are entering on their timesheets. He has found a software program that allows the company to monitor the computer usage of its remote employees without their knowledge. It shows time spent on the computer, number of keystrokes, types of applications used, Internet access, and web sites visited. Allen feels that this program will allow him to identify non-productive employees and correlate employee work with their actual timesheets.

Allen wants John to download the software to the employees' computers when they log on to the main system, and he doesn't want the employees to know anything about its purpose. Allen instructs John to just tell the employees' that the software is just an enhancement to the remote access applications.

John is concerned because the software doesn't differentiate between work and personal use. It also doesn't differentiate between the employee and other family members who may use the computer. It simply collects data and reports it back to the company. Allen would be able to see what employees (and their families) do on their computers and the Internet when they are not working. John feels that by not informing the employees that their systems are being monitored, he is violating their privacy. He isn't sure what to do.

To help John figure out what to do, we would first identify the stakeholders. They are:

1. John
2. Allen
3. The employees
4. The employees' families
5. The company

Each has a stake in the action that will be taken. We must also identify the relevant facts. We are not interested in the ethical principles involved, nor are we making any judgments at this time. We are simply interested in making certain that all of the facts are known. Facts are different than opinions and suppositions. Here are the relevant facts:

1. John is the systems administrator.
2. Allen is his boss and head of MIS and HR.
3. The employees work at home using their own computers.
4. Employees log onto the company's system from their personal computers.
5. Family members may also use the computers.

6. Employees fill out timesheets of their time spent working in order to get paid.
7. Allen wants software that monitors the computer usage surreptitiously installed.
8. The software will help identify "loafers" who are not productive.
9. The software does not differentiate between users.
10. The software does not differentiate between work and personal activity.
11. Allen has instructed John to install the software.

There may be other facts as well, but these appear to be the relevant ones. Notice that there are no opinions or expressions of feelings, such as "John thinks the software may violate employee privacy." At this point, we are not going to make any ethical judgments; we simply want to ensure that we are aware of all of the facts. We are not yet ready to determine if something is right or wrong, good or bad.

If we haven't missed anything important, we can be confident that we understand who is affected and what the facts are. We can then begin to apply ethical principles to help us identify the appropriate course of action.

Michael P. Harden

Chapter Thirty-One: Applying Ethical Principles

In the first section of this book we discussed the different ethical theories that have developed over time and how those ethical theories define ethical (or unethical) behavior. In making an ethical decision, we must be fully aware of how these various ethical theories help to shape our ultimate decision by providing us with a logical analysis of the all of the aspects of our ethical dilemma.

We often apply one or more of these ethical theories in our decision-making process without really knowing that we are doing it. We make judgments all of the time based on what we think is right or wrong, or what we "feel" in our gut to be morally correct. If we have a strong moral foundation, the chances are pretty good that we will do the right thing. However, in business situations that may have several different stakeholders, multiple considerations, and numerous possible outcomes, the process of determining the most ethical action is often more complex, and the stakes could be very high. This simply means that we must be more methodical in our decision-making and more attentive to the conflicting interests involved.

By using an approach that is based on a solid foundation of ethical principles and following a step-by-step process, we are better equipped to make decisions that will result in the best possible moral outcome, i.e., the most defensible action.

In the first section of this book, we discussed the following theories:

- Teleological Theories
  o Utilitarianism
  o The Social Contract
- Deontological Theories
  o Kantian Theory
  o Duty Theory
- Justice and Fairness

In applying these theories so we can solve ethical dilemmas, we must look at the stakeholders, the facts, and the actions we can take, and how ethical theories affect these components.

Quick and Easy

In any possible ethical dilemma, we can first apply the law. This is the quickest and easiest test we can perform. We can simply ask ourselves: "Does the action violate the law?" The reasons for this quick test are obvious. If something violates the law, there is no need to worry about whether it is ethical or not. Although there is often debate that something might violate the law but still be ethical, it doesn't apply in a situation such as this. We are not concerned about an illegal act being ethical, although we are often concerned about a lawful act being unethical. Our assumption in the business world is that unlawful acts, whether we agree with the law or not, are violations of the public trust, subject to penalties, and patently wrong. No director, business executive, or employee should ever violate the law and jeopardize themselves and their companies with criminal or civil sanctions regardless of how they feel about the particular law in question. So if the act violates the law, we need go no further in our analysis. We simply refrain from taking the illegal action, or we report the action to the authorities. As an example, if a coworker or supervisor asks you to dump several barrels of toxic waste in the local garbage dump, you do not need to analyze the ethical implications of this action. It is against the law, and for that reason alone you must refrain from taking that action. If you see a coworker loading several new laptop computers into the trunk of her car one evening after work, and the next day she reports them as stolen, you do not need to determine the ethical implications of her actions. She has broken the law, and that is all you need to know to take action.

If the behavior we are analyzing does not violate the law, it may still be unethical. Often, actions that are legal may be unethical. For example, it may not be illegal to moonlight and do outside work for one of your company's clients, but it certainly appears to be unethical. In cases where the law is not clear or where the action is not illegal but appears to be unethical, there are numerous professional guidelines that can help clarify the ethical implications of the issues. Accountants, doctors, lawyers, engineers, and many other professions have written guidelines that are published and posted on their respective association web sites. They are also available in handbooks and membership packets. If we suspect that an ethical dilemma exists in our professional capacity, we can quickly check the professional guidelines for clarification. For those of us who may not be members of a profession, we have other sources that can assist us. In many cases, our employer will have a code of conduct that we can turn to. It may be found in the employee handbook or posted outside the cafeteria. In any case, we can always check with our company's code of conduct, the Human Resources Manager, or in a larger company, the ethics officer or corporate counsel.

Some of the questions we can ask ourselves are: Does this action violate professional standards? Does it violate any professional codes of ethics? Does this action violate corporate policies? Does it violate the corporate code of conduct?

These various sources may not be available or helpful in identifying the particular ethical dilemmas that exist, so we may want to apply some of our casual tests. We are basically checking to see if the actions "appear" to be unethical. Do they pass the "Mom" test? How about the "Shush" test? Would you be proud telling your children about your behavior? Would your clients look down on your company if they knew what you were doing? Would you brag about your behavior or try to hide it?

These are the kinds of questions that can often help identify whether a particular behavior or course of action is or isn't ethical. Obviously, these casual tests are not foolproof. If we are fortunate, we may arrive at the conclusion that something isn't right by applying these casual tests. However, although these questions may alert us to possible ethical problems, they may only leave us with an uneasy feeling and no positive determination about the morality of the situation. When that happens, we must follow a more detailed and structured process.

The First Steps

The first step in ethical decision-making is to determine whether an ethical dilemma exists in the first place. In order to do this, we must go through several steps. These are:

1. **Identify all of the various stakeholders.** We must determine who will be affected by the decisions we must make. This quick exercise requires that we list any party that has some stake in the decision. Only by knowing all of the parties that are impacted by the decision or behavior, can we make a defensible decision. Sometimes there are more stakeholders than we originally perceived, and knowing this helps us to realize the repercussions of the various alternative actions we can take.

2. **Determine all of the relevant facts.** To be able to come up with a truly defensible ethical decision, we must be fully aware of all of the relevant facts. Otherwise, we may miss something that would have a significant effect on a stakeholder, or we could overlook a fact that would help us determine a viable course of action. Therefore, we must list all of the relevant facts — not speculation or opinions — but factual information. Armed with the list of stakeholders and the relevant facts, we can now move to the next step.

3. **Identify who will be harmed.** Since ethics deals primarily with *harm*, in this step, we must identify which of the stakeholders will be harmed by the actions or decisions. We can look at the various facts we have already listed, compare that to the list of stakeholders, and begin to develop an understanding of who will be harmed by the decisions we make. For example, if one of the facts is "Management wants to close the Chicago plant and move it to Mexico," we can see that several stakeholders will be nega-

tively impacted by this action. Employees will be harmed the most when they lose their jobs, but other stakeholders, such as the community (retailers, restaurants, etc.), local suppliers, the employees' families, and the local government (city, county, and school districts that rely on the tax base), will also be harmed.

4. **Identify who will benefit.** In the previous example, the stockholders of the company will likely benefit financially from the lower wages and cost basis in Mexico. The company will be more profitable, and that should drive up the stock value and/or increase the dividends. American consumers may also benefit if the lower costs are passed on in lower prices. And of course, the people of Mexico will benefit by having the new plant located in their country (new jobs, more or better wages, more tax revenues, etc.).

Since decisions typically result in some stakeholders being harmed while others benefit, the ethical dilemma is often ambiguous. Many questions present themselves. Who should be harmed and who should benefit? Do the benefits outweigh the harm? Do some stakeholders have a larger stake than others? Are some stakeholders' needs more important than others? Should they receive more consideration than the other stakeholders? Which alternatives provide the most benefit with the least amount of harm? Can some stakeholders accept more harm than others?

Because these questions are not easily answered, we now must apply the theories we discussed earlier in this book to help us identify the most appropriate solution(s). Using the ethical principles covered in the first section of this book, we can analyze the ethical dilemmas, answer the ambiguous questions, and develop alternative courses of action. Once this is accomplished, we can make a decision that is ethically defensible.

The Analysis

Once we have become familiar and comfortable with the various ethical theories we studied in the first section of this book, we can use our newfound skills to analyze possible alternative courses of action and their ethical impact.

Typically, as human beings, we are required to make decisions on a regular basis that have ethical implications. We use judgment, intuition, and notions of right and wrong to make our decisions. Using ethical theories is a way to enhance that decision-making ability. Applying solid ethical theories is a way to use a rational, logical process to enhance our decision-making skills so we can make better, more defensible ethical decisions.

Teleological Theories

One of the first steps in our logical process is to use the teleological theories we learned to assist us in analyzing the ethical outcomes of possible decisions or actions. Teleological theories hold that what makes an action right or wrong is determined strictly by the *consequences* of that action. The main teleological ethics theory is known as *utilitarianism*.

Utilitarianism provides us with a fairly objective method for making ethical decisions. We only have to ask ourselves whether the actions we are taking will generate benefits or harm to the greatest amount of stakeholders. In business situations we can look at our possible choices of actions and their likely consequences, and by determining whether those consequences produce the most good for the most stakeholders, we enhance our ability to make an ethical decision.

Utilitarianism works well in determining morally correct actions as long as the consequences of the action are easily measured. Sometimes it is hard to determine how the consequences may affect all of the various stakeholders involved. Utilitarianism is basically a balancing act — an attempt at balancing the level of harm vs. the level of benefit. And because of this balancing act, it is not always clear as to which consequences are good and which ones are bad. Therefore, we must ensure that the results of an action are something we can easily measure.

In the utilitarian approach to analysis, we must ask ourselves questions like this: Who is being harmed? Who is benefiting? Do the benefits outweigh the harm? Are more stakeholders being benefited than are being harmed? By working our way through these kinds of questions, we can logically begin to determine the consequences of any actions we may take. Using a utilitarian approach doesn't always yield a quick answer, but it certainly provides us with a great deal of information for consideration. If we can begin to assess the likely results of our actions — the consequences — we are beginning to narrow down our possible range of alternative decisions.

The reason we cannot rely on utilitarian principles alone is that if we follow the strictest definition of utilitarianism, we can easily justify morally wrong actions. Remember from previous chapters, in a utilitarian world, the practice of slavery can be justified as morally acceptable because it offers great benefits to a lot of people, but harms only a small number of people. So we must be careful when we use only utilitarian principles to justify our actions without weighing other factors as well.

We are also concerned with the *Social Contract*. Basically, social contract theory argues that we are all motivated by our own selfish interests, and it is these selfish interests that compel us to create a moral world in which to live. In business, if we had no moral rules that we could operate under, we would all be subject to the actions of others who were only trying to fulfill their own selfish interests. We would have to deal with a constant state of war between competing self-interests. Since this environment is not in our best interests, our own selfishness motivates us to adopt a set of rules that protects us from being hurt by others. These rules may prohibit lying, cheating, or stealing.

In a business situation, it is in our mutual interests to follow morally binding rules that protect us from the selfish interests of others. For example, it is in the mutual best interests of Company A and Company B to not cheat each other. This social contract says that Company A gives up its right to cheat Company B, and Company B agrees to the same. By transferring these rights to each other, both companies become obligated to not cheat the other. We realize that if we break our mutually beneficial rules and hurt someone, we will probably be hurt by others in return. So for selfish reasons, we abide by the rules we create.

The social contract helps to eliminate uncertainty and suspicion. It makes us feel more secure. We create a moral obligation for everyone to not harm each other. Since the contract exists as a mutual obligation to protect us all, violating the social contract is a highly unethical and immoral act. It creates insecurity and uncertainty.

When we look at ethical dilemmas, we must ask ourselves whether the actions we are analyzing violate the trust imposed on us by the social contract. Do the actions satisfy only self-interests? Will the actions cause suspicion or create a breach of the mutually beneficial rules under which we operate? Do our actions violate our moral obligations to the other stakeholders?

Using the obligations of the social contract as a way to determine the morality of our actions is another step that contributes to the overall analysis of an ethical dilemma.

Deontological Theories

In contrast to the teleological approach, deontological theories of ethics propose that the consequences are irrelevant in making an ethical decision. The deontological approach emphasizes the nature of the action itself or the rule governing the behavior. While teleological theories such as utilitarianism place the ethical emphasis on the *ends*, deontological theories place the ethical emphasis on the *means*. Deontological theory is more concerned with the *motive* behind the action rather than the result of the action.

As an example, suppose two salaried workers who aren't eligible for overtime volunteer to work late to fix a problem with a new product. One worker does it because he believes in maintaining the company's image of superb quality and also doesn't want to hurt any customers who bought the product. The other worker stays late to impress the boss and to avoid going home to his unruly kids and nagging wife. Although both of their efforts result in helping the company, the motives of the two volunteers are distinctly different. One is motivated by a sense of *duty*, while the other is motivated by a self-serving need. The first is a morally good action while the latter is a morally bad action. This is why we can use deontological theory as a tool to determine the ethicality of an action.

Deontologists believe that people should act from a sense of duty or obligation. These rules are absolute. For instance, if I tell the truth because I know it is the right thing for me to do and not because I am afraid of being caught in a lie, then I am basing my action on a duty, and that makes it morally correct. If I tell the truth only because I fear being caught lying, then my action does not come from a sense of duty but from a sense of self-protection, thereby making it morally wrong. In previous chapters, we discussed the seven absolute rules of duty proposed by W.D. Ross. They are:

1. Duties of fidelity — The duty to keep our promises and to always tell the truth.
2. Duties of reparation — The duty to provide compensation to people when we have injured or harmed them.
3. Duties of gratitude — The duty to return favors to people who have done things for us.
4. Duties of justice — The duty to ensure that goods are distributed fairly according to people's merits.
5. Duties of beneficence — The duty to do whatever we can to improve the condition of other people.
6. Duties of self-improvement — The duty to improve ourselves in regards to intelligence and virtue.
7. Duties of nonmaleficence — The duty to avoid harming others.

When we are analyzing ethical dilemmas, we can ask ourselves whether the actions involved uphold these duties. The answer should help identify whether an ethical dilemma exists and help guide us to an appropriate course of action. There are also other deontological theories we can use to help formulate an ethically defensible decision.

One of the deontological theories we use is Emmanuel Kant's Categorical Imperative. Kant believed that moral action should be based on reason and not on consequences. In fact, to Kant, consequences were irrelevant to the morality of the decision or action. Kant believed that an action should be taken because it is the right thing to do, because it has a basis in reason, and that rational people would do it from a sense of duty or moral obligation. The categorical imperative is an absolute command that has nothing to do with someone's desires or any other subjective considerations. A categorical imperative is something that *must* be done from a sense of duty. For example, "Do not cheat," or "Tell the truth," are imperatives that Kant would propose we must follow because it is our duty as rational beings to follow them. We treat categorical imperatives as if they were unquestionable truths.

The true test of a categorical imperative is whether it can be viewed in universal terms. We must ask ourselves what would happen if everyone behaved this way. For example, if we look at the categorical imperative "I must tell the truth," we can see how this might be universalized. Suppose no one ever told the truth. What would the world be like if everyone lied all of the time? Obviously, there would be no trust. We would not be able to accept anything as being true. Our business dealings would always be suspect. We would be suspicious of everything we are told. We would be unable to conduct business in a rational manner if we couldn't believe anything we were told. On the other hand, suppose that everyone told the truth. What would the world be like if that happened? Obviously, we would be able to trust everyone and always know that what we are being told is the truth. All of our decisions could be made with correct and reliable information. It would be a wonderful world in which to conduct business.

There is a second component to Kant's theory that takes the categorical imperative even further. Kant also believed that we should make ethical decisions based on respect for other people. Kant proposed that we must never treat people as a means to an end, but as an end in themselves. We cannot use people for our own gains. This principle requires respect for others. Although we do use other people everyday in our work environments (we have secretaries, clerks, janitors, drivers, and other employees), we must always look at others as more than objects or things. In Kant's categorical imperative, we make moral decisions by asking ourselves whether our actions will show respect for other people and not use those people for our own gains.

As an example, if a car salesman, trying to meet his monthly quota and obtain his commission, sells an unsuspecting customer a "new" car that was actually a lemon that had been returned by its previous owner, then he has treated that customer as a *means* to satisfying his own self-interests. The salesman's action also shows no respect for the rights or wellbeing of the individual involved.

So Kant's categorical imperative tells us that we must look for universality and consistency in behavior, i.e., what would it be like if everyone did this all of the time? Kant also proposes that we must treat people with respect and not use them to satisfy our own self-interests. Applying these principles to an ethical dilemma forces us to ask these kinds of questions: What would our environment be like if everyone conducted themselves this way? What if this happened all of the time? What would be the benefits to society (and our business) if everyone behaved this way? Would we be able to conduct business if everyone acted this way? Does this course of action show respect for the individual involved? Will the actions demonstrate disrespect to anyone? Am I, or anyone else, treating the person or stakeholder as a means to an end? Are we using the stakeholder to satisfy some self-interest?

Duty Theory

Duty theory expresses the notion that all of us have absolute obligations or duties to behave toward others in a certain way, to avoid harming others, to keep our promises, and to respect the rights of others. There is a definite correlation of duties with rights. What this means is simply that if a person has a right, then other people have a duty to respect that right. As an example, if an employer has a right to expect its employees to work a full shift for the wages they are paid, then the employees have a duty to respect that right and not slack off and hide behind the building playing cards during their shift. Another example would be that employees have a right to know that their phone calls are being monitored, so the employer has a correlating duty to inform them that they are being monitored. Obviously, duties and rights are inexorably tied together. You cannot have one without the other.

In analyzing ethical dilemmas, we can apply the principles of duties and rights against the relevant facts and stakeholders. We can ask ourselves: What are the rights of the various stakeholders involved? What rights are being violated, and for which stakeholders? If there are rights involved, then what are the corresponding duties of the other stakeholders to uphold those rights? Are those stakeholders ignoring their duties?

We also discussed several different natural rights in previous chapters. Based on those natural rights theories, we know that we have a right to own property. We have a right to privacy. We have a right to the fruits of our labor. We have a right to be left alone. We have a right not to be harmed. We have a right to be informed. In analyzing whether an ethical dilemma exists, we must determine whether an action is violating one or more of these natural rights.

Justice and Fairness

We often use the terms *justice* and *fairness* interchangeably because we tend to view justice as being fair in our decisions and treating everyone equally. We typically use the principle of justice when we are dealing with the distribution of something. This might be how we distribute profits to shareholders, benefits to employees, or discounts to our customers. Since the principle of justice often deals with the fairness of distribution, and most business decisions involve how something is distributed (for example, jobs, resources, benefits, wages, workload, dividends, stock options, supplies, materials, etc.), then the principle of justice is particularly relevant to business.

Reasonable people acknowledge that distributing everything on a completely equal basis is unworkable in real life. We accept that differences in what someone receives should be justified by differences that are *relevant* to the basis for the distribution. For example, if an employee works harder or longer than others, then that employee should be paid more on a proportional basis. If a shareholder invests more capital than other shareholders, then he should be entitled to more dividends than the others, proportionate to the amount of stock he owns. If a customer buys more products than other customers, then that customer should be entitled to better discounts than the other customers. This principle also infers that if there are no relevant differences between individuals, then there should be no differences in the equality of distribution. Basically, if two people are performing the same job, working the same amount of hours, and are equally productive, then they should be paid the same.

When the principles of justice and fairness are violated, it is often due to one of two factors: *favoritism* or *discrimination*.

When an employer shows some kind of favoritism to an employee or customer, the principle of fairness and justice is violated because someone receives a benefit that is not justified on some relevant difference. Other employees or customers will not consider this fair. On the other hand, if an employer discriminates against someone, they are depriving that employee of something without basing that decision on a relevant difference. Favoritism bestows unequal benefits to someone and discrimination imparts unequal harm to someone. Neither situation is fair based on the principle of justice. When one or the other occurs, we have an *injustice*.

Using the concepts of justice and fairness, we can analyze a situation or course of action by asking ourselves questions such as: Does this action treat everyone equally? If it does not, is the difference in treatment justified by some *relevant* differences? Does this action demonstrate or promote favoritism for certain stakeholders? Does this action or behavior demonstrate or promote discrimination towards certain stakeholders?

Virtue Theory

Virtues are universal characteristics that can be useful in any situation. Virtues are character traits that "good" people follow. These traits provide us with great benefits in both our personal and our business lives. Some of them are:

- Honesty
- Courage
- Generosity
- Compassion
- Loyalty
- Dependability
- Self-control
- Benevolence
- Tolerance
- Courtesy
- Fairness

Most ethical philosophers believe that moral decisions can be made by practicing virtuous behavior in our interactions with other people. We must ask ourselves whether the actions in question are demonstrative of virtuous behavior.

Other Factors

We must also attempt to identify whether other factors are involved as well. We can look for issues such as the obligation of reciprocity, goal displacement, ethical relativism, and agency theory. One or more of these issues may be present and helping to create the ethical dilemma we are analyzing. We should always look closely at a potential ethical dilemma to determine whether one or more of these phenomena are at work. Conversely, we must ensure that any decision we make is not based on one of these ethically flawed situations.

A Final Step

Once we have gone through this process, we have one final check that we can do. We can use the dialectic approach to refine our ethical arguments. We have used several ethical theories and principles to arrive at a decision that satisfies these ethical requirements. If we are still unsure about our decision, we can take the last step of refining our arguments. We do this by using the dialectic technique. The dialectic method requires questions and answers as a form of arguing for a claim. Our continued questioning of an argument helps us to expose gaps in that argument so that we can then reformulate the argument to close the gaps. By doing so, we can eventually arrive at an argument that has a strong and solid footing to defend its original claim. This is a form of philosophical analysis that forces us to thoroughly evaluate our claims. By questioning our own conclusions (or the conclusions of others), we can refine a decision to the most defensible argument.

Process Summary

We have now studied the process that allows us to fully analyze a situation, identify any potential ethical dilemmas, and come to a decision by applying the ethical principles in this book. As a summary, here is the process we have gone through:

Check the law. Does the action in question violate any laws or government regulations? If it does, then there is no point going any further. The action is illegal and must be treated as such.

If the law is unclear, or it doesn't specifically prohibit the behavior, then we can check it against any applicable professional standards or codes of conduct. Accountants, attorneys, doctors, and many other professions have written codes of conduct for their professions. These will often give specific guidelines on different behaviors, i.e., what should and should not be done.

We can also seek guidance by checking any corporate or organizational codes of conduct or corporate policies. Our employers will often have such codes of conduct or policies that tell us what behavior is prohibited.

We can also do some quick casual tests to determine if there may be an ethical dilemma. We can look at any possible ethical dilemma and ask ourselves questions such as these:

- What would my mother say if she knew I was doing this?
- Would I brag about this behavior?
- Would I want to hide this behavior from my children, co-workers, or friends?
- Would I want to have this behavior revealed on the national news or in the local newspaper?
- Does it feel wrong?
- Does it violate the Golden Rule?
- Would I want my clients to know about this?

The answers to these questions can be very insightful. If the answers to these questions set off alarms in our heads, then we can assume that something may be wrong.

If, after doing this, we now feel uncomfortable or unsure about whether a certain action is ethical, we can follow a more formal process that will take us through an analysis of the issues by applying traditional ethical principles and concepts.

First, we must identify all of the various stakeholders. We must determine who will be affected by the decisions we will make. Only by knowing all of the parties that are impacted by the decision or behavior, can we make a defensible decision. Knowing who is involved helps us to realize the repercussions of the various alternative actions we can take.

Second, we must determine the relevant facts. To be able to come up with a defensible ethical decision, we must be aware of all of the relevant facts. Therefore, we must list all of the relevant facts — not speculation or opinions — but factual information. These facts will help us later when we apply ethical principles.

Third, we need to identify who will be harmed. Since ethics deals primarily with harm, we must identify which of the stakeholders will be harmed by the actions or decisions. We can look at the various facts we have already listed, compare that to the list of stakeholders, and begin to develop an understanding of who will be harmed by the decisions we make.

Fourth, we must identify who will benefit. In any decision, there are always competing interests at stake. Different stakeholders may have interests that are completely opposite those of other stakeholders. Therefore, if one class of stakeholder is harmed, some other stakeholders will certainly benefit. Ethical decision-making is almost always a matter of determining who will be harmed and who will benefit, and to what extent.

Once we have gone through these four basic steps, we can apply ethical principles to the stakeholders and facts. We do this by asking questions about the action or behavior we are analyzing. Those questions are based on the different ethical principles we have studied. Typically, we would do this in a logical order, beginning with the simplest ethical theories — those that deal with consequences.

Apply Teleological Theories

Teleological theories instruct us to look at the consequences of an action. To do so, we can look at the two major consequential theories: utilitarianism and the social contract. The utilitarian theory proposes that we provide the greatest good to the most people. In essence, we must harm as few stakeholders as possible in order to benefit the greatest number of stakeholders. To apply the utilitarian theory to an action or behavior, we can ask ourselves these types of utilitarian questions:

- Who is being harmed?
- Who is benefiting?
- Does the amount of benefit outweigh the harm?
- Are more people (stakeholders) benefiting than are being harmed?

This is a good first step in the process, but it doesn't always yield an argument that can help us with our decision. Utilitarian arguments don't always provide us with the best answers, just a place to start.

That is why we typically use the utilitarian approach coupled with other ethical theories.

Another teleological theory we can use is the theory of the social contract. The social contract is our unwritten moral obligation to others. It helps to eliminate uncertainty and suspicion and makes us feel more secure. It affirms that we have a moral obligation to not harm each other. The contract exists as a mutual obligation to protect us all, and violating the social contract is a highly unethical and immoral act because it creates insecurity and uncertainty. To determine if the social contract is being violated with a specific action or behavior, we can ask ourselves the following types of questions:

- Do the actions we are analyzing violate the trust imposed on us by the social contract?
- Do the actions satisfy only self-interests?
- Will the actions cause suspicion or create a breach of the mutually beneficial rules we operate under?
- Do the actions violate a certain stakeholder's moral obligations to the other stakeholders?

Apply Deontological Theories

Deontological theory is more concerned with the motive behind the action rather than the consequences of the action. It deals with *why* we do something. There are several deontological theories we can use to analyze the actions that are in question.

Kant's categorical imperative tells us that we must look for universality and consistency in behavior, so we would ask questions such as these:

- What would it be like if everyone did this all of the time?
- What would be the benefits to our business if everyone behaved this way?
- Would we be able to conduct business if everyone acted this way?

Kant also proposed that we must treat people with respect and not use them to satisfy our own self-interests. Applying this principle to an ethical dilemma forces us to ask these kinds of questions:

- Does this course of action show respect for the individuals involved?
- Will the actions demonstrate disrespect to anyone?
- Am I, or anyone else, treating the person or stakeholder as a means to an end?
- Are we using the stakeholder to satisfy some self-interest?

Another deontological theory we can use in our analysis is duty theory. Duty theory says that all of us have absolute obligations or duties to behave toward others in a certain way, to avoid harming others, to keep our promises, and to respect the rights of others. There is also a definite correlation of duties with rights. Simply stated, this means that if a person has a right, then other people have a duty to respect that right. In analyzing ethical dilemmas, we can apply the principles of duties and rights against the relevant facts and stakeholders. We can ask ourselves these kinds of questions to see if duty theory is being violated:

- What are the rights of the various stakeholders involved?
- What rights are being violated, and for which stakeholders?
- If there are rights involved, then what are the corresponding duties of the other stakeholders to uphold those rights?
- Are those stakeholders ignoring their duties?

A secondary, but no less important aspect of duties and rights is the concept of natural rights. Based on natural rights theories, we know that we have a right to own property, a right to privacy, a right to the fruits of our labor, a right to be left alone, a right not to be harmed, and a right to be informed. In analyzing whether an ethical dilemma exists, we must ask ourselves:

- Does an action violate one or more of these natural rights, and for which stakeholders?
- If so, who is responsible for violating these rights?

Applying the Concepts of Justice and Fairness

We can also apply the principles of justice and fairness. Since the principle of justice often deals with the fairness of distribution, and most business decisions involve how something will be distributed (for example, jobs, resources, benefits, wages, workload, dividends, stock options, supplies, materials, etc.), then the principle of justice is particularly relevant to business.

We can acknowledge that distributing everything on a completely equal basis is unworkable in real life. We accept the axiom that differences in what someone receives should be justified by differences that are relevant to the basis for the distribution. This principle also infers that if there are no relevant differences between individuals, then there should be no differences in the equality of distribution. When the principles of justice and fairness are violated, it is often due to either favoritism or discrimination. Favoritism bestows unequal benefits to someone and discrimination imparts unequal harm to someone. Neither situation is fair based on the principle of justice.

Using the concepts of justice and fairness, we can analyze a situation or course of action by asking ourselves questions such as these:

- Does this action treat everyone equally?
- If it does not, is the difference in treatment justified by some relevant differences?
- Does this action demonstrate or promote favoritism for certain stakeholders?
- Does this action or behavior demonstrate or promote discrimination towards certain stakeholders?

Applying Virtue Theory

We can also look at a situation and the possible courses of action, and use virtue theory to help us determine an appropriate course of action. We can do this by asking ourselves questions such as:

- Which virtues apply to this behavior, e.g., honesty, compassion, courage, generosity, loyalty, or dependability?
- Does the action demonstrate virtuous behavior?
- Which virtues that apply to this behavior, are absent?

Using the Dialectic

We can also refine our arguments. Once we have gone through this process, we have one final check we can do — we can use the dialectic approach to refine our ethical arguments. Our continued questioning of an argument helps us to expose gaps in that argument, and then we can reformulate the argument to close the gaps. By doing so, we can eventually arrive at an argument that has a strong and solid footing to defend its original claim. By questioning our own conclusions, we can refine our decision so it has the most defensible arguments possible, thoroughly analyzed and thought out. We can also apply this technique to the decisions of others to determine the strength of their arguments or to force them to refine their arguments.

Michael P. Harden

Chapter Thirty-Two: The Decision

The key to ethical decision-making is weighing the facts and stakeholders' interests against the various ethical principles we have discussed in previous chapters. Once that process has taken place, we should be able to arrive at a decision that is defensible and based on the ethical principles we have used in our analysis. Throughout the process, we have asked many questions that have helped point out where ethical problems exist. The answers to our questions should have illuminated the ethical issues and helped us focus on the correct or best ethical course of action. It needs to be noted that this process is not a mathematical formula that requires us to score answers or tabulate results. Rather, it is an intuitive process that forces us to rely on our knowledge of ethical theories and the relevant facts involved in the particular situation. If we know and understand the ethical principles that form the foundation for ethical decision-making, we can make our decisions with greater ethical insight. This results in a lower probability of making a bad decision that could cause problems for our employers or for ourselves.

Each question we ask ourselves about an action or behavior helps to define the ethical issues at stake and focuses us on the most appropriate course of action. In some cases we may experience an epiphany, in other cases it may be more of a building process where each answer builds upon the previous answer to help us finally arrive at the best moral course of action. Once we have done this a few times, it begins to become intuitive.

It is commonly accepted that several people can look at the same situation and come to several completely different courses of action. In each case, each person thinks that his decision is the most ethical action. Nevertheless, by going through a process of applying each of the various ethical theories and using the results of the application of those theories to formulate a course of action, we are assured of being able to explain why our decision is the best ethical decision, and if need be, defend that decision with ethical clarity.

Michael P. Harden

Chapter Thirty-Three: Codes of Conduct

A code of conduct (or a code of ethics) is a written statement that spells out what an organization expects from its members. A code of conduct specifies the minimum ethical standards of behavior required in an organization. Every company and every organization should have one. In the 2000 National Business Ethics Survey, nearly 90 percent of the employees surveyed stated that their companies have some form of written ethical standards such as a code of conduct. Moreover, 65 percent of the survey respondents said that their organizations have some type of training about its ethical standards (ethics training). This is up significantly from previous years and is definitely a good trend.

Many companies think that developing and implementing a code of conduct is all that is necessary, but codes of conduct by themselves, are not sufficient to foster an ethical environment. Ethical standards are ignored and violated every day in many organizations (for many of the reasons previously stated in this book). Expecting employees to religiously follow a set of ethical guidelines without establishing the proper ethical environment for them is a disappointment waiting to happen. Although a code of ethics will have some positive influence on many employees, it is worthless without the rigorous support of management, the proper corporate culture, and regular training.

A code of ethics alone cannot guarantee that people will do the right thing. Therefore, management needs to foster an environment that promotes ethical behavior. There are numerous ways in which this can be done. Here is a list of proactive steps that will help ensure an ethical environment:

Codes should include broad guidance as well as specific policies. A code of conduct may list specific ethical standards such as "employees may not accept gifts from vendors," but it should also include broad behavioral guidelines such as "respect the rights of others," "obey the law," "treat others fairly," and "avoid harming others." Establishing broad guidelines helps to set a tone that fosters ethical behavior. Many of these guidelines can be based on ethical theories and virtues.

Enforce the code fairly and consistently. Employees need to know that the code covers everyone, and that everyone will be held to it. Waivers from the code must never be granted, especially to management. This sets the wrong example and shows that not all members of the organization are held to the same standards. Lack of enforcement or selective enforcement will dilute the effectiveness of the code.

Set the example. Management must demonstrate the proper ethical tone at every level. Employees should be able to point to a manager and know that his or her integrity is without question. Therefore, managers must be trained on how to make ethical decisions in order to gain the respect of their employees, as well as to solve ethical dilemmas.

Hire and keep the right people. Since a rotten apple can create an environment that fosters broader unethical behavior, it is important to hire ethical people and get rid of those that are not. By ensuring, to the best of management's ability, that people with sound ethical principles are hired, the chances of having an environment that promotes ethical behavior is enhanced. When people are identified as being corrupt or unethical, they should be terminated.

Take steps to prevent an unethical culture from developing. Managers must ensure that phenomena such as suboptimization, goal displacement, agency theory, and competitive pressures don't result in ethical lapses. Management must be sensitive and attentive as to how these different conditions influence ethical lapses and create a culture of dishonesty.

Conduct ethical training. To ensure that managers and employees understand the organization's ethical policies and that they are capable of identifying ethical dilemmas and resolving them, formal ethics training should be conducted regularly. By providing employees with the correct tools to identify that an ethical dilemma exists, and also teaching them ethical principles and decision-making techniques, they are more likely to make ethically defensible decisions and avoid trouble. A solid ethics training program is a great insurance policy to help avoid lawsuits, litigation costs, and personnel problems that drain resources and hinder productivity.

Establish an ethics officer position. Typically, an ethics officer will develop ethical programs and training, and keep up-to-date on ethical issues within the organization. That position can also be used as an independent channel of communications for reporting ethical violations. If the company cannot afford to dedicate a full-time position to this function, it can appoint an existing officer (typically in human resources or the corporate counsel's office) to fulfill this important role as an additional duty. Companies need to think of ethics as a management discipline that requires a skilled person to be responsible for it.

Promote whistle-blowing. Companies that create environments where potential whistle-blowers are encouraged to come forward without the fear of retribution are less likely to see whistle-blowers go outside of the company to air their claims. Also, since a true whistle-blower identifies corruption, inefficiencies, and mismanagement, encouraging this kind of information will ultimately benefit the company in the long run. Management must begin to see whistle-blowers as corporate assets rather than liabilities.